Miss Mur

and Other Stories

Other Volumes in the Black Women Writers Series
Series Editor: Deborah E. McDowell

Marita Bonner/*Frye Street and Environs*
Octavia E. Butler/*Kindred*
Alice Childress/*Like One of the Family*
Frances E. W. Harper/*Iola Leroy*
Gayl Jones/*Corregidora; Eva's Man*
Ann Petry/*The Street; The Narrows*
Carlene Hatcher Polite/*The Flagellants*

Miss Muriel and Other Stories

Ann Petry

BEACON PRESS   BOSTON

Beacon Press
25 Beacon Street
Boston, Massachusetts 02108-2800

Beacon Press books
are published under the auspices of
the Unitarian Universalist Association of Congregations.

96 95   8 7 6 5 4

Library of Congress Cataloging-in-Publication Data
Petry, Ann Lane
   Miss Muriel and other stories / Ann Petry.
      p. cm. — (Black women writers series)
   Reprint. Originally published: Boston : Houghton Mifflin, 1971.
   ISBN 0-8070-8311-9
   I. Title.   II. Series.
[PS3531.E933M57 1971]
813'.54 — dc19   88-47664

This book is for Walter J. Petry

Contents

Miss Muriel   1

The New Mirror   58

Has Anybody Seen Miss Dora Dean?   89

The Migraine Workers   112

Mother Africa   126

The Bones of Louella Brown   163

Olaf and His Girl Friend   181

Like a Winding Sheet   198

The Witness   211

Solo on the Drums   235

The Necessary Knocking on the Door   243

In Darkness and Confusion   252

Doby's Gone   296

Miss Muriel
and Other
Stories

Miss Muriel

ALMOST EVERY DAY, Ruth Davis and I walk home from school together. We walk very slowly because we like to talk to each other and we don't get much chance in school or after school either. We are very much alike. We are both twelve years old and we are freshmen in high school and we never study — well, not very much, because we learn faster than the rest of the class. We laugh about the same things and we are curious about the same things. We even wear our hair in the same style — thick braids halfway down our backs. We are not alike in one respect. She is white and I am black.

Yesterday when we reached the building that houses my father's drugstore, we sat down on the front steps — long wooden steps that go all the way across the front of the building. Ruth said, "I wish I lived here," and patted the steps though they are very splintery.

Aunt Sophronia must have heard our voices, because she came to the door and said, "I left my shoes at the shoemaker's this morning. Please go and get them for me," and she handed me a little cardboard ticket with a number on it.

"You want to come with me, Ruth?"

"I've got to go home. I'm sure my aunt will have things for me to do. Just like your aunt." She smiled at Aunt Sophronia.

I walked partway home with Ruth and then turned back and went up Petticoat Lane toward the shoemaker's shop. Mr. Bemish, the shoemaker, is a little white man with gray hair. He has a glass eye. This eye is not the same color as his own eye. It is a deeper gray. If I stand too close to him, I get a squeamish feeling because one eye moves in its socket and the other eye does not.

Mr. Bemish and I are friends. I am always taking shoes to his shop to be repaired. We do not own a horse and buggy and so we walk a great deal. In fact, there is a family rule that we must walk any distance under three miles. As a result, our shoes are in constant need of repair, the soles and heels have to be replaced, and we always seem to be in need of shoelaces. Quite often I snag the uppers on the bull briars in the woods and then the tears have to be stitched.

When I went to get Aunt Sophronia's shoes, Mr. Bemish was sitting near the window. It is a big window and he has a very nice view of the street. He had on his leather apron and his eyeglasses. His glasses are small and they have steel rims. He was sewing a shoe and he had a long length of waxed linen thread in his needle. He waxes the thread himself.

I handed him the ticket and he got up from his workbench to

get the shoes. I saw that he had separated them from the other shoes. These are Aunt Sophronia's store shoes. They had been polished so that they shone like patent leather. They lay alone, near the front of the table where he keeps the shoes he has repaired. He leaned toward me and I moved away from him. I did not like being so close to his glass eye.

"The lady who brought these shoes in. Who is she?"

I looked at him and raised one eyebrow. It has taken me two months of constant practice in front of a mirror to master the art of lifting one eyebrow.

Mr. Bemish said, "What's the matter with you? Didn't you hear what I said? Who was that lady who brought these shoes in?"

I moved further away from him. He didn't know it but I was imitating Dottle Smith, my favorite person in all the world. Dottle tells the most wonderful stories and he can act and recite poetry. He visits our family every summer. Anyway, I bowed to Mr. Bemish and I bowed to an imaginary group of people seated somewhere on my right and I said, "Gentlemen, be seated. Mr. Bones, who was that lady I saw you with last night?" I lowered the pitch of my voice and said, "That wasn't no lady. That was my *wife*."

"Girlie —"

"Why do you keep calling me girlie? I have a name."

"I cannot remember people's names. I'm too old. I've told you that before."

"How old are you, Mr. Bemish?"

"None of your business," he said pettishly. "Who —"

"Well, I only asked in order to decide whether to agree with you that you're old enough to be forgetful. Does the past seem more real to you than the present?"

Mr. Bemish scowled his annoyance. "The town is full of children," he said. "It's the children who bring the shoes in and come and get them after I've fixed them. They run the errands. All those children look just alike to me. I can't remember their names. I don't even try. I don't plan to clutter up my mind with a lot of children's names. I don't see the same children that often. So I call the boys boy, and I call the girls girlie. I've told you this before. What's the matter with you today?"

"It's spring and the church green is filled with robins looking for worms. Don't you sometimes wish you were a robin looking for a worm?"

He sighed. "Now tell me, who was that lady that brought these shoes in?"

"My Aunt Sophronia."

"Sophronia?" he said. "What a funny name. And she's your aunt?"

"Yes."

"Does she live with you?"

Mr. Bemish's cat mewed at the door and I let her in. She is a very handsome creature, gray with white feet, and really lovely fur. "May-a-ling, May-a-ling," I said, patting her, "where have you been?" I always have the feeling that if I wait, if I persist, she will answer me. She is a very intelligent cat and very responsive.

"Does your aunt live with you?"

"Yes."

"Has she been living with you very long?"

"About six months, I guess. She's a druggist."

"You mean she knows about medicine?"

"Yes, just like my father. They run the store together."

Mr. Bemish thrust his hands in Aunt Sophronia's shoes and held them up, studying them. Then he made the shoes walk

along the edge of the table, in a mincing kind of walk, a caricature of the way a woman walks.

"She has small feet, hasn't she?"

"No." I tried to sound like my mother when she disapproves
of something.

He flushed and wrapped the shoes in newspaper, making a
very neat bundle.

"Is she married?"

"Who? Aunt Sophronia? No. She's not married."

Mr. Bemish took his cookie crock off the shelf. He lives in
the shop. Against one wall he has a kitchen stove, a big black
iron stove with nickel fenders and a tea kettle on it, and there is
a black iron sink with a pump right near the stove. He cooks
his meals himself, he bakes bread, and usually there is a stew
bubbling in a pot on the stove. In winter the windows of his
little shop frost over, so that I cannot see in and he cannot see
out. He draws his red curtains just after dusk and lights his
lamps, and the windows look pink because of the frost and the
red curtains and the light shining from behind them.

Sometimes he forgets to draw the curtains that separate his
sleeping quarters from the rest of the shop and I can see his
bed. It is a brass bed. He evidently polishes it, because it
shines like gold. It has a very intricate design on the headboard
and the footboard. He has a little piece of flowered carpet in
front of his bed. I can see his white china pot under the bed. A
dark suit and some shirts hang on hooks on the wall. There is a
chest of drawers with a small mirror in a gold frame over it, and
a washbowl and pitcher on a washstand. The washbowl and
pitcher are white with pink rosebuds painted on them.

Mr. Bemish offered me a cookie from the big stoneware
crock.

"Have a cookie, girlie."

He makes big thick molasses cookies. I ate three of them without stopping. I was hungry and did not know it. I ate the fourth cookie very slowly and I talked to Mr. Bemish as I ate it.

"I don't think my Aunt Sophronia will ever get married."

"Why not?"

"Well, I never heard of a lady druggist before and I don't know who a lady druggist would marry. Would she marry another druggist? There aren't any around here anywhere except my father and certainly she couldn't marry him. He's already married to my mother."

"She looks like a gypsy," Mr. Bemish said dreamily.

"You mean my Aunt Sophronia?"

Mr. Bemish nodded.

"She does not. She looks like my mother and my Aunt Ellen. And my father and Uncle Johno say they look like Egyptian queens."

They are not very tall and they move quickly and their skins are brown and very smooth and their eyes are big and black and they stand up very straight. They are not alike though. My mother is business-minded. She likes to buy and sell things. She is a chiropodist and a hairdresser. Life sometimes seems full of other people's hair and their toenails. She makes a hair tonic and sells it to her customers. She designs luncheon sets and banquet cloths and guest towels and sells them. Aunt Ellen and Uncle Johno provide culture. Aunt Ellen lectures at schools and colleges. She plays Bach and Beethoven on the piano and organ. She writes articles for newspapers and magazines.

I do not know very much about Aunt Sophronia. She works

in the store. She fills prescriptions. She does embroidery. She reads a lot. She doesn't play the piano. She is very neat. The men who come in the store look at her out of the corner of their eyes. Even though she wears her hair skinned tight back from her forehead, and wears very plain clothes, dresses with long, tight sleeves and high necks, but still looks like — well, like an Egyptian queen. She is young but she seems very quiet and sober.

Mr. Bemish offered me another cookie. "I'll eat it on my way home to keep my strength up. Thank you very much," I said primly.

When I gave the shoes to Aunt Sophronia, I said, "Mr. Bemish thinks you look like a gypsy."

My mother frowned. "Did he tell you to repeat that?"

"No, he didn't. But I thought it was an interesting statement."

"I wish you wouldn't repeat the things you hear. It just causes trouble. Now every time I look at Mr. Bemish I'll wonder about him —"

"What will you wonder — I mean —"

She said I must go and practice my music lesson and ignored my question. I wonder how old I will be before I can ask questions of an adult and receive honest answers. My family always finds something for me to do. Are they not using their power as adults to give orders in order to evade the questions?

That evening, about five o'clock, Mr. Bemish came in the store. I was sitting on the bench in the front. It is a very old bench. The customers sit there while they wait for their prescriptions to be filled. The wood is a beautiful color. It is a deep, reddish brown.

Mr. Bemish sat down beside me on the bench. His presence

irritated me. He kept moving his hand up and down the arms of the bench, up and down, in a quick, nervous movement. It is as though he thought he had an awl in his hand, and he was going in and out making holes in leather and then sewing, slipping a needle in and out, as he would mend a saddle or a pair of boots.

My father looked at him over the top of his glasses and said, "Well, Bemish, what can I do for you?"

"Nothing. Nothing at all. I just stopped in to pass the time of day, to see how you all were —" His voice trailed away, softly.

He comes every evening. I find this very annoying. Quite often I have to squeeze myself onto the bench. Pritchett, the sexton of the Congregational church — stout, red-faced, smelling of whiskey — rings the bell for a service at seven o'clock and then he, too, sits in the front of the store, watching the customers as they come and go until closing time. He eyed Mr. Bemish rather doubtfully at first, but then ignored him. When the sexton and Mr. Bemish were on the bench, there was just room enough for me to squeeze in between them. I didn't especially mind the sexton, because he usually went to sleep, nodding and dozing until it was time to close the store. But Mr. Bemish doesn't sit still — and the movement of his hands is distracting.

My mother finally spoke to my father about Mr. Bemish. They were standing in the back room. "Why does Mr. Bemish sit out there in the store so much?" she asked.

"Nothin' else to do."

She shook her head. "I think he's interested in Sophronia. He keeps looking around for someone."

My father laughed out loud. "That dried-up old white man?"

The laughter of my father is a wonderful sound — if you know anything about music you know he sings tenor and you know he sings in the Italian fashion with an open throat and you begin to smile, and if he laughs long enough, you laugh too, because you can't help it.

"Bemish?" he said. And he laughed so hard that he had to lean against the doorjamb in order to keep his balance.

Every night right after supper, Mr. Bemish sits in the store rubbing the arm of the bench with that quick, jerking motion of his hand, nodding to people who come in, sometimes talking to them, but mostly just sitting.

Two weeks later I walked past his shop. He came to the door and called me. "Girlie," he said, beckoning.

"Yes, Mr. Bemish?"

"Is your aunt with the peculiar name still here — that is, in town, living with you?"

"Yes, she is, Mr. Bemish."

"Don't she ever go in the drugstore?"

"Not after five o'clock, Mr. Bemish. My father doesn't approve of ladies working at night. At night we act just like other people's families. We sit around the table in the dining room and talk, and we play checkers, and we read and we —"

"Yes, yes," he said impatiently. "But don't your aunt ever go anywhere at night?"

"I don't think so. I go to bed early."

"Do you think —" And he shook his head. "Never mind, girlie, never mind," and he sighed. "Here — I just made up a fresh batch of those big cookies you like so well."

I walked down Petticoat Lane toward the drugstore eating one of Mr. Bemish's thick molasses cookies. I wished I had taken time to tell him how cozy our downstairs parlor is in the winter. We have turkey-red curtains at the windows too, and we pull the window shades and draw the curtains, and there is a very thick rug on the floor and it is a small room, so the rug completely covers the floor. The piano is in there and an old-fashioned sofa with a carved mahogany frame and a very handsome round stove and it is warm in winter; and in the summer when the windows are open, you can look right out into the back yard and smell the flowers and feel the cool air that comes from the garden.

The next afternoon, Mr. Bemish came in the drugstore about quarter past three. It was a cold, windy afternoon. I had just come from school and there was a big mug of hot cocoa for me. Aunt Sophronia had it ready and waiting for me in the back room. I had just tasted the first spoonful; it was much too hot to gulp down, and I leaned way over and blew on it gently, and inhaled the rich, chocolatey smell of it. I heard my aunt say, "Why, Mr. Bemish, what are you doing out at this hour?"

"I thought I'd like an ice cream soda." Mr. Bemish's voice sounded breathless, lighter in weight, and the pitch was lower than normal.

I peeked out at him. He was sitting near the fountain in one of the ice cream parlor chairs. He looked very stiff and prim and neater than usual. He seemed to have flattened his hair closer to his skull. This made his head appear smaller. He was holding his head a little to one side. He looked like a bird but I cannot decide what bird — perhaps a chickadee. He drank the soda neatly and daintily. He kept looking at Aunt Sophronia.

He comes every day now, in the middle of the afternoon. He should have been in his shop busily repairing shoes or making boots, or making stews and cookies. Instead, he is in our store, and his light gray eye, the one good eye, travels busily over Aunt Sophronia. His ears seem to waggle when he hears her voice, and he has taken to giggling in a very silly fashion.

He always arrives about the same time. Sometimes I sit in one of the ice cream parlor chairs and talk to him. He smells faintly of leather, and of shoe polish, and of wax, and of dead flowers. It was quite a while before I could place that other smell — dead flowers. Each day he stays a little longer than he stayed the day before.

I have noticed that my father narrows his eyes a little when he looks at Mr. Bemish. I heard him say to my mother: "I don't like it. I don't want to tell him not to come in here. But I don't like it — an old white man in here every afternoon looking at Sophronia and licking his chops — well, I just don't like it."

Aunt Sophronia took a sudden interest in the garden. In the afternoon, after school, I help her set out plants and sow seed. Our yard is filled with flowers in the summer; and we have a vegetable garden that in some ways is as beautiful as the flowers — it is so neat and precise-looking. We keep chickens so that we can have fresh eggs. And we raise a pig and have him butchered in the fall.

When the weather is bad and we cannot work in the garden, Aunt Sophronia and I clean house. I do not like to clean house but I do like to sort out the contents of other people's bureau drawers. We started setting Aunt Sophronia's bureau in order. She showed me a picture of her graduating class from Pharmacy College. She was the only girl in a class of boys. She was black and the boys were white. I did not say anything about this difference in color and neither did she. But I did try to find out what it was like to be the only member of the female sex in a class filled with males.

"Didn't you feel funny with all those boys?"

"They were very nice boys."

"Oh, I'm sure they were. But didn't you feel funny being the only girl with so many young men?"

"No. I never let them get overly friendly and we got along very well."

I looked at the picture and then I looked at her and said, "You are beautiful."

She put the picture back in her top drawer. She keeps her treasures in there. She has a collar made of real lace, and a pair of very long white kid gloves, and a necklace made of gold nuggets from Colorado that a friend of my mother's left to Aunt Sophronia in her will. The gloves and the collar smell like our garden in August when the flowers are in full bloom and the sun is shining on them.

Sometimes I forget that Aunt Sophronia is an adult and that she belongs in the enemy camp, and I make the mistake of saying what I have been thinking.

I leaned against the bureau and looked down into the drawer, at the picture, and said, "You know, this picture reminds me of the night last summer when there was a female moth, one of those huge night moths, on the inside of the screen door, and all the male moths for miles around came and clung on the outside of the screen, making their wings flutter, and you know, they didn't make any sound but it was kind of scary. Weren't you —"

Aunt Sophronia closed the drawer with a hard push. "You get a broom and a dustpan and begin to sweep in the hall," she said.

On Saturday morning, after I finished washing the breakfast dishes and scrubbing the kitchen floor, I paid a call on Mr. Bemish. He was cleaning his house, too. He had taken down the red curtains that hung at the windows all winter, and the red curtains that hung in front of his bed, separating his sleeping quarters from the rest of his shop, and he was washing these curtains in a big tub at the side of his house. He was making a terrific splashing and the soapsuds were pale pink. He had his sleeves rolled up. His arms are very white and stringy-looking.

"Too much red for summer, girlie. I've got to get out the green summer ones."

He hung them on the line and poured the wash water out on the ground. It was pink.

"Your curtains ran, didn't they?" I looked at a little pink puddle left on top of a stone. "If you keep washing them, they'll be pink instead of red."

His own eye, the real eye, moved away from me, and there was something secret, and rather sly, about his expression. He said, "I haven't seen your aunt in the store lately. Where is she?"

"She's been busy fixing the garden and cleaning the house. Everybody seems to be cleaning house."

"As soon as I get my green curtains put up, I'm going to ask your aunt to come have tea."

"Where would she have tea with you?"

"In my shop."

I shook my head. "Aunt Sophronia does not drink tea in people's bedrooms and you have only that one room for your shop and there's a bed in it and it would be just like —"

"I would like to have her look at some old jewelry that I have and I thought she might have tea."

"Mr. Bemish," I said, "do you like my Aunt Sophronia?"

"Now, girlie," he said, and he tittered. "Well, now, do you think your aunt likes me?"

"Not especially. Not any more than anybody else. I think you're too old for her and besides, well, you're white and I don't think she would be very much interested in an old white man, do you?"

He frowned and said, "You go home. You're a very rude girl."

"You asked me what I thought, Mr. Bemish. I don't see why

you get mad when I tell you what I think. You did ask me, Mr. Bemish."

I followed him inside his shop. He settled himself near the window and started to work on a man's boot. It needed a new sole and he cut the sole out of leather. I looked out the front window. There is always enough breeze to make his sign move back and forth; it makes a sighing noise. In the winter if there's a wind, the sign seems to groan because it moves back and forth quickly. There is a high-laced shoe painted on the sign. The shoe must once have been a deep, dark red, but it has weathered to a soft rose color.

Mr. Bemish is my friend and I wanted to indicate that I am still fond of him though I disapprove of his interest in Aunt Sophronia. I searched for some topic that would indicate that I enjoy talking to him.

I said, "Why don't you have a picture of a man's boot on your sign?"

"I prefer ladies' shoes. More delicate, more graceful —" He made an airy gesture with his awl and simpered.

I went home and I told Aunt Sophronia that Mr. Bemish is going to ask her to have tea with him.

"Will you go?"

"Of course not," she said impatiently.

Aunt Sophronia did not have tea with Mr. Bemish. He sees her so rarely in the store that he finally came in search of her.

It is summer now and the Wheeling Inn is open for the season. The great houses along the waterfront are occupied by their rich owners. We are all very busy. At night after the store is closed, we sit in the back yard. On those warm June nights, the fireflies come out, and there is a kind of soft summer light, composed of moonlight and starlight. The grass is thick underfoot and the air is sweet. Almost every night my mother and my father and Aunt Sophronia and I, and sometimes Aunt Ellen and Uncle Johno, sit there in the quiet and in the sweetness and in that curious soft light.

Last night when we were sitting there, Mr. Bemish came around the side of the house. There was something tentative in the way he came toward us. I had been lying on the grass and I sat up straight, wondering what they would do and what they would say.

He sidled across the lawn. He didn't speak until he was practically upon us. My mother was sitting in the hammock under the cherry tree, rocking gently back and forth, and she didn't see him until he spoke. He said, "Good evening." He sounded as though he was asking a question.

We all looked at him. I hoped that someone would say: "What are you doing in our back yard, our private place, our especially private place? You are an intruder, go back to your waxed thread and your awl, go back to your house and your cat." Nobody said anything.

He stood there for a while, waiting, hesitant, and then he bowed and sat down, cross-legged, on the grass near Aunt Sophronia. She was sitting on one of the benches. And he sat so close to her that her skirt was resting on one of his trouser legs. I kept watching him. One of his hands reached toward her skirt and he gently fingered the fabric. Either she felt this or the motion attracted her attention, because she moved away from him, and gathered her skirt about her, and then stood up and said, "The air is making me sleepy. Good night."

The next afternoon I took a pair of my father's shoes to Mr. Bemish to have the heels fixed. My father wears high-laced black shoes. I left them on Mr. Bemish's work table.

"You can get them tomorrow."

I did not look right at him. I leaned over and patted May-a-ling. "She has such a lovely name, Mr. Bemish. It seems to me a name especially suited for a cat."

Mr. Bemish looked at me over the top of his little steel-rimmed glasses. "You've got a nice back yard," he said.

"I don't think you should have been in it."

"Why not?" he asked sharply. "Did anybody say that I shouldn't have been in it?"

"No. But the front part of the building, the part where the drugstore is, belongs to everybody. The back part of the building, and upstairs in the building, and the yard are ours. The yard is a private part of our lives. You don't belong in it. You're not a part of our family."

"But I'd like to be a part of your family."

"You can't get to be a part of other people's families. You have to be born into a family. The family part of our lives is just for us. Besides, you don't seem to understand that you're the wrong color, Mr. Bemish."

He didn't answer this. He got up and got his cookie crock and silently offered me a cookie.

After I returned from the shoe shop, I sat on the wooden steps that run across the front of the drugstore. I was trying to decide how I really feel about Mr. Bemish. I always sit at the far end of the steps with my back against the tight board fence. It is a very good place from which to observe the street, the front of the store, the church green. People walk past me not noticing that I am there. Sometimes their conversations are very unusual. I can see a long way down the path that bisects the green. It is a dirt path and not too straight. The only straight paths in town are those in front of the homes of people who have gardeners.

From where I sat I could see a man approaching. He was strolling down the path that crosses the church green. This is a most unusual way for a man to walk in Wheeling in the summer. It is during the summer that the year-round residents earn their living. They mow lawns, and cut hedges, and weed gardens, and generally look after the summer people. Able-bodied men in Wheeling walked fast in summer.

This tall, broad-shouldered man was strolling down the path. He was wearing a white suit, the pants quite tight in the leg, and he had his hands in his hip pockets, and a stiff straw hat, a boater, on the back of his head.

I sat up very straight when I discovered that this was a very dark-colored man. I could not imagine where he came from. He could not possibly have been a butler or a waiter, even if he had wanted to and spent a whole lifetime in trying. He would never have been able to walk properly — he would always swagger, and who ever heard of a swaggering butler or a waiter who strolled around a table?

As he came nearer, I saw that he had a beard, an untidy shaggy beard like the beard of a goat. His hair was long and shaggy and rough-looking too. Though he was tall, with wide shoulders, the thick rough hair on his head and the goat's beard made his head and face look too big, out of proportion to his body.

When he saw me, he came straight toward me. He bent over me, smiling, and I moved back away from him, pressing against the fence. His eyes alarmed me. Whenever I think about his eyes, I close mine, trying to shut his out. They are reddish brown and they look hot, and having looked into them, I cannot seem to look away. I have never seen anyone with eyes that color or with that strange quality, whatever it is. I described them as looking "hot," but that's not possible. It must be that they are the color of something that I associate with fire or heat. I do not know what it is.

"You lost?" he said.

"No. Are you?"

"Yup. All us black folks is lost." He said this in a husky, unmusical voice, and turned away and went in the store.

I went in the store, too. If this unusual-looking man with the goat's beard got into a discussion of "all us black folks is lost" with my father, I wanted to hear it.

My father said, "How-de-do?" and he made it a question.

The bearded man nodded and said, "The druggist in?"

"I'm the druggist."

"This your store?"

"That's right."

"Nice place you got here. You been here long?"

My father grunted. I waited for him to make the next move in the game we called Stanley and Livingstone. All black strangers who came into our store were Livingstones — and it was up to the members of our family to find out which lost Mr. Livingstone or which lost Mrs. Livingstone we had encountered in the wilds of the all-white town of Wheeling. When you live in a town where there aren't any other black people, naturally you're curious when another black person shows up.

I sat down in the front of the store and waited for my father to find out which Mr. David Livingstone he was talking to and what he was doing in our town. But my father looked at him with no expression on his face and said, "And what did you want?"

The man with the goat's beard fished in the pocket of his tight white pants. In order to do this, he thrust his leg forward a little to ease the strain on the fabric, and thus he gave the impression that he was pawing the ground. He handed my father a piece of paper.

"I got a prescription for a lotion —"

"It'll take a few minutes," my father said, and went in the back room.

The bearded man came and sat beside me.

"Do you live here in Wheeling?" I asked.

"I work at the inn. I'm the piano player."

"You play the piano?"

"And sing. I'm the whole orchestra. I play for the dinner hour. I play for all those nice rich white folks to dance at night. I'll be here all summer."

"You will?"

"That's right. And I've never seen a deader town."

"What's your name?"

"Chink."

"Mr. Chink —"

"No," he said, and stood up. "Chink is my first name. Chink Johnson."

Mr. Johnson is a restless kind of man. He keeps moving around even when he is sitting still, moving his feet, his hands, his head. He crosses his legs, uncrosses them, clasps his hands together, unclasps them.

"Why are you having a prescription filled?"

"Hand lotion. I use it for my hands."

My father came out of the back room, wrapped up a bottle, and said, "Here you are."

Chink Johnson paid him, said good-bye to me, and I said, "Good-bye, Chink."

"What's his name?"

"Chink Johnson. He plays the piano at the inn."

Chink Johnson seems to me a very interesting and unusual man. To my surprise, my father did not mention our newest Mr. Livingstone to the family. He said nothing about him at all. Neither did I.

Yet he comes in the drugstore fairly often. He buys cigarettes and throat lozenges. Sometimes he drives over from the inn in a borrowed horse and carriage. Sometimes he walks over. My father has very little to say to him.

He doesn't linger in the store, because my father's manner is designed to discourage him from lingering or hanging around. But he does seem to be looking for something. He looks past the door of the prescription room, and on hot afternoons the door in the very back is open and you can see our yard, with its beautiful little flower gardens, and he looks out into the yard, seems to search it. When he leaves he looks at the house, examining it. It is as though he is trying to see around a corner, see through the walls, because some sixth sense has told him that there exists on the premises something that will interest him, and if he looks hard enough, he will find it.

My mother finally caught a glimpse of him as he went out the front door. She saw what I saw — the goat's beard in silhouette, the forward thrust of his head, the thick shaggy hair — because we were standing in the prescription room looking toward the door.

"Who was that?" she asked, her voice sharp.

"That's the piano player at the inn," my father said.

"You've never mentioned him. What is his name?"

"Jones," my father said.

I started to correct him but I was afraid to interrupt him because he started talking fast and in a very loud voice. "Light-

foot Jones," he said. "Shake Jones. Barrelhouse Jones." He
started tapping on the glass case in front of him. I have never
heard him do this before. He sings in the Congregational
church choir. He has a pure, lyric tenor voice, and he sings all
the tenor solos — the "Sanctus," "The Heavens Are Telling."
You can tell from his speaking voice that he sings. He is always humming or singing or whistling. There he was with a
pencil in his hand, tapping out a most peculiar rhythm on the
glass of a showcase.

"Shake Jones," he repeated. "Rhythm in his feet. Rhythm in
his blood. Rhythm in his feet. Rhythm in his blood. Beats out
his life, beats out his lungs, beats out his liver, on a piano," and
he began a different and louder rhythm with his foot. "On a pi-
an-o. On a pi-an-o. On a pi —"

"Samuel, what is the matter with you? What are you talking
about?"

"I'm talkin' about Tremblin' Shakefoot Jones. The piano
player. The piano player who can't sit still and comes in here
lookin' around and lookin' around, prancin' and stampin' his
hoofs, and sniffin' the air. Just like a stallion who smells a mare
— a stallion who —"

"Samuel! How can you talk that way in front of this child?"
My father was silent.

I said, "His name is Chink Johnson."

My father roared, terrible in his anger, "His name is Duke.
His name is Bubber. His name is Count, is Maharajah, is King
of Lions. I don't give a good goddamn what he calls himself. I
don't want him and his restless feet hangin' around. He can let
his long feet slap somebody else's floor. But not mine. Not
here —"

He glared at me and glared at my mother. His fury silenced

us. At that moment his eyes were red-brown just like Chink Jones, no, Johnson. He is shorter, he has no beard, but he had at that moment a strong resemblance to Chink.

I added to his fury. I said, "You look just like Chink Johnson."

He said, "Ah!!! . . ." He was so angry I could not understand one word he said. I went out the front door and across the street, and sat on the church steps and watched the world go by and listened to the faint hum it made as it went around and around.

I saw Mr. Bemish go in the drugstore. He stayed a long time. That gave me a certain pleasure because I knew he had come to eat his ice cream soda, mouthful by mouthful, from one of our long-handled ice cream soda spoons, and to look at Aunt Sophronia as he nibbled at the ice cream. He always looks at her out of the corners of his eyes, stealing sly little glances at her. I knew that Aunt Sophronia would not be in the store until much later and that he was wasting his time. It was my father's birthday and Aunt Sophronia was in the kitchen baking a great big cake for him.

If Mr. Bemish had known this, he might have dropped in on the birthday celebration, even though he hadn't been invited. After all, he had sidled into our back yard without being invited and our yard is completely enclosed by a tight board fence, and there is a gate that you have to open to get in the yard, so that entering our yard is like walking into our living room. It is a very private place. Mr. Bemish is the only person that I know of who has come into our yard without being invited, and he keeps coming, too.

After Mr. Bemish left the store, I crossed the street and sat outside on the store steps. It was hot. It was very quiet. Old

Lady Chimble crossed the church green carrying a black silk umbrella, and she opened it and used it as a sunshade. A boy went by on a bicycle. Frances Jackins (we called her Aunt Frank), the black cook in the boardinghouse across the street, arrived carrying something in a basket. She is always cross and usually drunk. She drinks gin. Mother says this is what has made Aunt Frank's lips look as though they were turned inside out and she says this is called a "gin lip." They are bright red, almost like a red gash across the dark skin of her face. I want very much to ask Aunt Frank about this — how it feels, when it happened, etc. — and someday I will, but I have not as yet had a suitable opportunity. When she is drunk, she cannot give a sensible answer to a sensible question, and when she is sober, or partially sober, she is very irritable and constantly finds fault with me. She is absolutely no relation to us; it is just that my mother got in the habit of calling her Aunt Frank many years ago and so we all call her that. Because I am young, she tries to boss me and to order me around, and she calls me Miss in a very unpleasant, sarcastic way.

She is a very good cook when she is sober. But when she is drunk, she burns everything, and she is always staggering across the street and stumbling up our back steps, with bread pans filled with dough which would not rise because she had forgotten the yeast, and with burned cakes and pies and burned hams and roasts of beef. When she burns things, they are not just scorched; they are blackened and hardened until they are like charcoal.

Almost every night she scratches at our back door. I have sharper hearing than everybody else; I can hear people walking around the side of the house when no one else has heard them — anyway, I always hear her first. I open the door suddenly and very fast, and she almost falls into the kitchen and stands there swaying, and fouling our kitchen with the sweetish smell of gin and the dank and musty odor of her clothes.

She always has a dip of snuff under her upper lip and she talks around this obstruction, so that her voice is peculiar. She speaks quickly to keep the snuff in place, and sometimes she pauses and works her upper lip, obviously getting the snuff in some special spot. When she comes to the back door at night, she puts the basket of ruined food just inside the door, on the floor, and says to my mother, "Here, Mar-tha, throw this away. Throw it a-way for me. Give it to the hens. Feed it to the pig —"

She turns all two-syllable words into two separate one-syllable words. She doesn't say "Martha" all in one piece. She separates it, so that it becomes "Mar-tha"; she doesn't say "away," but "a-way." It is a very jerky kind of speech.

I am always given the job of burying the stuff in the back yard, way down in the back. I dig a hole and throw the black-ened mess into it and then cover it with lime to hasten decom-position and discourage skunks and dogs.

Sometimes I hide behind the fence and yell at her on her way back across the street:

> Ole Aunt Frankie
> Black as tar
> Tried to get to heaven
> In a 'lectric car.
> Car got stalled in an underpass,
> Threw Aunt Frankie right on her ass.

Whenever I singsong this rhyme at her, she invariably tries to climb over the fence, a furious drunken old woman, threatening me with the man's umbrella that she carries. I should think she would remember from past performances that she cannot possibly reach me. But she always tries. After several futile efforts, she gives up and goes back to the boardinghouse across the street. A lot of old maids and widows live there. No gentlemen. Just ladies. They spend their spare time rocking on the front porch, and playing whist, and looking over at the drugstore. Aunt Frank spends her spare time in the kitchen of the boardinghouse, rocking and emptying bottle after bottle of gin.

But on the day of my father's birthday, she was sober; at least, she walked as though she were. She had a basket on her arm with a white napkin covering its contents. I decided she must have made something special for my father's supper. She went in the drugstore, and when she came out, she didn't have the basket. She saw me sitting on the steps but she ignored me.

Aunt Sophronia came and stood in the window. She had washed the glass globes that we keep filled with blue, red, and yellow liquid. She was wearing a dark skirt and a white blouse. Her hair was no longer skinned tight back from her forehead; it was curling around her forehead, perhaps because she had been working in the garden, bending over, and the hairpins that usually hold it so tightly in place had worked themselves loose. She didn't look real. The sun was shining in the window and it reflected the lights from the jars of colored water back on her face and her figure, and she looked golden and rose-colored and lavender, and it was as though there were a rainbow moving in the window.

Chink Johnson drove up in his borrowed horse and carriage. He stood and talked to me and then started to go in the store, saw Aunt Sophronia, and stood still. He took a deep breath. I could hear him. He took off the stiff straw hat that he wore way back on his head and bowed to her. She nodded, as though she really didn't want to, and turned away and acted as though she were very busy.

He grabbed my arm and actually pinched it.

"What are you doin'?" I said angrily. "What is the matter with you? Let go my arm."

"Shut up," he said impatiently, pinching harder. His fingers felt as though they were made of iron. "Who is that?"

I pried his fingers loose and rubbed my arm. "Where?"

"In the window. Who is that girl in the window?"

"That's my Aunt Sophronia."

"Your aunt? Your aunt?"

"Yes."

He went in the store. One moment he was standing beside me and the next moment he had practically leaped inside the store.

I went in too. He was leaning in the window, saying, "Wouldn't you like to go for a walk with me this Sunday?"

She shook her head.

"Well, couldn't you go for a ride with me? I'll call for you —"

Aunt Sophronia said, "I work every day."

"Every day?" he said. "But that's not possible. Nobody works every day. I'll be back tomorrow —"

And he was gone. Aunt Sophronia looked startled. She didn't look angry, just sort of surprised.

I said, "Tomorrow and tomorrow and tomorrow —" And I thought, well, she's got two suitors now. There's this Shake Jones Livingstone, otherwise known as Chink Johnson, and there's Mr. Bemish. I do not think I would pick either one. Mr. Bemish is too old even though he is my friend. I think of Chink Johnson as my friend too, but I do not think he would make a good husband. I tried to decide why I do not approve of him as a husband for Aunt Sophronia. I think it is because Aunt Sophronia is a lady and Chink Johnson is — well — he is not a gentleman.

That night at supper we celebrated my father's birthday. At that hour nobody much came in the store. Pickett, the sexton, sat on the bench in the front and if anybody came in and wanted my father, he'd come to the back door and holler for him.

There was a white tablecloth on the big, oak dining room table, and we used my mother's best Haviland china and the sterling silver knives and forks with the rose pattern, and there was a pile of packages by my father's plate, and there were candles on the cake and we had ice cream for dessert. My old enemy, Aunt Frank, had delivered Parker House rolls for his birthday and had made him a milk-panful of rice pudding, because my father has always said that when he dies he hopes it will be because he drowns in a sea composed of rice pudding, that he could eat rice pudding morning, noon, and night. Aunt Frank must have been sober when she made the pudding, for it was creamy and delicious and I ate two helpings of it right along with my ice cream.

I kept waiting for Aunt Sophronia to say something about Chink Johnson. He is a very unusual-looking man and we've never had a customer, black or white, with that kind of beard. She did not mention him. Neither did I. My father has never mentioned him — at least not at the table. I wonder if my father hopes he will vanish. Perhaps they are afraid he will become a part of the family circle if they mention him.

Now Chink Johnson has become a part of the family circle, and he used the same method that Mr. Bemish used. He just walked into the yard and into the house. I was upstairs and I happened to look out of the window, and there was Chink Johnson walking up the street. He opened our gate, walked around the side of the house and into our back yard. I hurried to the back of the house and looked out the window and saw him open the screen door and go into the kitchen. He didn't knock on the door either, he just walked in.

For the longest time I didn't hear a sound. I listened and listened. I must have stood still for fifteen minutes. Then I heard someone playing our piano. I knew it must be Chink Johnson because this was not the kind of music anyone in our house would have been playing. I ran downstairs. My mother had been in the cellar, and she came running up out of the cellar, and my father came hurrying over from the drugstore. We all stood and looked and looked.

Chink was sitting at our piano. He had a cigarette dangling from his lower lip, and the smoke from the cigarette was like a cloud — a blue-gray, hazy kind of cloud around his face, his eyes, his beard — so that you could only catch glimpses of them through the smoke. He was playing some kind of fast, discordant-sounding music and he was slapping the floor with one of his long feet and he was slapping the keys with his long fingers.

Aunt Sophronia was leaning against the piano looking down at him. He did not use music when he played, and he never once looked at the keyboard, he just kept looking right into Aunt Sophronia's eyes. I thought my father would tell Chink to go slap somebody else's floor with his long feet, but my mother gave him one of those now-don't-say-a-word looks and he glared at Chink and went back to the drugstore.

Chink stayed a long time; he played the piano, he sang, or rather I guess you would say he talked to the music. It is a very peculiar kind of musical performance. He plays some chords, a whole series of them, and he makes peculiar changes in the chords as he plays, and then he says the words of a song — he doesn't really sing, but his voice does change in pitch to, in a sense, match the chords he is playing, and he does talk to a kind of rhythm which also matches the chords. I sat down beside him and watched what he was doing, and listened to the words he said, and though it is not exactly music as I am accustomed to hearing it, I found it very interesting. He told me that what he does with those songs is known as the "talkin' blues." Only he said *"talk*in' " and he made "blues" sound like it was two separate words; not just a two-syllable word, but two distinct words.

I have been trying to play the piano the way he does but I get nothing but terrible sounds. I pretend that I am blind and keep my eyes closed all the time while I feel for chords. He must have a special gift for this because it is an extremely difficult thing that he is doing and I don't know whether I will ever be able to do it. He has a much better ear for music than I have.

Chink Johnson comes to see Aunt Sophronia almost every day. Sometimes when I look out in the back yard, Mr. Bemish is out there too. He always sits on the ground, and at his age, I should think it might give him rheumatism. He must be a very brave little man or else his love for Aunt Sophronia has given him great courage. I say this because Chink Johnson is very rude to Mr. Bemish and he stares at him with a dreadfully cruel look on his face. If I were small and slender and old like Mr. Bemish, I would not sit in the same yard with a much bigger, much younger man who obviously did not want me there.

I have thought a great deal about Mr. Bemish. I like him. He is truly a friend. But I do not think he should be interested in Aunt Sophronia — at least not in a loving kind of way. The thing that bothers me is that I honestly cannot decide whether I object to him as a suitor for her because he is white or because he is old. Sometimes I think it is for both reasons. I am fairly certain it isn't just because he's old. This bothers me. If my objections to him are because he's white (and that's what I told him, but I often say things that I know people do not want to hear and that they particularly do not want to hear from someone very much younger than they are), then I have been "trained" on the subject of race just as I have been "trained" to be a Christian. I know how I was trained to be a Christian — Sunday school, prayers, etc. I do not know exactly how I've been "trained" on the subject of race. Then why do I feel like this about Mr. Bemish?

Shortly after I wrote that, I stopped puzzling about Mr. Bemish because summer officially started — at least for me. It is true that school has been out for a long time, and we are wearing our summer clothes, and the yard is filled with flowers — but summer never really gets under way for me until Dottle Smith comes for his yearly visit.

Dottle and Uncle Johno went to school together. They look sort of alike. They are big men and they are so light in color they look like white men. But something in them (Dottle says that it is a "cultivated and developed and carefully nourished hatred of white men") will not permit them to pass for white. Dottle teaches English and elocution and dramatics at a school for black people in Georgia, and he gives lectures and readings during the summer to augment his income. Uncle Johno is the chief fund-raising agent for a black school in Louisiana.

I believe that my attitude towards Mr. Bemish stems from
Dottle Smith. And Johno. They are both what my father calls
race-conscious. When they travel on trains in the South, they
ride in Jim Crow coaches until the conductor threatens to have
them arrested unless they sit in the sections of the train reserved for whites. They are always being put out of the black
sections of waiting rooms, and warned out of the black sections
of towns, and being refused lodgings in black rooming houses
on the grounds that they would be a source of embarrassment
— nobody would be able to figure out why a white man
wanted to live with black people, and they would be suspected
of being spies, but of what kind or to what purpose, they have
never been able to determine.

I have just reread what I have written here, and I find that
I've left out the reason why I am writing so much about Dottle.
Yesterday afternoon when I came back from an errand, there
was a large, heavy-looking bag — leather, but it was shaped
like a carpetbag — near the bench where the customers sit
when they wait for prescriptions. I recognized it immediately.
I have seen that bag every summer for as far back as I can
remember. I wondered if Dottle had come alone this time or if
he had a friend with him. Sometimes he brings a young man
with him. These young men look very much alike — they are
always slender, rather shy, have big dark eyes and very smooth
skin just about the color of bamboo.

I looked at Dottle's big battered old bag sitting on the floor
near the bench, and I could almost see him, with his long curly
hair, and I could hear him reciting poetry in his rich, buttery
voice. He can quote all the great speeches from *Hamlet, Macbeth, Richard II*, and he can recite the sonnets.

I loved him. He was lively and funny and unexpected.

Sometimes he would grab my braid and shout in his best Shakespearean voice, "Seize on her Furies, take her to your torments!"

I looked at Dottle's battered bag and I said to my father, "Is he alone? Or has he got one of those pretty boys with him?"

My father looked at me over the top of his glasses. "Alone."

"How come he to leave his bag here?"

"Well, the Ecckles aren't home. Ellen's gone on vacation —"

"Why does Aunt Ellen always go on vacation when Dottle comes?"

My father ignored this and went on talking. "Johno's gone to Albany collecting money for the school."

"Where is Dottle now?"

"I'm right here, sugar," and Dottle Smith opened the screen door and came in. He looked bigger than he had the summer before. He hugged me. He smelled faintly of lavender.

"You went and grew, honey," he said, and took off his hat and bowed. It was a wide-brimmed Panama, and he had on a starched white shirt, and a flowing Byronic kind of black tie, and I looked at him with absolute delight. He was being a Southern "cunnel" and he was such an actor — I thought I could see lace at his wrists, hear mockingbirds sing, see a white-columned mansion, hear hoofbeats in the distance, and hear a long line of slaves, suitably clad as footmen and coachmen and butlers and housemen, murmur, "Yes, massah. Yes, massah." It was all there in his voice.

"Why, in another couple years I'll be recitin' poetry to you. How's your momma? This summer I'll have to teach you how to talk. These Yankah teachers you've got all talk through their noses. They got you doin' the same thing —"

For two whole days I forgot about Chink Johnson and Mr.

Bemish and Aunt Sophronia. Dottle liked to go fishing and crabbing; he liked to play whist; and he could tell the most marvelous stories and act them out.

The very next day Dottle and Uncle Johno and I went crabbing. We set out early in the morning with our nets and our fishing lines and the rotten meat we used for bait, and our lunch and thermos bottles with lemonade in them. It was a two-mile walk from where we lived to the creek where we caught crabs.

There was a bridge across the creek, an old wooden bridge. Some of the planks were missing. We stood on this bridge or sat on it and threw our lines in the water. Once in a great while a horse and wagon would drive across and set the planks to vibrating. Johno and Dottle would hop off the bridge. But I stayed on and held to the railing. The bridge trembled under my feet, and the horse and wagon would thunder across, and the driver usually waved and hollered, "I gotta go fast or we'll all fall in."

The water in the creek was so clear I could see big crabs lurking way down on the bottom; I could see little pieces of white shells and beautiful stones. We didn't talk much while we were crabbing. Sometimes I lay flat on my stomach on the bridge and looked down into the water, watching the little eddies and whirlpools that formed after I threw my line in.

Before we ate our lunch, we went wading in the creek. Johno and Dottle rolled up the legs of their pants, and their legs were so white I wondered if they were that white all over, and if they were, how they could be called black. We sat on the bank of the creek and ate our lunch. Afterward Dottle and Johno told stories, wonderful stories in which animals talk, and there are haunted houses and ghosts and demons, and old black preachers who believe in heaven and hell.

They always started off the same way. Dottle would say to Johno, "Mr. Bones, be seated."

Though I have heard some of these stories many, many times, Dottle and Johno never tell them exactly the same. They change their gestures; they vary their facial expressions and the pitch of their voices.

Dottle almost always tells the story about the black man who goes in a store in a small town in the South and asks for Muriel cigars. The white man who owns the store says (and here Johno becomes an outraged Southern white man), "Nigger, what's the matter with you? Don't you see that picture of that beautiful white woman on the front of this box? When you ask for them cigars, you say *Miss* Muriel cigars!"

Though Uncle Johno is a good storyteller, he is not as good, not as funny or as dramatic, as Dottle. When I listen to Dottle I can see the old black preacher who spent the night in a haunted house. I see him approaching the house, the wind blowing his coattails, and finally him taking refuge inside because of the violence of the storm. He lights a fire in the fireplace and sits down by it and rubs his hands together, warming them. As he sits there, he hears heavy footsteps coming down the stairs (and Dottle makes his hand go thump, thump, thump on the bank of the creek) and the biggest cat the old man has ever seen comes in and sits down, looks at the old preacher, looks around, and says, "Has Martin got here yet?" The old man is too startled and too nervous to answer. He hears heavy footsteps again — thump, thump, thump. And a second cat, much bigger than the first one, comes in, and sits down right next to the old preacher. Both cats stare at him, and then the second cat says to the first cat, "Has Martin got here yet?" and the first cat shakes his head. There is something so speculative in their glance that the old man gets more and more uneasy. He wonders if they are deciding to eat him. The wind howls in the chimney, puffs of smoke blow back into the room. Then another and bigger cat thumps down the stairs. Finally there are six enormous cats, three on each side of him. Each one of these cats has asked the same question of the others — "Martin got here yet?" A stair-shaking tread begins at the top of the stairs, the cats all look at each other, and the old man grabs his hat, and says to the assembled cats, "You tell Martin ah been here but ah've gone."

I clapped when Dottle finished this story. I looked around thinking how glad I am he is here and what a wonderful place this is to listen to stories. The sun is warm but there is a breeze and it blows through the long marsh grass which borders the creek. The grass moves, seems to wave. Gulls fly high overhead. The only sound is the occasional cry of a gull and the lapping of water against the piling of the bridge.

Johno tells the next story. It is about an old black preacher and a rabbit. The old man tries to outrun an overfriendly and very talkative rabbit. The rabbit keeps increasing in size. The old man runs away from him and the rabbit catches up with him. Each time the rabbit says, "That was some run we had, wasn't it, brother?" Finally the old man runs until he feels as though his lungs are going to burst and his legs will turn to rubber, and he looks back and doesn't see the rabbit anywhere in sight. He sits down on a stone to rest and catch his breath. He has just seated himself when he discovers the rabbit sitting right beside him, smiling. The rabbit is now the same size as the preacher. The rabbit rolls his eyes and lisps, "That wath thome run we had, wathn't it?" The old man stood up, got ready to run again, and said, "Yes, that was some run we had, brother, but" — he took a deep breath — "you ain't *seen* no runnin' yet."

After they finished telling stories, we all took naps. Dottle and Johno were wearing old straw hats, wide-brimmed Panamas with crooked, floppy brims. Dottle had attached a piece of mosquito netting to his, and it hung down across his shoulders. From the back he looked like a woman who was wearing a veil.

When we woke up it was late in the afternoon and time to start for home. I ran part of the way. Then I sat down by the side of the road, in the shade, and waited until they caught up with me.

Dottle said, "Sugar, what are you in such a hurry for?"

I said, laughing, "Miss Muriel, you tell Martin I been here but I've gone and that he ain't *seen* no runnin' yet."

I got home first. Chink Johnson was in the store. When Dottle and Johno arrived, I introduced Chink to my uncles, Johno and Dottle. They didn't seem much impressed with each other. Johno nodded and Dottle smiled and left. Chink watched Dottle as he went toward the back room. Dottle has a very fat bottom and he sort of sways from side to side as he walks.

Chink said, "He seems kind of ladylike. He related on your mother's side?"

"He's not related at all. He's an old friend of Uncle Johno's. They went to school together. In Atlanta, Georgia." I sounded very condescending. "Do you know where that is?"

"Yeah. 'Nigger, read this. Nigger, don't let sundown catch you here. Nigger, if you can't read this, run anyway. If you can't run — then vanish. Just vanish out.' I know the place. I came from there."

My father was standing outside on the walk talking to Aunt Frank, so I felt at liberty to speak freely and I said, "Nigger, what are you talkin' about you want Muriel cigars. You see this picture of this beautiful redheaded white woman, nigger, you say *Miss* Muriel."

Chink stood up and he was frowning and his voice was harsh. "Little girl, don't you talk that way. I talk that way if I feel like it but don't you ever talk that way."

I felt as though I had been betrayed. One moment he was my friend and we were speaking as equals and the next moment, without warning, he is an adult who is scolding me in a loud, harsh voice. I was furious and I could feel tears welling up in my eyes. This made me angrier. I couldn't seem to control my weeping. Recently, and I do not know how it happened, whenever I am furiously angry, I begin to cry.

Chink leaned over and put his hand under my chin, lifted my face, saw the tears and he kissed my cheek. His beard was rough and scratchy. He smelled like the pine woods, and I could see pine needles in his hair and in his beard, and I wondered if he and Aunt Sophronia had been in the woods.

"Sugar," he said gently, "I don't like that Miss Muriel story. It ought to be told the other way around. A black man should be tellin' a white man, 'White man, you see this picture of this beautiful black woman? *White* man, you say *Miss* Muriel!' "

He went out of the store through the back room into the yard just as though he were a member of the family. It hadn't taken him very long to reach this position. Almost every afternoon he goes for a walk with Aunt Sophronia. I watch them when they leave the store. He walks so close to her that he seems to surround her, and he has his head bent so that his face is close to hers. Once I met them strolling up Petticoat Lane, his dark face so close to hers that his goat's beard was touching her smooth brown cheek.

My mother used to watch them too, as they walked side by side on the dirt path that led to the woods — miles and miles of woods. Sometimes he must have said things that Aunt Sophronia didn't like, because she would turn her head sharply away from him.

I decided that once you got used to his beard and the peculiar color and slant of his eyes, why you could say he had an interesting face. I do not know what it is about his eyes that makes me think of heat. But I know what color they are. They are the color of petrified wood after it's been polished, it's a red brown, and that's what his eyes are like.

I like the way he plays the piano, though I do not like his voice. I cannot get my mother to talk about him. My father grunts when I mention Chink's name and scowls so ferociously that it is obvious he does not like him.

I tried to find out what Aunt Sophronia thought of him. Later in the day I found her in the store alone and I said, "Do you like Chink Johnson?"

She said, "Run along and do the supper dishes."

"But do you?"

"Don't ask personal questions," she said, and her face and neck flushed.

She must have liked him though. She not only went walking with him in the afternoon, but on Sunday mornings he went to church with her. He wore a white linen suit and that same stiff straw hat way back on his head. He brought her presents — a tall bottle of violet eau de cologne, a bunch of Parma violets made of silk, but they looked real. On Sundays, Aunt Sophronia wore the violets pinned at her waist and they made her look elegant, like a picture in a book.

I said, "Oh, you look beautiful."

My mother said, dryly, "Very stylish."

We all crossed the street together on Sunday mornings. They went to church. I went to Sunday school. Sunday school was out first and I waited for them to come down the church steps. Aunt Sophronia came down the church steps and he would be so close behind her that he might have been dancing with her and matching his leg movements to hers. Suddenly he was in front of her and down on the path before she was and he turned and held out his hand. Even there on the sidewalk he wasn't standing still. It is as though his feet and his hands are more closely connected to his heart, to his central nervous system, than is true of other people, so that during every waking moment he moves, tapping his foot on the floor, tapping his fingers on a railing, on somebody's arm, on a table top. I wondered if he kept moving like that when he was asleep, tapping quarter notes with his foot, playing eighth notes with his right hand, half notes with his left hand. He attacked a piano when he played, violated it — violate a piano? I thought, violate Aunt Sophronia?

He stood on the dirt path and held out his hand to Aunt Sophronia, smiling, helping her down the church steps.

"Get your prayers said, sugar?" he said to me.

"Yes. I said one for you and one for the family. Aunt Sophronia, you smell delicious. Like violets —"

"She does, doesn't she?"

We walked across the street to the drugstore, hand in hand. Chink was in the middle and he held one of my hands and one of Aunt Sophronia's. He stays for dinner on Sundays. And on Sunday nights we close the store early and we all sit in the back yard, where it is cool. Mr. Bemish joins us in the yard. At dusk the fireflies come out, and then as the darkness deepens, bats swoop around us. Aunt Sophronia says, "Oooooh!" and holds on to her head, afraid one might get entangled in her hair.

Dottle took out one of his big white handkerchiefs and tied it around his head, and said in his richest, most buttery voice, "One of the nocturnal or crepuscular flying mammals constituting the order Chiroptera."

Dottle sprawled in a chair and recited poetry or told long stories about the South — stories that sometimes had so much fear and terror and horror in them that we shivered even though the air was warm. Chink didn't spend the evening. He sat in one of the lawn chairs, tapping on the arm with his long flexible fingers, and then left. Mr. Bemish always stays until we go in for the night. He takes no part in the conversation, but sits on the ground, huddled near Aunt Sophronia's skirts. Once when a bat swooped quite close, Aunt Sophronia clutched his arm.

Sometimes Dottle recites whole acts from *Macbeth* or *Hamlet* or all of the Song of Solomon, or sometimes he recites the loveliest of Shakespeare's sonnets. We forget about the bats swooping over our heads, ignore the mosquitoes that sting our ankles and our legs, and sit mesmerized while he declaims, "Shall I compare thee to a summer's day?"

The summer is going faster and faster — perhaps because of the presence of Aunt Sophronia's suitors. I don't suppose Dottle is really a suitor, but he goes through the motions. He picks little bouquets for her — bachelor buttons and candytuft — and leaves them on the kitchen table. He always calls her Miss Sophronia. If we are outdoors and she comes out to sit in the yard, he leaps to his feet, and bows and says, "Wait, wait. Befo' you sit on that bench, let me wipe it off," and he pulls out an enormous linen handkerchief and wipes off the bench. He is always bowing and kissing her hand.

By the middle of August it was very hot. My father had the store painted, and when the blinds were taken down, the painter found whole families of bats clinging together in back of the blinds. Evidently they lived there. I couldn't get hold of one, although I tried. They were the most peculiar-looking creatures. They looked almost like a person who wears glasses all the time and then suddenly goes without them, they have a kind of peering look.

Chink Johnson is always in our house or in the store or in the yard or going for walks with Aunt Sophronia. Whenever he is not violating the piano at the inn, he is with Aunt Sophronia —

He taught her how to dance — in the back yard, without any music, just his counting and clapping his hands. His feet made no sound on our thick grass. On two different sunny afternoons, he gave her dancing lessons, and on the third afternoon, he had her dancing. She was laughing and she was lively-looking and she looked young. He persuaded her to take off her shoes and she danced in her bare feet. Fortunately, nobody knows this but me.

He took her fishing. When they came back, she was quite sunburned but her eyes were shining as though they held the reflected light from the sun shining on water.

Just in that one short summer he seemed to take on all kinds of guises — fisherman, dancer, singer, churchgoer, even delivery boy.

One morning someone knocked at the back door and there was Chink Johnson with our grocery order, saying to my Aunt Sophronia, "Here's your meat, ma'am, and your vegetables," touching his hat, bowing, unloading the crate of groceries, and then sitting down at the kitchen table as though he owned it, drinking a cup of coffee that no one had offered him, just pouring it out of the enamel pot that stays on the stove, finding cream and sugar himself, and sitting there with his legs thrust way out in front of him, and those terribly tight pants he wears looking as though they were painted on his thighs.

Sometimes when he sits in our kitchen, he laughs. His laughter is not merry. When my father laughs, the sound makes you laugh, even when you don't know what he is laughing about.

When Chink Johnson laughs, I look away from him. The sound hurts my ears. It is like the ugly squawk of some big bird that you have disturbed in the woods and it flies right into your face, pecking at your eyes.

It has been a very interesting summer. I have begun to refer to it in the past tense because there isn't much left of a summer by the middle of August. One Thursday afternoon, Aunt Sophronia and I saw that other ladies liked Chink Johnson too.

Thursday afternoon is traditionally maid's day off and Chink Johnson drove the maids from the inn into town, in a wagon, late in the day. He stopped in front of the store with a wagon full of girls in long skirts, giggling, leaning against him, a kind of panting excitement in that wagon, their arms around him; they whispered to him; they were seized by fits of laughter, shrieks of laughter.

They came in the store and bought hairnets and hairpins and shampoo and Vaseline and hair tonics and cough medicines and court plaster and a great many items that they did not need because it was a pleasure to be spending money, and to be free of the tyranny of the housekeepers' demands — or so my mother said — some young and attractive, some not so young, about ten of them.

Aunt Sophronia was in the store and she waited on them, studying them. Every once in a while one would go to the door, and yell, "We'll be out in a minute, Chink. Just a little while!" and wave at him and throw kisses at him.

Then they were gone, all at once, piling into the wagon, long full skirts in disarray. One of them sat in Chink's lap, laughing, looking up into his face, and saying, "Let's go in the woods. Chink, take us in the woods. I'll help drive."

Aunt Sophronia and I stood in the doorway and watched them as they drove off, going toward the pine woods. The wagon seemed to be filled with wide skirts, and ruffled petticoats, all suddenly upended because Chink said, "Giddup, there!" and hit the horse with the whip, cracked it over the horse's ears, and the horse started off as though he were a race-horse.

It was late when they went past the store, going home. Sitting in the back yard, we could hear the horse racing, and the girls squealing and laughing, and Chink singing a ribald song, about "Strollin', and Strollin'."

Dottle stopped right in the middle of a poem and Mr. Bemish straightened up so that he was not quite so close to Aunt Sophronia's skirts. It was like having Chink Johnson right there in the back yard with us — the rough, atonal voice, the red-brown eyes that looked hot, literally hot, as though if you touched them you would have to withdraw your fingers immediately because they would be scorched or singed or burned, the jutting beard, the restless feet and hands.

We sat absolutely still. We could hear the rattling of the wagon, the clop-clop of the horse's hoofs and above it the laughter of the girls, and dominating that sound, Chink Johnson's voice lifted in song. Even after they were so far away we could not possibly hear them, these sounds seemed to linger in the air, faint, far-off.

It was a warm night, brilliant with light from the moon. I pictured the girls as sitting on top of Chink, all around him, on his arms, in his lap, on his shoulder, and I thought the prettiest one should be perched on his head.

Dottle lit a cigar and puffed out clouds of bluish smoke and said, "I never heard the mating call of the male so clearly sounded on a summer's night." He laughed so hard that he had to get out one of his big handkerchiefs and dab his eyes with it.

Aunt Sophronia got up from the bench so fast that she brushed against Mr. Bemish, almost knocking him over. He lost his balance and regained it only because he supported himself with one hand on the ground. She must have known that she had very nearly upset him but she went marching toward the house, her back very straight and her head up in the air, and she never once looked back.

Dottle said, "Have I offended her?"

My mother said, "It's late. It's time we went in."

Mr. Bemish must have gone home when we went in the house, but he was back in the yard so early the next morning he might just as well have spent the night. Dottle and I were standing in the kitchen, looking down at the back yard. He was drinking coffee out of a mug and I was eating a piece of bread and butter. Our back yard is a pretty sight on a summer morning. It is filled with flowers, and birds are singing, and the air is very cool; and there is a special smell, a summer smell compounded of grass and dew on the grass and flowers, and the suggestion of heat to come later in the day.

We looked out the door and there was Mr. Bemish down on

his knees in front of Aunt Sophronia. She was sitting on the bench and she looked horrified, and she seemed to have been in the act of trying to stop him, one hand extended in a thrusting-away motion. I thought: His pants legs will be very damp because there's still dew on the grass, and how did he get here so early, and did he know that she would be sitting on the bench almost before sunup?

"Ah, girlie, girlie!" he said, on his knees in our back yard, kneeling on our thick, soft grass. "Will you marry me?"

"No!"

"Is it," he said, "because I am old?" and his voice went straight up in pitch just like a scale. "I'm not old. I'm not old. Why, I can still jump up in the air and click my heels together three times!"

And he did. He got up off his knees and he jumped up, straight up, and clicked his heels together three times, and landed on the grass, and there was just a slight thumping sound when he landed.

Aunt Sophronia said, "Mr. Bemish, Mr. Bemish, don't do that — don't do that — go away, go home —" And she ran toward the house and he started after her and then he saw us standing in the door, watching him, and he stood still. He shouted after her, "I'll put on my best coat and my best hat and you won't know me — I'll be back — and you won't know me —"

Dottle glared at him through the screen door and said, "You old fool — you old fool —"

Mr. Bemish hurried around the side of the house, pretending that he hadn't heard him.

I did not know when Mr. Bemish would be back, wearing his best coat and his best hat, but I certainly wanted to see him and, if possible, to witness his next performance. I decided that whenever Aunt Sophronia was in the store, I'd be in the store too.

When my father went to eat his dinner at twelve-thirty, Aunt Sophronia looked after the store. There weren't many people who came in at that hour; it was the dinner hour and Aunt Sophronia sat in the prescription room, with the door open, and read the morning newspaper. There was an old wooden chair by the window, in the prescription room. It had a faded painting across the back, a wooden seat, and back and arms. It was a very comfortable chair if you sat up straight, and Aunt Sophronia sat up very straight. She could look out of the window and see the church green, see the path that went up Petticoat Lane toward the pine woods, and she commanded a view of the interior of the store.

I don't think she saw Mr. Bemish when he entered. If she had, she would have gotten out of the chair immediately to wait on him. But she was reading the newspaper, and he came in very quietly. He was wearing a cutaway coat that was too long, and a pair of striped trousers, and he was carrying a silk hat in his hand, a collapsed silk hat. He stopped inside the door and put the hat in shape and then placed it carefully on his head. He looked like a circus clown who is making fun of the ringmaster, mocking him, making his costume look silly.

Mr. Bemish went straight through the store, and stood in front of Aunt Sophronia, and he jumped straight up in the air, like a dancer, and clicked his heels together three times. The bottles on the shelves rattled and the back room was filled with a pinging sound.

"Oh, my goodness," Aunt Sophronia said, frowning. "Oh, my goodness, don't jump like that." And she stood up.

My father came in through the back door and he said, "What's going on in here? What's going on in here?"

Mr. Bemish said, "I was just showing Miss Sophronia that I can still jump up in the air and click my heels together three times before I come back down again."

My father made a noise that sounded like "Boooooh!" but wasn't quite, and Mr. Bemish retreated, talking very fast. "I had asked Miss Sophronia if she would marry me and she said no, and I thought perhaps it was because she thinks I'm too old and not stylish enough and so I got dressed up and I was showing her I could still jump —"

"Get out of here! Get out of here! Get out of here!"

My father's voice kept rising and increasing in volume, and his face looked as though he were about to burst. It seemed to darken and to swell, to get bigger.

Aunt Sophronia said, "Oh, you mustn't talk to him like that —"

My father was moving toward Mr. Bemish, and Mr. Bemish was retreating, retreating, and finally he turned and ran out of the store and ran up Petticoat Lane with his long coattails flapping about his legs.

My father said, "I shouldn't have let him hang around here all these months. I can't leave this store for five minutes that I don't find one of these no-goods hangin' around when I come back. Not one of 'em worth the powder and shot to blow 'em to hell and back. That piano player pawin' the ground and this old white man jumpin' up in the air, and that friend of Johno's, that poet or whatever he is, all he needs are some starched petticoats and a bonnet and he'd make a woman — he's practically one now — and he's tee-heein' around, and if they were all put together in one piece, it still wouldn't be a whole man." My father shook his fist in the air and glared at Aunt Sophronia.

"I guess it's all my fault —" Aunt Sophronia sounded choked-up and funny.

My father said, "No, no, no, I didn't mean that," and patted her arm. "It's all perfectly natural. It's just that we're the only black people living in this little bit of town and there aren't any fine young black men around, only this tramp piano player, and every time I look at him I can hear him playing some rags and see a whole line of big-bosomed women done up in sequined dresses standin' over him, moanin' about wantin' somebody to turn their dampers down, and I can see poker games and crap games and —"

My mother came in through the back room. She said, "Samuel, why are you talking about gambling games?"

"I was trying to explain to Sophy how I feel about that piano player."

To my surprise, my mother said, "Has Sophronia asked you how you feel about Mr. Johnson?"

When my father shook his head, she said, "Then I don't think there is any reason for you to say anything about him. I need you in the garden. I want you to move one of my peonies."

I wonder what my mother would say if she knew how my father chased little Mr. Bemish out of his store. I wonder if Mr. Bemish will ever come back.

Mr. Bemish did come back. He came back the following Sunday. We were all in the store — Aunt Sophronia, and Dottle, and Chink and I.

Mr. Bemish sidled in through the door. He looked as though he expected someone to jump out at him and yell, "Go home!" But he came in anyway and he sat down beside me on the bench near the front of the store.

Chink was leaning on the cigar case, talking to Aunt Sophronia, his face very close to hers. I couldn't hear what he was saying, but he seemed to be trying to persuade her to do something, go for a walk, or something, and she was obviously refusing, politely but definitely. Dottle was standing near the back of the store, watching Chink.

Aunt Frank opened the store door, and she stood in the doorway holding the screen door open. She has a cross, sharp way of speaking, very fast and very unpleasant. She saw me and she said, "Where's Mar-tha?"

I wasn't expecting to see Aunt Frank in the store at that hour and I was so surprised that I didn't answer her.

"What's the mat-ter with you? Cat got your tongue? Didn't you hear what I said? Where's your moth-er?"

"She's over on the other side of the building, in the kitchen. She's having coffee with my father."

She scowled at Chink. "How long's that bearded man been in here talkin' to Sophy?"

Chink turned around and looked toward Aunt Frank. Aunt Sophronia started toward her, moving very fast out from behind the cigar case, saying, "Can I get something for you?"

As Aunt Frank stood there holding the door open, a whole flight of bats came in the store. I say a "flight" because I don't know what else to call a large-sized group of bats. They swooped down and up in a blind, fast flight.

Aunt Frank shrieked, "Ahhh! My hair, watch out for your hair! Ahhhhhh!" and stood up on the bench, and held her black fusty skirts close about her and then pulled them over her head. I decided she had confused mice and bats, that the technique for getting rid of mice was to stand on a chair and clutch one's skirts around one, that is, if you were a lady and pretended to be afraid of mice. I did learn that Aunt Frank was wearing carpet slippers made of dark gray felt, black cotton stockings, and under the outside layer of skirts there seemed to be a great many layers of black petticoats.

Dottle ran into the back room and held the door tightly shut. There is a glass in the door and he could look out at the rest of us as we dodged the bats. I could see his large pale face, and long hair, and I supposed he was as frightened as Aunt Frank that bats would get entangled in his hair, because he squealed, all the rich, buttery quality gone from his voice, just a high-pitched squealing.

Aunt Frank cautiously lowered the outer skirt, fumbled in a pocket, and took out a bottle — not a big bottle, but about the size of an eight-ounce cough medicine bottle — and she took two or three swigs from it, recorked it, and then re-covered her head.

Chink grabbed a newspaper and slapped at the bats as they circled. "Gotcha. Hi-hi-gotcha — hi-hi-gotcha — hi-hi!" and he folded the newspaper and belted them as they swished past him.

Mr. Bemish stared. I decided that he'd lived with bats and spiders and mice, well, not lived with perhaps, but was so accustomed to them that he could not understand why they should cause all this noise and confusion and fear. He ignored the bats entirely and went to the rescue of his lady love. He clasped Aunt Sophronia to his bosom, covering her head with his hands and arms and he kept murmuring comforting words. "Now, now, I won't let anything hurt you. Nothing can harm you." He took a deep breath and said, quite distinctly, "I love you, my darling. I love you, love you —"

Aunt Sophronia seemed to nestle in his arms, to cuddle closer to him, to lean harder every time a bat swooped past them.

Father came through the back room — he had to wrestle

Dottle out of the way before he could get through the door —
and he very sensibly held the screen door open, and what with
the impetus offered by Chink's folded newspaper, the bats
swooped outside.

It was really very exciting while it lasted, what with all the
shrieks and the swift movement of the bats. When I began to
really look around, the first thing I noticed was that Aunt Sophronia was still huddled in the protective arms of Mr. Bemish.
Dottle came out of the back room with his mouth pursed and
his cheeks were puffed out a little and I wouldn't have been
surprised if he had hissed at Mr. Bemish. He and Chink
headed straight toward Mr. Bemish. They are very tall men
and Mr. Bemish is short and slender, and as they converged on
him, one from the rear and the other from the side, he looked
smaller and older than ever.

Aunt Sophronia stepped away from Mr. Bemish. She moved
toward Chink. One side of her face was red where it had been
pressed hard against the wool of Mr. Bemish's coat.

All of a sudden my father's hand was resting on one of
Chink's shoulders. He has large, heavy hands and his hand
seemed to have descended suddenly and with great weight. He
said, "You'll not start any trouble in my store."

Aunt Frank said, "Bats! Bats!" She indicated that my father
was to help her down from the bench. She climbed down awkwardly, holding on to him. "Worse than bats," she said, and she
made a wide all-inclusive gesture that took in Chink and Dottle
and Mr. Bemish. "Where's Mar-tha?" she demanded. "She still
in the kitchen?"

My father nodded. He held the door open for Mr. Bemish
and Mr. Bemish scuttled out. Dottle and Chink went out too.

I found a dead bat on the floor and sat down on the bench at the front of the store to examine it. It had a very unpleasant smell. But it was such an interesting creature that I ignored the odor. It had rather large, pointed ears that I thought were quite charming. It had very sharp little claws. I could see why the ladies had screamed and covered their heads, because if those claws got entangled in their long hair, someone would have had to cut their hair to get a bat out of it. Aunt Frank's hair isn't long; it is like a sheep's wool, tight-curled and close to the skin or scalp. But I suppose a bat's sharp little claws and peculiar wings snarled up in that might create more of a problem than it would if caught in longer and less tightly curled hair.

The wings of the bat were webbed like the feet of ducks, with a thin membranelike tissue that was attached to the body, reaching from the front legs or arms to the back legs and attached to the sides. The body was small in comparison to the wide sweep of those curious wings. I stretched its wings out and they looked like the inside of an opened umbrella, and I couldn't help admiring them. I began to think of all the things I'd heard said about bats, "blind as a bat," and the word "batty" meaning crazy, and I tried to figure out why "batty." Probably because a bat's behavior didn't make sense to a human being — its fast, erratic flight would look senseless.

Then Aunt Frank's voice sounded right in my ear, and her horrible breath was in my nose, and she smelled worse than the bat. She said, "You throw that nasty thing away. You throw that nasty thing away."

I thrust the dead bat straight at her black and wrinkled face. "Look out," I yelled. "It'll suck your blood. It's still alive. Look out!"

She jumped away, absolutely furious. "You little vixen," she said, and squealed just like a pig. Then she saw my mother standing in the door of the prescription room. "Mar-tha," she commanded, "you come here and make her throw this nasty thing away. Make her throw it away. She's settin' here playin' with a dead bat."

My mother said, "If you want to look at the bat, take it outside or take it in the back room. You can't keep a dead bat here in the drugstore."

"This can't hurt her. It's dead."

She interrupted me. "Many people are afraid of bats. It doesn't make any difference whether the bats are dead or alive — they are still afraid of them."

I went outside and sat on the front steps and waited. There was a full moon and the light from it made the street and the houses and the church look as though they had been white-washed. I put the bat beside me on the step. I was going to wait for Aunt Frank, and when she came out of the store and started down the steps, I was going to put the dead stinking bat in one of the big pockets in her skirt — the pocket where she kept her bottle of gin. And when she got home and reached for a drink, I hoped she would discover, encounter, touch with her bony fingers, the corpse of "one of the nocturnal or crepuscular flying mammals constituting the order Chiroptera" as a token of my affection.

I must have waited there on the steps for two hours. My father began putting out the lights in the store. I stayed right there, anticipating the moment when my ancient enemy, Aunt Frank, would come stumbling around the side of the building.

And then — one moment I was sitting on the splintery front steps of the store, and the next moment I was running up Petticoat Lane, going just as fast as I could, because it had suddenly occurred to me that Chink Johnson and Dottle Smith had gone out of the drugstore right behind Mr. Bemish and they hadn't returned.

By the time I reached Mr. Bemish's shop, I was panting. I couldn't catch my breath.

Mr. Bemish's wagon was drawn up close to the side of the shop. The horse was hitched to it. Mr. Bemish was loading the headboard of his beautiful brass bed on the wagon. He was obviously moving — leaving town — at night. He walked in a peculiar fashion as though he were lame. He was panting too, and making hiccupping noises like someone who has been crying a long time, so long that no real sound comes out, just a kind of hiccupping noise due to the contractions of the throat muscles and the heaving of the chest.

As I stood there, he got the headboard on the wagon, and then he struggled with his mattress, and then the springs, and then he brought out his cobbler's bench.

Dottle and Chink stood watching him, just like two guards or two sheriffs. None of us said anything.

I finally sat down on the enormous millstone that served as Mr. Bemish's front step. I sat way off to one side where I wouldn't interfere with his comings and goings.

May-a-ling, his cat, rubbed against me and then came and sat in my lap, with her back to me, facing toward Mr. Bemish.

It didn't take him very long to empty the shop of his belongings. I couldn't help thinking that if we ever moved, it would take us days to pack all the books and the pictures and the china, and all our clothes and furniture. We all collected things. Aunt Sophronia did beautiful embroidery and she collected embroidered fabrics, and Mother collected old dishes and old furniture, and my father collected old glass bottles and old mortars, and they all collected books, and then all the rooms had furniture and there were all kinds of cooking pots. No one of us would ever get all of his belongings in one wagon.

Mr. Bemish came out of the shop and walked all around the little building with that peculiar stiff-legged gait. Apparently the only item he'd overlooked was his garden bench. He had trouble getting it in the wagon, and I dumped May-a-ling on the ground and went to help him.

One of Dottle's meaty hands gripped my braid. "He can manage."

I twisted away from him. "He's just a little old man and he's my friend and I'm going to help him."

Chink said, "Leave her alone."

Dottle let go of my hair. I helped put the bench in the wagon, and then went inside the shop with him, and helped him carry out the few items that were left. Each time I went inside the shop with Mr. Bemish I asked him questions. We both whispered.

"Where are you going, Mr. Bemish?"

"Massachusetts."

"Why?"

He didn't answer. His hiccups got worse.

I waited until we'd taken down the green summer curtains and carefully folded them, and put them in the little trunk that held some of his clothes, and put his broom and his dustpan and his tall kitchen cooking stool on the wagon, before I repeated my question. His hiccups had quieted down.

"Why are you leaving, Mr. Bemish?" I whispered.

"They were going to sew me up."

"Sew you up. Did you say — sew you up?"

"Yes."

"Where?" I said, staring at him, thinking: Sew up? Sew up what — eyes, nostrils, mouth, ears, rectum? "They were trying to scare you, Mr. Bemish. Nobody would sew up a person, a human being, unless it was a surgeon — after an operation —"

He shook his head. "No," he whispered. "I thought so too, but — no, they meant it — with my own waxed thread —"

"Did they —"

"Hush! Hush!"

We used this little piece of flowered carpet to wrap his wash-bowl and pitcher in and then put the whole bulky package it made on the wagon. We went back inside to make sure that we hadn't forgotten anything. The inside of his shop looked very small and shabby and lonely. There wasn't anything left except his stove and he obviously couldn't take that. It was a very big, handsome stove and he kept it quite shiny and clean.

"Can you keep a secret?" he whispered, standing quite close to me. He smelled old and dusty and withered like dried flowers.

I nodded.

He handed me a small velvet bag. "Hide it, girlie," he whispered. "It's some old jewelry that belonged to my mother. Give it to Miss Sophronia at Christmas from me." He patted my arm.

We went outside and he took down the sign with the lady's high-laced shoe painted on it, and put it on the wagon seat. He climbed in the wagon, picked up the reins.

"May-a-ling, May-a-ling," he called. It was the most musical sound I have ever heard used to call a cat. She answered him instantly. She mewed and jumped up on the wagon seat beside him. He clucked to the horse and they were off.

I waited not only until they were out of sight, but until I

could no longer hear the creak of the wagon wheels and the clop-clop of the horse's hoofs, and then I turned and ran.

Chink said, "Wait a minute —"

Dottle said, "You don't understand —"

I stopped running just long enough to shout at them, "You both stink. You stink like dead bats. You and your goddamn Miss Muriel —"

The New Mirror

My MOTHER SAID, "Where is your father?" She was standing outside the door of the downstairs bathroom. Even if she had been farther away, I would have understood what she said, because her voice had a peculiar quality just this side of harshness, which made it carry over longer distances than other people's voices.

From inside the bathroom, I said, "He's in the back yard listening to the bees."

"Please tell him that breakfast is ready."

"Right away," I said. But I didn't tell him right away. I didn't move. We had had a late, cold spring, with snow on the ground until the end of April. Then in May the weather turned suddenly warm and the huge old cherry trees in our yard blossomed almost overnight. There were three of them, planted in a straight line down the middle of the back yard. As soon as the sun was up, it seemed as though all the honeybees in Wheeling, New York, came to the trees in swarms. Every sunny morning, my father stood under one of those bloom-filled cherry trees and listened to the hum of the bees. My mother knew this just as well as I did, but she was sending a bathroom dawdler to carry a message to a cherry-tree dawdler so that she would finally have both of us in the dining room for breakfast at the same time.

I spent the next ten minutes looking at myself in the new plate-glass mirror that had been hung over the basin just the day before. A new electrical fixture had been installed over the mirror. My mother had had these changes made so that my father could shave downstairs. She said this would be more convenient for him, because it placed him closer to the drugstore while he shaved. Our drugstore was in the front of the building where we lived.

The bathroom walls were white, and under the brilliant, all-revealing light cast by the new fixture I looked like all dark creatures impaled on a flat white surface: too big, too dark. My skin was a muddy brown, not the clear, dark brown I had always supposed it to be. I turned my head and the braid of hair that reached halfway down my back looked like a thick black snake. It even undulated slightly as I moved. I grabbed the braid close to my head and looked around for a pair of scissors, thinking I would cut the braid off, because it was an absolutely revolting hair style for a fifteen-year-old girl. But there weren't any scissors, so I released my grip on the braid and took another look at myself — head-on in the glittering mirror. I decided that the way I looked in that white-walled bathroom was the way our family looked in the town of Wheeling, New York. We were the only admittedly black family in an all-white community and we stood out; we looked strange, alien. There was another black family — the Granites — but they claimed to be Mohawk Indians. Whenever my father mentioned them, he laughed until tears came to his eyes, saying, "Mohawks? Ha, ha, ha. Well, five or six generations of Fanti tribesmen must have caught five or six generations of those Mohawk females named Granite under a bush somewhere. Ha, ha, ha."

He never said things like that in the drugstore. He and my mother and my aunts kept their private lives and their thoughts about people inside the family circle, deliberately separating the life of the family from the life of the drugstore. But it didn't work the other way around, for practically everything we did was decided in terms of whether it was good or bad for the drugstore. I liked the store, and I liked working in it on Saturdays and after school, but it often seemed to me a monstrous, mindless, sightless force that shaped our lives into any old pattern it chose, and it chose the patterns at random.

I turned out the light and went to tell my father that breakfast was ready. He was standing motionless under the first big cherry tree. He had his back turned, but I could tell from the way he held his head that he was listening intently. He was short, and seen from the back like that, his torso looked as though it had been designed for a bigger man.

"Yoo-hoo!" I shouted, as though I were calling someone at least two hundred feet away from me. "Break-fast. Break-fast." In my mind, I said, "Sam-u-el, Sam-u-el." But I didn't say that out loud.

He did not turn around. He lifted his hand in a gesture that pushed the sound of my voice away, indicating that he had heard me and that I was not to call him again.

I sat down on the back steps to wait for him. Though the sun was up, it was cool in the yard. The air was filled with a delicate fragrance that came from all the flowering shrubs, from the cherry blossoms and the pear blossoms, and from the small plants — violets and daffodils. A song sparrow was singing somewhere close by. I told myself that if I were a maker of perfumes I would make one and call it "Spring," and it would smell like this cool, sweet, early-morning air and I would let only beautiful young brown girls use it, and if I could sing I would sing like the song sparrow and I would let only beautiful young brown boys hear me.

When we finally went into the house and sat down to breakfast, my father said (just as he did every spring) that the honeybees buzzed on one note and that it was E-flat just below middle C but with a difference. He said he had never been able to define this in the musical part of his mind and so had decided that it was the essential difference in the sound produced by the buzzing of a bee and the sound produced by a human voice lifted in song. He also said that he wouldn't want to live anywhere else in the world except right here in Wheeling, New York, in the building that housed our drugstore, with that big back yard with those cherry trees in it, so that in the spring of the year, when the trees were in full bloom, he could stand under them smelling that cherry-blossom sweet air and listening to those bees holding that one note — E-flat below middle C. Then he said, "When I was out there just now, that first cherry tree was so aswarm with life, there were so many bees moving around bumping into the blossoms and making that buzzing sound, that hum . . . " He touched his forehead lightly with one of his big hands, as though he were trying to stimulate his thinking processes. "You know, I could have sworn that tree spoke to me."

I leaned toward him, waiting to hear what he was going to say. I did not believe the tree had said anything to him, but I wanted to know what it was he *thought* the tree had said. It seemed to me a perfect moment for this kind of revelation. We had just finished eating an enormous breakfast: grapefruit and oatmeal and scrambled eggs and sausage and hot cornmeal muffins. This delicious food and this sunny room in which we had eaten it were pleasant segments of the private part of our life, totally separated from the drugstore, which was the public part. I relished the thought that the steady stream of white customers who went in and out of our drugstore did not know what our dining room was like, did not even know if we had one. It was like having a concealed weapon to use against your enemy.

The dining room was a square-shaped, white-walled room on the east side of the building. The brilliant light of the morning sun was reflected from the walls so that the whole room seemed to shimmer with light and the walls were no longer white but a pale yellow. I thought my father looked quite handsome in this room. His skin was a deep reddish brown and he was freshly shaved. He had used an after-shave lotion, and it gave his face a shiny look. He was bald-headed, and in this brilliantly sunlit room the skin on his face and on his head looked as though it had been polished.

The dining room table was oak. It was square, well suited to the square shape of the room. The chairs had tall backs and there was a design across the top of each one. The design looked as though it had been pressed into the wood by some kind of machine.

My mother sat at one end of the table and my father sat at the other end, in armchairs. I sat on one side of the table, and my Aunt Sophronia sat on the other side. She was my mother's youngest sister. She and my mother looked very much alike, though she was lighter in color than my mother. They were both short, rather small-boned women. Their eyes looked black, though they were a very dark brown. They wore their hair the same way — piled up on top of their heads. My mother's hair was beginning to turn gray, but Aunt Sophronia's was black. There was a big difference in their voices. Aunt Sophronia's voice was low-pitched, musical — a very gentle voice.

My aunt and my mother and father were drinking their second cups of coffee and I was drinking my second glass of milk when my father said he thought the cherry tree had spoken to him. They both looked at him in surprise.

I asked, "What did the tree say?"

"It bent down toward me and it said . . ." He paused, beckoned to me to lean toward him a little more. He lowered his voice. "The tree said, 'Child of the sun — '" He stopped talking and looked directly at me. In that sun-washed room, his eyes were reddish brown, almost the same color as his skin, and I got the funny feeling that I had never really looked right at him before, and that he believed the tree had said something to him, and I was shocked. He whispered, "The tree said, 'It will soon be time to go and open the drugstore!'"

I scowled at him and he threw his head back and laughed, making a roaring, explosive sound. It was just as though he had said, "Got you, you idiot — you — ha, ha, ha." He opened his mouth so wide I could see his gums, red and moist, see the three teeth that he had left, one in the upper jaw and two in the lower jaw, even see his tonsils. I began muttering to him in my mind, "How do you chew your food, old toothless one with the red-brown skin and the bald head. Go up, thou bald head. Go up, thou bald-headed black man."

Right after breakfast, I helped my father open the drugstore for the day. I was still annoyed that he had been able to fool me into thinking he believed a cherry tree had spoken to him, but I so enjoyed working in the drugstore that I would not deny myself that pleasure simply because he had deliberately talked nonsense and I had been stupid enough to believe him.

He swept the floor with a big soft-bristled broom. Then he went outside and swept off the long, wooden steps that ran all the way across the front of the building. He left the front door open, and the cool, sweet-smelling early-morning air dispelled the heavy odor of cigars, the sticky vanilla smell from the soda fountain and the medicinal smell of the prescription room — part alcohol, part spicy things, part disinfectant.

I put change in both the cash registers — the one in the store proper and the one behind the fountain. The fountain was in a separate room, rather like a porch with a great many windows. I put syrups in the fountain — chocolate, Coca-Cola, root beer, lemon, cherry, vanilla. The chocolate syrup had a mouth-watering smell, and the cherry and the lemon syrups smelled like a fruit stand on a hot summer day, but the root beer and the Coca-Cola syrups smelled like metal.

Our black and white cat sat in the doorway and watched my father. The cat yawned, opening his mouth wide, and I could see his wonderful flexible pink tongue and his teeth — like the teeth of a tiger, only smaller, of course. I wondered if cats ever became practically toothless, like my father. He wouldn't have cavities filled because he said all that silver or amalgam or gold or whatever it was, and all that X-raying that butter-fingered dentists do, and all that use of Novocain was what made people develop cancer of the jaw. When his teeth hurt and the dentist said the pain was due to a big cavity, he simply had the tooth pulled out without an anesthetic. Once I asked him if it hurt to have teeth pulled without Novocain or gas. He said, "Of course it hurts. But it is a purely temporary hurt. The roots of my teeth go straight down and it is a very simple matter to pull them out. I've pulled some of them out myself."

I sorted the newspapers, looked at the headlines, quickly skimmed the inside of the Buffalo News. I saw a picture of a man, obviously an actor, wearing a straw hat. I wanted the picture because of his tooth-revealing grin, and I reminded myself to cut it out. The newspapers that didn't sell were returned for credit. Quite often I snipped out items that interested me. I always hunted for articles that dealt with the importance of chewing food thoroughly, and for pictures of men with no teeth, and for pictures of very handsome men exposing a great many teeth. I intended to leave this particular picture on the prescription counter, where my father would be sure to see it.

When Aunt Sophronia came to work at nine o'clock, the store was clean and it smelled good inside. Like my father, she was a pharmacist, and when he was not in the store, she was there. She wore dark skirts and white shirtwaists when she was working, and she put on a gray cotton store coat so that people would know she worked in the store and would not think she was a customer.

One other person worked in the drugstore — Pedro, a twelve-year-old Portuguese boy. He was supposed to arrive at nine on Saturdays and Sundays. He was always prompt and the first stroke of the town clock had not yet sounded when he came hurrying into the store. He was a very sturdily built boy, with big dark eyes. He had an enormous quantity of tangled black hair. He couldn't afford to have his hair cut at the barbershop, so my father cut it for him. The first time I saw him cutting Pedro's hair out in the back room, I asked him if he knew how to cut hair.

He said, "No."

I said, "Well, how do you know what to do?"

"I don't," he said, snipping away with the scissors. "But I can shorten it some. Otherwise, he'll look like a girl."

Though Pedro was fond of all of us, he had a special feeling about my father. He told my father that he would like to stay in the store all the time — he could sleep in the back room, and all he needed was a blanket and a mattress and he could bring those from home, and he would provide his own food and clothes. There were eleven kids in his family, and I imagine he preferred being part of a family in which there were fewer people, and so decided to become a member of our family. My father wouldn't let him sleep in the back room, but Pedro did manage to spend most of his waking hours (when he wasn't in school, of course) at the store. He provided his own food. He ate oranges, sucking out the juice and the pulp. He hung a big smoked sausage from one of the rafters in the back room and sliced off pieces of it for his lunch. He loved fresh pineapple, and he was always saying that the only thing in the world he'd ever steal if he couldn't get it any other way would be a ripe pineapple.

At one minute after nine, my father went to the post office. When he left, he was holding some letters that he was going to mail. I thought his hand looked big and very dark holding all those white envelopes. I went to the door and watched him as he walked up the street, past the elm trees, past the iron urn on the village green, past the robins and the tender green young grass on each side of the gravel path. He had a stiff straw hat tilted just a little toward the back of his head. As he moved off up the street, he was whistling "Ain't goin' to study war no more, no more, no more."

We were so busy in the store that morning that I did not realize what time it was until my mother called up to find out why my father had not been home for his noon meal. There was such a sharp line of demarcation between house and store that my mother always telephoned the drugstore when she had a message for my father.

Aunt Sophronia answered the phone. I heard her say, "He's not in the store right now — he's probably in the cellar. We'll send him right along." After she hung up the receiver, she said, "See if your father is in the cellar unpacking stock or way down in the yard burning rubbish."

He wasn't in the cellar and he wasn't in the back yard. The burner was piled high with the contents of the wastebasket from the prescription room (junk mail, empty pillboxes, old labels) and the contents of the rubbish box from the fountain (straws, paper napkins, Popsicle wrappers).

All three cherry trees were still filled with bees, and they were buzzing on their one note. I walked from one tree to the next, pausing to listen, looking up into the white blossoms, and the trees seemed to be alive in a strange way because of the comings and goings of the bees. As I stood there, I felt it would be very easy to believe that those trees could speak to me.

I went back to the drugstore, and Aunt Sophronia said, "You didn't see him?"

"No. And I don't think he ever came back from the post office. Each time someone asked for him, I thought he was in the back room or down in the cellar or outside in the yard. And each time, whoever it was wanted him said they'd come back later, and I never really had to look for him."

"I'll call the post office and ask if he's picked up our packages, and that way I'll find out if he's been there without actually saying that we're looking for him."

I could hear her end of the conversation, and obviously he hadn't been in the post office at all that morning. She hung up the telephone and called the railroad station and asked if Mr. Layen had been there to get an express package. The station-master had a big booming voice, and I could hear him say, "No." Aunt Sophronia said, "You would have seen him if he had been at the station?" He said, "I certainly would."

Pedro and I wanted to go and look for my father. Aunt Sophronia snapped at us, saying, "Don't be foolish. Where would you look? In the river? In the taverns? Your father wouldn't kill himself, and he doesn't drink . . ."

She frightened me. She had frightened Pedro, too; he was pale and his eyes looked bigger. I had thought my father was late for dinner because he had stopped somewhere to talk and got involved in a long-winded conversation, and that if Pedro and I had walked up or down the street we would have found him and told him his dinner was ready. Aunt Sophronia obviously thought something dreadful had happened to him. Now we began to think so, too.

We kept waiting on the customers just as though there was no crisis in our family. I kept saying to myself, "Your father dies, your mother dies, you break your leg or your back, you stand in a pool of cold sweat from a fever, you stand in a pool of warm blood from a wound, and you go out in the store and smile and say, 'Fine, just fine, we're all fine, nothin's ever wrong with us cull-ed folks.' "

Whenever the store was empty, my aunt would say nervously, "What could have happened to him?" And then clear her throat two or three times in quick succession — a sure sign that she was upset and frightened. Later in the afternoon she said in a queer way, just as though he had passed out of our lives and she was already reminiscing about him, "He did everything at exactly the same time every day. He always said that was the only way you could run a store — have a certain time for everything and stick to it."

This was true. He opened the drugstore promptly at eight, he went to get the mail promptly at nine, and he ate his dinner at twelve. At four in the afternoon, he drank a bottle of Moxie — the only soda pop that he regarded as fit for human consumption. (He said if that were ever taken off the market he would have to drink tea, which upset his stomach because it was a drink suited to the emotional needs of the Chinese, the East Indians, the English, the Irish, and nervous American females, and it had, therefore, no value for him, representing as he did a segment of a submerged population group only a few generations out of Africa, where his ancestors had obviously been witch doctors.)

On Sundays he went to church. He went in through the rear entrance and into the choir loft from the back about two minutes after the service started. There was a slight stir as the ladies of the choir and the other male singer (a tall, thin man who sang bass) rearranged themselves to make room for him. He sang a solo almost every Sunday, for he had a great big, beautiful tenor voice. On Sundays he smelled strongly of aftershave lotion, and on weekdays he smelled faintly of after-shave lotion.

My aunt kept saying, "Where would he go? Where would he go?"

I said, "Maybe he went to Buffalo." I didn't believe this, but she'd have to stop clearing her throat long enough to contradict me.

"What would he go there for? Why wouldn't he say so? How would he get there?"

"He could go on the bus," I said. "Maybe he went to get new eyeglasses. He buys his eyeglasses in the five-and-ten. He likes five-and-tens."

"He hates buses. He says they smell and they lurch."

I laughed. "He says they stink and they lurch in such a way they churn the contents of your belly upside down." She made no comment, so I said again, "He buys his glasses in the five-and-ten in Buffalo and —"

"What?" she said. "I don't believe it."

"It's true. You ask Mother. She said that the last time they went to Buffalo . . ." I tried to remember how long ago that would have been.

"Well?"

"Well, Mother said she wanted to get a new hat and he said that he'd be in the five-and-ten, and there was Samuel and an old black man with him, and they were bent practically double over a counter. She told me, 'Your father had piece of newspaper in his hand and he had on a pair of glasses, and he was looking at this newspaper, saying, "No, not strong enough," and he moved on and picked up another pair of glasses and put them on and said, "Let's see. Ah! Fine!" Then he turned to this old black man, a dreadful-looking old man, ragged and dirty and unshaven and smelling foully of whiskey, and he said to him, "You got yours?" ' Mother said, 'Samuel, whatever are you doing?' Even when she told it, she sounded horrified. He said, 'I'm getting my glasses.' Then he asked the old man if he'd got his, and the old man nodded and looked at Mother and sort of slunk away. I suppose she had on one of those flowered hats and white gloves. Mother said she looked at the counter and there were rows and rows of glasses and they were all fifty cents apiece. And that's what Samuel uses — that's what he's always used. He says that he doesn't need special lenses, that he hasn't anything unusual the matter with his eyes. All he needs is some magnifying glass so that he can see to read small printed matter, and so that's why he buys his glasses in the five-and-ten." I stopped talking.

My aunt didn't say anything. She frowned at me.

So I started again. "He gets two pair at a time. Sometimes he loses them. Sometimes he breaks them. You know he likes to push them up high on top of his forehead, out of the way when he isn't using them, and his bald head is always greasy or sweaty and the glasses slide off on the floor and quite often they break. Didn't you know that?"

She said, "No, and I wish you'd stop calling your father Samuel." She went to wait on a customer.

I sat down on the high stool in front of the prescription counter. I didn't believe that my father had gone to Buffalo. He wouldn't go away without leaving any message. I wondered if he'd been kidnapped, and dismissed the idea as ridiculous. Something must have happened to him.

My mother called the store again, and right afterward Aunt Sophronia told Pedro to go in through the kitchen door and get coffee and sandwiches that Mrs. Layen had made and bring them into the store. We ate in the back room, one at a time. We didn't eat very much. I didn't like the smell of the coffee. It has always seemed to me that the human liver doesn't like coffee, that it makes the liver shiver. But all my family drank

coffee and so did Pedro, and they didn't like to have me tell
them how I felt about it.

I sat in the back room with that liver-shivering smell in my
nose and looked out the back door. It was a pleasant place to sit
and eat. It was a big room, and the rafters in the ceiling were
exposed. True, there was a lot of clutter — pots and pans and
mops and brooms, and big copper kettles stuck in corners or
hanging from the rafters, and piles of old newspapers and magazines stacked on empty cartons. The walls were lined with
small boxes that contained herbs. Some wholesale druggist had
thrown them out, and my father had said he'd take them, because a dried herb would be good a hundred years from now; if
it were properly dried, it would not lose its special properties.
The back room always smelled faintly of aromatic substances
— a kind of sneeze-making smell. The door was open, and I
could look out into the back yard and see the cherry trees and
the forsythia and all the flowering shrubs and the tender new
grass.

We were very busy in the store all that afternoon. At five
o'clock, my mother came in through the back door and sat
down in the prescription room. She kept looking out of the window, toward the green. She had on a hat — a dark blue straw
hat with small white flowers across the front — and her best
black summer suit and white gloves. She was obviously dressed
for an emergency, for disaster, prepared to identify Samuel
Layen in hospital or morgue or police station.

The customers came in a steady stream. They bought the
afternoon papers, cigarettes, tobacco. Men on their way home
from work stopped to get ice cream for dessert. As the afternoon wore along, the shadows from the elm trees lengthened

until they were as long as the green was wide. The iron urn in
the middle looked chalk white. As the daylight slowly diminished, the trunks of the trees — that great expanse of trunk
without branches, characteristic of the elms — seemed to be
darkening and darkening.

I turned on the lights in the store and the student lamp on
the prescription counter. It wasn't really quite dark enough to
justify turning on the lights and I thought my aunt would say
this, but she didn't. She asked my mother if she would like a
glass of ginger ale.

"That would be very nice, thank you," my mother said. Her
voice was deeper and harsher, and its carrying quality seemed
to have increased.

"Pedro, get Mrs. Layen a glass of ginger ale."

When Pedro brought the ginger ale, Mother took a sip of it
and then put it on the windowsill. It stayed there — bubbles
forming, breaking, breaking, forming, breaking, until finally it
was just a glass of yellowish liquid sitting forgotten on the windowsill.

When there weren't any customers in the store, we all went
into the prescription room and sat down and waited with my
mother. We sat in silence — Pedro and Aunt Sophronia and my
mother and I. I kept thinking, But my father wouldn't leave us
of his own free will. Only this morning at breakfast he said he
wouldn't want to live anywhere else in the world except right
here where we live. It could be suicide, or he could have been
murdered. Certainly not kidnapped for ransom. What do we
own? We don't own a car. There's the old building where we
live and there's the store with its ancient mahogany-colored fixtures and glass-enclosed cases and the fountain room. But if it
were all put together with our clothes and our household goods

— pots and pans and chairs and tables and sofas and beds and mirrors — it wouldn't add up to anything to kidnap a man for.

Then I thought, Perhaps he left my mother for another woman. Preposterous. He was always saying that the first time he saw her she was sixteen and he decided right then and there he was going to marry her; she had big, black, snappy eyes, and her skin was so brown and so beautiful. His friends said he would be robbing the cradle, because he was twenty-four. He did marry her when she was eighteen. He said that whenever he looked at her he always thought, Black is the color of my true love's hair.

Aunt Sophronia said, "Perhaps we should put something in the newspaper — something . . . "

My mother said, "No," harshly. "The Layens would descend like a horde of locusts, crying, 'Samuel! Samuel! Samuel!' No. They all read the Buffalo *Recorder* and they would be down from Buffalo before we could turn around twice. Sometimes I think they use some form of astral projection. No. We won't put anything in the newspapers, not even if . . ."

I knew she was going to say, or had stopped herself from saying, "even if he is dead," though I did not see how she could keep an account of his death out of the newspapers.

My mother said my father's family was like a separate and warlike tribe — arrogant, wary, hostile. She thought they were probably descended from the Watusi. In Buffalo, they moved through the streets in groups of three or four. She always had the impression they were stalking something. Their voices were very low in pitch, almost guttural, and unless you listened closely you got the impression they were not speaking English but were simply making an accented sound — uh-uh-uh-*uh* — that only they could understand.

Whenever my great-grandfather, the bearded patriarch of the family, went out on the streets of Buffalo, he was accompanied by one of his grandsons, a boy about fourteen, tall, quick-moving. The boy was always given the same instructions: "Anything happen to your grandfather, anybody say anything to him, you come straight back here, straight back here." "Anybody say anything to him" meant if anyone called him "out of his name." If this occurred, my mother said the boy would go straight home with the old man and emerge in the company of Uncle Joe, Uncle Bill, Uncle Bobby, Uncle John, Uncle George, my father, Aunt Kate, and Aunt Hal — all of them hellbent on vengeance.

They had lived in New Jersey — they always said "Jersey" — at the foot of a mountain they called Sour Mountain. When they first came to New York State, they lived in Albany. The whole clan — Great-Grandma, Great-Grandpa, Grandma and Grandpa, and all eight children including my father, Samuel, and a baby — came to Albany on one of the Hudson River boats. They had six ducks in wooden cages going splat all over the deck, a huge, woolly black dog — ancestry unknown, temper vicious — and six painted parlor chairs that Great-Grandma insisted on bringing with her. The men and boys wore black felt hats, and the skin on their faces and hands was almost as dark as the felt of the hats. They wore heavy black suits that Great-Grandma had made for them. Whenever anyone approached them on the boat, they executed a kind of flanking motion and very quickly formed a circle, the men facing the outside, the women on the inside.

My mother once told she knew all the details about the arrival of these black strangers in Albany, because her family had known a black man who worked on the Hudson River boats and he had told her father about it. When the boat approached the dock, it had to be maneuvered into position, and so it started to move back down the river. It did not go very far, but there was an ever-increasing length of water between the boat and the dock. The sun was out, the brass railings gleamed in the sunlight, and the white paint sparkled as the boat edged away from the dock. The dark-skinner, fierce-looking men held a conference. The old bearded man who was my great-grandfather gave a cry — a trumpeting kind of cry — and took a long running leap off the boat and landed on the dock, hitting it with his cane and bellowing, "You ain't takin' us back now, you know! Throw that baby down to me! Throw that baby down to me!" There were outraged cries from the people on the deck. One of the Layens threw the baby down to the old man and he caught it. He glared up at the scowling deckhands and the staring people and shouted, "Ain't goin' to take us back now, you know! We paid to get here. Ain't going to take us back now. Jump!" he roared. "All of you, jump!"

My mother said the black man told her father this story, and he ended it by saying, "You know, those people jumped off that boat — even the women. They picked up all their stuff, even those damn ducks and that vicious dog and those chairs, and they took these long running leaps and landed on the dock. I never saw anything like it. And that old bearded black man kept walking up and down on the dock, hitting it with his cane, and he's got this baby, dangling it by one foot, and he's hollering out and hollering out, 'We paid to get here! Ain't goin' to take us back now, you know!' "

I sat in the prescription room staring at my mother and thinking again, If my father died, she would not tell his family? Even if he died? She would be afraid to tell them for fear they would arrive in Wheeling and attack all the inhabitants — they would be as devastating as a gang of professional stranglers. Old as he was now, my great-grandfather wouldn't ride in an automobile and he didn't like trains, so he would probably walk down to Wheeling from Buffalo, muttering to himself, intractable, dangerous, his beard quivering with rage, his little eyes blazing with the light of battle.

Customers kept coming into the store. Pedro and I waited on them. Once, when we were both behind the tobacco counter, he said, "I could just walk around in the town and look for him. I wouldn't tell people he was lost."

I shook my head. "Aunt Sophronia wouldn't like it."

Each time the phone rang, I answered it. I left the door of the phone booth open, so they could all hear what I said, in case it was some kind of news about my father. It never was. It was always somebody who wanted some of his chocolate syrup, or his special-formula cold cream, or his lotion for acne. I kept saying the same thing in reply. "He isn't here right now. We expect him, we expect him. When? Later. We expect him later."

There was an automatic closing device on the screen door which kept it from banging shut. It made a hissing sound when the door was opened. Each time we heard that hiss, we all looked toward the door expectantly, thinking perhaps this time it would be Samuel. Finally, Aunt Sophronia turned on a small radio on the prescription counter. There was a great deal of static, voices came in faintly, and there was a thin thread of music in the background — a confusion of sounds. I had never known my aunt to turn on the radio in the store. My father said that only certain kinds of decaying drugstores had radios blatting in them, and that the owners turned them on hoping to distract the customers' attention away from the leaks in the roof, the holes in the floor, the flyblown packages, and the smell of cat.

Aunt Sophronia sat on the high stool in front of the prescription counter, bent forward a little, listening. We all listened. My mother looked down at her hands, Pedro looked at the floor, Aunt Sophronia looked at the black and white linoleum on the counter. I thought, We're waiting to hear one of those fudge-voiced announcers say that a short thick-bodied black man has been found on the railroad track, train gone over him, or he's been found hanging or shot or drowned. Why drowned? Well, the river's close by.

I practiced different versions of the story. "Young woman finds short, thick-bodied, unidentified black man." "School children find colored druggist in river." "Negro pharmacist lost in mountains." "Black man shot by white man in love duel." Colored druggist. Negro pharmacist. Black man. My father? I hovered in the doorway listening to the radio — world news roundup, weather, terrible music. Nothing about unidentified black men.

Aunt Sophronia turned toward my mother and said something in a low voice.

"Police?" my mother said in a very loud voice, and repeated it. "Police?"

"He's been gone since nine o'clock this morning. What else can we do except call the police?"

"No!" My mother's voice was louder and harsher than I had ever heard it. "There's no need to go to the police. We don't know where Samuel is, but if we wait patiently we'll find out." Her eyes were open very wide and they glistened. It occurred to me that they might be luminous in the dark, like a cat's eyes.

"He might have had an accident."

"We would have been informed," my mother said firmly. "His name is engraved on the inside of his watch. His name is on his shirt and on his underwear and his handkerchiefs. I mark everything with indelible ink."

"But if it happened in Buffalo —"

"If what happened? What are you talking about?"

Aunt Sophronia began to cry. Right there in the prescription room. She made so much noise you could hear her out in the store. I was appalled. The private part of our life had suddenly and noisily entered the public part — or perhaps it was the other way around. When people cry and try to talk at the same time, their words come out jerkily and they have to speak between the taking of big convulsive breaths, and so they cannot control the volume of their speech and they shout, and that is what my quiet-voiced Aunt Sophronia was doing. She was shouting right there in the drugstore. Someone came into the store and turned to look toward the prescription room to see what was going on. Pedro ran out of the room to wait on the customer.

"I'm just as fond of him as you are!" Aunt Sophronia shouted between sobs and gasps and agonized-sounding crying noises. "Just as worried as you are! You can't just sit there and let him disappear! And not do anything about it!"

My mother stood up, looked at me, and said, "Call a taxi." Then she turned to my aunt and said, "We will go to the Tenyeck Barracks and discuss this with the state police." Her voice was pitched so low and it was so loud that it sounded like a man's voice.

When the town taxi came, I stood in the doorway and watched them go down the front steps. It was perfectly obvious that my aunt had been crying, for her eyelids were red and swollen. My mother looked ill. They both seemed to have shrunk in size. They were bent over and so looked smaller and shorter than they actually were. When they reached the sidewalk, they turned and glanced up at me. I felt like crying, too. The flowered hat had slipped so far back on my mother's head that it made her look as though she were bald. Aunt Sophronia had a yellow pencil stuck in her hair, and she had put on an old black coat that hung in the back room. The coat was too big for her; the sleeves were too long and it reached almost to her ankles. Under it, she was still wearing the gray cotton store coat. They looked like little old women — humble, questing, moving slowly. When they turned, I could see the white part of their eyes under the irises, and I had to look away from them.

Aunt Sophronia said, "If there are any prescriptions, I'll fill them later." Then she took my mother by the arm and they went toward the taxi. The driver got out and held the door open for them and closed it behind them.

I wondered what my mother would say to the state police. "My husband is missing. He is a short, broad-shouldered black man, bald-headed, forty-eight years old?" Would the state police snicker and say, "Yes, we would hardly expect you, with your dark brown skin, to be married to a white man. Wearing what when last seen?" "Light gray summer suit and polka-dot bow tie, highly polished black shoes." The gravel path that bisects the village green was very dry this morning — no mud. So there would still have been polish on his shoes. But not if he were drowned. But who would drown him, and why? Might have drowned himself. Drowned himself? Surely she will say that he has only three teeth, three teeth only — one in the upper jaw and two in the lower jaw.

Then I thought, But why did they have to *go* to the police? Why couldn't they have telephoned? Because someone might have overheard the conversation. So what difference would that make? Did they think the police would send out a silent and invisible bloodhound to hunt for the black druggist from Wheeling? Did they think the police would send out invisible men to search the morgues in Buffalo, to fish for a fresh black corpse in the streams and coves and brooks in and around Wheeling?

We didn't even hunt for him the way white people would have hunted for their father. It was all indirect. Has he been to the post office? . . . "Oh, oh, oh." Has he been to the railroad station to pick up an express package? . . . "I see, I see, I see."

Between customers I thought, We've even infected Pedro, who is Portuguese, with this disease, whatever it is. Why did we have to hunt for my father this way? Because there is something scandalous about a disappearance, especially if it is a black man who disappears. Could be caused by a shortage of funds (What funds? His own?), a shortage of narcotics, unpaid bills, a mistake made in a prescription — scandal, scandal, scandal. Black druggist, mixed up with police, disappears. Mixed up with police.

It wasn't until Miss Rena Randolph handed me an empty prescription bottle to be refilled that I realized what my aunt had done. I held the sticky bottle in my hand, the label all over gravy drips, as my father was wont to say, and I thought, Why, I'm in charge of the drugstore and I am only fifteen. The only other person working in the store is Pedro, and he is only twelve. All my life I'd heard conversations about "uncovered" drugstores — drugstores without a pharmacist on the premises. For the first time, our store was "uncovered." Suppose something happened . . .

Miss Randolph leaned against the counter and coughed and

coughed and coughed. "I won't need it until morning," she said, pointing at the bottle that I held. "I have more at home. I always keep two bottles ahead."

My father told me once that he thought she looked as though she had just been dug up out of her grave. She was a very unhealthy-looking old woman. She was tall and very thin. Her skin was gray, her clothes were gray, and her hair was gray. But her teeth were yellow. She wore eyeglasses with no rims. Just last week when my father was refilling this same prescription for her, he said, "I don't know what Doc keeps giving her this stuff for. Perfectly obvious what's the matter with her, and this isn't going to cure it."

"What *is* the matter with her?" I asked.

He shrugged his shoulders and said evasively, "Your guess is just as good as mine — or Doc's."

"I can get it in the morning," she repeated now.

"Yes, ma'am. It will be ready in the morning."

"Quiet in here tonight. Where's your aunt?"

"Outside," I said, and the way I said it made it sound as though I meant "transported" or "sold down the river."

She looked around the store as though she were a stranger, seeing it for the first time. She said, "It's a nice night. I suppose she's working in the garden."

After Miss Randolph left, I looked around the store, too. What had she seen that made her say it was a nice night and that my aunt would be working in the garden? You couldn't really see what was on the shelves — just the gleam of bottles and jars inside the dark-mahogany, glass-enclosed cases. The corners lay in deep shadow. It might have been a conjurer's shop, except, of course, for the cigarettes and the candy and the soda fountain. The bottles gleaming darkly along the walls could have held wool of bat and nose of Turk, root of the mandrake and dust of the toad. I went out in the back room and looked into the yard. It seemed to go on forever, reaching into a vast, mysterious distance, unexplored, silent — not even the twitter of a bird. It was pitch black. I couldn't see the blossoms on the cherry trees, I couldn't tell what shape the yard was. But I now knew what was wrong with Miss Rena Randolph. She was crazy.

As the evening wore along, we got fewer and fewer customers. They bought cigarettes and cigars, candy, magazines. Very few cars went past. The town clock struck nine, and this surprised me, because I hadn't realized it was so late. My father always closed the store at nine-thirty. I had never closed it — or opened it, for that matter. I did not know where the keys to the front door were kept. I watched the clock, wondering what I should do at nine-thirty.

At quarter past nine, there was only one customer in the store — a woman who had purchased a box of candy. I was wrapping it up for her when someone pulled the screen door open with an abrupt, yanking movement and Pedro said, "Ah —"

I looked up and saw my father standing in the doorway, swaying back and forth, his arms extended. As I watched, he reached out and supported himself by leaning against the doorjamb. His appearance was so strange, he seemed so weak, so unlike himself, that I thought, He's been wounded. I peered at him, hunting for bruises on his face or his hands. As he entered the store, he kept looking around, blinking. He was wearing his light gray suit, and his newest boater hat, and the bow tie that I remembered. But the tie was twisted around to one side and it was partly untied, and his suit looked rumpled and so did his shirt.

I escorted the customer to the door, held it open for her, and then went to my father and said, "We — we didn't know where you were. Are you all right?"

He patted my hand. He said, "Look," and he smiled, revealing a set of glittering, horrible, wolfish-looking false teeth. There was a dribble of dried blood at the corner of his mouth. "I got my teeth."

I could barely understand what he said. He sounded as though he were speaking through or around a formidable obstruction that prevented his tongue and his lips from performing their normal function. The teeth glistened like the white porcelain fixtures in the downstairs bathroom.

I said, "Oh," weakly.

Pedro patted my father's arm. He said, "I worried —"

"Am I always going to sound like this?"

"I don't think so," I said.

He went into the prescription room and sat down in the chair by the window. Pedro stood beside him. I sat down on the high stool in front of the counter.

"Where's Sophy?"

I jumped off the stool. "They've gone to the police. I must telephone them —"

"Police? Police?" He made whistling noises when he said this. "Jesus Christ! For what?"

"They thought you were lost. I've got to call the Barracks —"

"Lawth?" he said, angrily. "Loweth?" he roared. "Lowerth? How could I we lowerth?" He stopped talking, reached up and took out the new false teeth, and wrapped them in his handkerchief. When he spoke again, he sounded just like himself. "I

read about this place in Norwich where they take all your teeth
out at once and put the false teeth in — make them for you and
put them in all the same day. That's where I was. In Norwich.
Getting my teeth. How could I get lost?"

"Oh!" I said and put my hand over my mouth, keeping the
pain away. "Didn't it hurt? Don't the teeth hurt?"

"Hurt?" he shouted. "Of course they hurt!"

"But why didn't you tell Mother you were going?"

"I didn't think I'd be gone more than two hours. I got on a
bus up at the corner, and it didn't take long to get there. They
pulled the teeth out. Then they took impressions. They
wouldn't let me have the teeth right away, said they had to wait
to make sure the jaw had stopped bleeding, and so the whole
process took longer than I thought it would."

"What made you finally get false teeth?" I didn't think it was
pictures of the Valentino types, with their perfect white teeth,
that I'd left around for him to see, and I didn't think it was the
sight of Gramps Fender, the old man who took care of the
house next door and whose false teeth hung loose in his mouth,
or the fact that my Aunt Sophronia and my mother kept talking
about the importance of chewing as an aid to the digestion of
food. So if it wasn't any of these things, then what was it?

He sighed and said that that morning, while he was shaving,
he had run through a solo he was to sing in church on Sunday.
He stood in front of that new plate-glass mirror in the downstairs bathroom under all that brilliant white light, and he
opened his mouth wide, and he saw himself in the mirror — the
open mouth all red and moist inside, and the naked gums with a
tooth here and there, and it was the mouth of an idiot out of
Shakespeare, it was the mouth of the nurse in *Romeo and Juliet*,
the mouth of the gravediggers in *Hamlet*, but most shocking of

all, it was the mouth of Samuel Layen. This was what the congregation looked at and into on Sunday mornings. He said he couldn't bear the thought that that was what all those white people saw when he sang a solo. If he hadn't seen his mouth wide open like that in the new mirror under that new light . . .

I thought, But the congregation couldn't possibly see the inside of his mouth — he's in the choir loft when he sings, and he's much too far away from them. But I didn't say this.

He said it was while he was standing under the first cherry tree, looking up at the sky and listening to the hum of the bees, that he decided he would take a bus and head for Norwich and get himself some false teeth that very day without saying anything about it to anyone. He put the teeth back in his mouth and turned to Pedro and said, in that mumbling, full-of-pebbles voice, "How do I look?" and he smiled.

Pedro said, "You look beautiful, Mr. Layen," and touched him gently on the shoulder.

I went into the phone booth and closed the door. I started to dial the number of the state police. It was on a card up over the phone, along with the telephone numbers of the local doctors and the firehouse. I hesitated. The phone booth smelled of all its recent users — of cigar smoke, perfume, sweat. I felt as constrained as though all of these people were in the booth with me: politicians, idle females, workmen. I couldn't imagine myself saying, "We thought my father was missing. He's been gone all day and my mother and my aunt have now reported him as missing, but he's back." Why didn't I feel free to say this? Was it the presence of those recent users of the phone booth, who might ask, "Where'd he go?" "Has he done this before?" "Has he got a girl friend?" I dialed the number, and a gruff voice said, "State Police. Tenyeck Barracks. Officer O'Toole speaking."

I didn't know what to say to him, so I didn't say anything.

The voice sounded loud, impatient, in my ear. *"Hullo! Hello? Speak up! Speak up!"*

If I said that we thought my father was missing but he isn't, he's found, he's back, then wouldn't this Officer O'Toole want to know where he'd been? I said, "Well—"

The voice said, "Hello? Hello?" and "Yes?" and "What is it?" It was a very gruff voice and it had a barking quality.

I shook my head at the voice. I was not free to speak openly to that gruff policeman's voice. I thought, Well, now, perhaps the reason my father hadn't wanted to replace his teeth was that one of the images of the black man that the white man carries around with him is of white teeth flashing in a black and grinning face. So my father went toothless to destroy that image. But then there is toothless old Uncle Tom, and my old black mammy with her head rag is toothless, too, and without teeth my father fitted *that* image of the black man, didn't he?

So he was damned either way. Was he not? And so was I. And so was I.

Then I thought, Why bother? Why not act just like other people, just this once, just like white people — come right out and say the lost is found. My hand, my own hand, had in response to some order from my subconscious reached for a pencil that was securely fastened to a nail in the booth, tied there by a long red string. The pencil hung next to a big white pad. This was where we wrote down telephone orders. I was doodling on the big white pad. The skin on my hand was so dark in contrast to the white pad that I stared, because that was the second time that day that I had taken a good look at the color of my skin against something stark white. I looked at my dark brown hand and thought, Throw that baby down to me, you ain't goin' to take us back now, you know; all of us people with this dark skin must help hold the black island inviolate. I said, "This is Mr. Layen's daughter, at Layen's Drugstore in Wheeling. Mrs. Layen and her sister, Miss Bart, are on their way over there. Will you tell them that Mr. Layen found his watch —"

"Found his watch? He lost it, did he? Valuable watch, I suppose. Wait a minute. They're just coming up the steps now, just coming in the door. Wait a minute. I'll let you talk to Mrs. Layen yourself."

Everybody knew us for miles around. We were those rare laboratory specimens the black people who ran the drugstore in the white town of Wheeling, New York, only black family in town except for the Granites, who, ha, ha, ha —

"Wait a minute," the gruff, barking voice said again.

I closed my eyes and I could see my mother and my aunt — two bent-over little women, going up the steps of the state-police barracks in Tenyeck, humble, hesitant, the whites of their eyes showing under the irises.

My mother's voice sounded in my ear. "Yes?" Harsh, loud.

I said, "Father is so happy. He found his watch. He thinks he dropped it in Norwich, where he went to get his new false teeth." It sounded as though he'd always had false teeth — or at least Officer O'Toole, who was undoubtedly listening in, would think so.

Has Anybody Seen Miss Dora Dean?

ONE AFTERNOON LAST WINTER, when the telephone rang in my house in Wheeling, New York, I started not to answer it; it was snowing, I was reading a book I had been waiting for weeks to get hold of, and I did not want to be disturbed. But it seemed to me that the peals of the bell were longer, more insistent than usual, so I picked up the phone and said, "Hello."

It was Peter Forbes — and neither that name nor any other is the actual one — and he was calling from Bridgeport. He said abruptly, and wheezily, for he is an asthmatic, "Ma is terribly ill. Really awfully sick."

He paused, and I said I was very sorry. His mother, Sarah Forbes, and my mother had grown up together in a black section of Bridgeport.

Peter said, "She's got some dishes she wants you to have. So will you come as soon as you can? Because she is really very sick."

I had heard that Sarah, who was in her seventies, was not well, but I was startled to learn that she was "terribly ill," "really very sick." I said, "I'll come tomorrow. Will that be all right?"

"No, no," he said. "Please come today. Ma keeps worrying about these dishes. So will you please come — well, right away? She is really terribly, terribly ill."

Knowing Sarah as well as I did, I could understand his insistence. Sarah had an unpleasant voice; it was a querulous, peevish voice. When she was angry or irritated, or wanted you to do something that you did not want to do, she talked and talked and talked, until finally her voice seemed to be pursuing you. It was like a physical pursuit from which there was no escape.

I said, "I'll leave right away," and hung up.

It took me three hours to drive from Wheeling to Bridgeport, though the distance is only forty-five miles. But it is forty-five miles of winding road — all hills and sharp curves. The slush in the road was beginning to freeze, and the windshield wiper kept getting stuck; at frequent intervals I had to stop the car and get out and push the snow away so that the wiper could function again.

During that long, tedious drive, I kept thinking about Sarah and remembering things about her. It was at least two years since I had seen her. But before that, over a period of twenty years, I had seen her almost every summer, because Peter drove over to Wheeling to go fishing, and his mother came too. She usually accompanied him whenever he went out for a ride. He would leave her at my house, so that she could visit with me while he and his two boys went fishing.

I thoroughly enjoyed these visits, for Sarah could be utterly charming when she was so minded. She was a tall woman with rather bushy black hair that had a streak of gray near the front. Her skin was a wonderful reddish brown color and quite unwrinkled, in spite of her age. She would have been extremely attractive if she hadn't grown so fat. All this fat was deposited on her abdomen and behind. Her legs had stayed thin, and her feet were long and thin, and her head, neck, and shoulders were small, but she was huge from waist to knee. In silhouette, she looked rather like a pouter pigeon in reverse. Her legs were not sturdy enough to support so much weight, and she was always leaning against doors, or against people, for support. This gave her an air of helplessness, which was completely spurious. She had a caustic sense of humor, and though she was an old woman, if something struck her as being funny, she would be seized by fits of giggling just as if she were a very young and silly girl.

I knew a great deal about Sarah Forbes. This knowledge stemmed from a long-distance telephone call that she made to my mother thirty-three years ago, when I was nine years old. I overheard my mother's side of the conversation. I can still repeat what she said, word for word, even imitating the intonation, the inflection of her voice.

In those days we lived in the building that housed my father's drugstore, in Wheeling. Our kitchen was on the ground floor, behind the store, and the bedrooms were upstairs, above it. Just as other children sat in the family living room, I sat in the drugstore — right near the front window on a bench when the weather was cold, outside on the wooden steps that extended across the front of the building when the weather was warm. Sitting outside on those splintery steps, I could hear everything that went on inside. In summer, the big front door of the store stayed wide open all day, and there was a screen door with fancy scrollwork on all the wooden parts. There were windows on either side of the door. On each window my father had painted his name in white letters with the most wonderful curlicues and flourishes, and under it the word "Druggist." On one window it said "Cold Soda," and on the other window "Ice Cream," and over the door it said "Drug Store."

Whether I sat inside the store or outside it, I had a long, sweeping view of the church, the church green, and the street. The street was as carefully composed as a painting: tall elm trees, white fences, Federal houses.

If I was sitting outside on the steps, listening to what went on in the store, no one paid any attention to me, but if I was sitting inside on the bench near the window, my mother or my father would shoo me out whenever a customer reached the really interesting part of the story he was telling. I was always being shooed out until I discovered that if I sat motionless on the bench, with a book held open in front of me, and did not glance up, everyone forgot about me. Occasionally, someone would stop right in the middle of a hair-raising story, and then my father would say, "Oh, she's got her nose in a book. She's just like she's deaf when she's got her nose in a book. You can say anything you want to and she won't hear a word." It was like having a permanent season ticket in a theater where there was a continuous performance and the same play was never given twice.

My special interest in Sarah dates from a rainy afternoon

when I was sitting inside the store. It was a dull afternoon — no customers, nothing, just the busy sound of rain dripping from the eaves, hitting the wooden steps. The wall telephone rang, and my mother, wiping her hands on her apron, came to answer it from the kitchen, which was just behind the prescription room of the store. Before she picked up the receiver, she said, "That's a long-distance call. I can tell by the way the operator is ringing. That's a long-distance call."

I sat up straight, I picked up my book and I heard the tinkling sound of money being dropped in at the other end. Then I heard my mother saying, "Why, Sarah, how are you? . . . What? What did you say? . . . Found him? Found him where?" She listened. "Oh, *no!*" She listened again. "Oh, my dear! Why, how dreadful! Surely an accident. You think — !" A longer period of listening. "Oh, no. Why that's impossible. Nobody would deliberately —" She didn't finish what she was going to say, and listened again. "A letter? Forbes left a letter? Tear it up! You mustn't let anyone know that —" There was a long pause. "But you must think of Peter. These things have an effect on — Excuse me."

She turned and looked at me. I had put the book down on the bench, and I was staring straight at her, breathing quite fast and listening so intently that my mouth was open.

She said, "Go out and play."

I kept staring at her, not moving, because I was trying to figure out what in the world she and Sarah Forbes had been discussing. What had happened that no one must know about?

She said again, her voice rising slightly, "Go out and play."

So I went the long way, through the back of the store and the prescription room and the kitchen, and I slammed the back door, and then I edged inside the prescription room again, very quietly, and I heard my mother say, "He must have had a heart attack and fallen right across the railroad tracks just as the train was due. That's the only possible explanation. And, Sarah, burn that letter. Burn it up!" She hung up the phone, and then she said to herself, "How dreadful. How perfectly dreadful."

Whether Sarah took my mother's advice and burned Forbes' letter I do not know, but it became common knowledge that he had committed suicide, and his death was so reported in the Bridgeport newspapers. His body had been found on the railroad tracks near Shacktown, an outlying, poverty-stricken section of Bridgeport, where the white riffraff lived and the lowest brothels were to be found. He was the only person that my father and my mother and my aunts had ever known who had killed himself, and they talked about him endlessly — not his suicide but his life as they had known it. His death seemed to have put them on the defensive. They sounded as though he had said to them, "This life all of us black folk lead is valueless; it is disgusting, it is cheap, it is contemptible, and I am throwing it away, so that everyone will know exactly what I think of it." They did not say this, but they sounded perplexed and uneasy whenever they spoke of Forbes, and they seemed to feel that if they could pool their knowledge of him they might be able to reach some acceptable explanation of why he had killed himself. I heard Forbes and Sarah discussed, off and on, all during the period of my growing up.

I never saw Forbes. The Wingates, an enormously wealthy white family for whom he worked, had stopped coming to Wheeling before I was born, and he had stopped coming there too. But I heard him described so often that I knew exactly what he looked like, how he sounded when he talked, what kind of clothes he wore. He was a tall, slender black man. He was butler, social secretary, gentleman's gentleman. When Mr. Wingate became ill, he played the role of male nurse. Then, after Mr. Wingate's death, he ran the house for Mrs. Wingate. He could cook, he could sew, he could act as coachman if necessary; he did all the buying and all the hiring.

The Wingates were summer residents of Wheeling. Their winter home was in Bridgeport. In Wheeling, they owned what they called a cottage; it was an exact replica of an old Southern mansion — white columns, long graveled driveways, carefully maintained lawns, brick stables, and all within six hundred feet of Long Island Sound.

During the summer, Forbes rode a bicycle over to my father's drugstore every pleasant afternoon. He said he needed the exercise. Whenever I heard my family describing Forbes, I always thought how dull and uninteresting he must have been. There would never be anything unexpected about him, never anything unexplained. He would always move exactly as he was supposed to when someone pulled the proper strings. He was serious, economical, extremely conservative — a tall, elegant figure in carefully pressed black clothes and polished shoes. His voice was slightly effeminate, his speech very precise. Mrs. Wingate was an Episcopalian and so was Forbes.

But one day when my father was talking about Forbes, some six months after his death, he suddenly threw his head back and laughed. He said, "I can see him now, bicycling down the street, with those long legs of his pinched up in those straight tight pants he wore, pumping his legs up and down, and whistling 'Has Anybody Seen Miss Dora Dean?' with his coattails flying in the wind. I can see him now." And he laughed again.

At the time, I could not understand why my father should have found this funny. Years later, I learned that the tune Forbes whistled was one that Bert Williams and George Walker, a memorable team of black comedians, had made famous along with their cakewalk. They were singing "Dora Dean" in New York in about 1896. Dora Dean, the girl of the song, played the lead in a hit show called "The Creole Show," which was notable for a chorus of sixteen beautiful brown girls. I suppose it amused my father to think that Forbes, who seemed to have silver polish in his veins instead of good red blood, should be whistling a tune that suggested cakewalks, beautiful brown girls, and ragtime.

Mrs. Wingate's name entered into the discussions of Forbes because he worked for her. It was usually my mother who spoke of Mrs. Wingate, and she said the same thing so often that I can quote her: "Mrs. Wingate always said she simply couldn't live without Forbes. She said he planned the menus, he checked the guest lists, he supervised the wine cellar — he did everything. Remember how she used to come into the store and say he was her mind, her heart, her hands? That was a funny thing to say, wasn't it?" There would be a pause, and then she would say, "Wasn't it too bad that she let herself get so fat?"

It was from my mother that I learned what Mrs. Wingate looked like. She was short and blond, and her face looked like the face of a fat china doll — pink and white and round. She used rice powder and rouge to achieve this effect. She bought these items in our drugstore. The powder came wrapped in thin white paper with a self stripe, and the rouge came in little round cardboard boxes, and inside there was a round, hard cake of reddish powder and a tiny powder puff to apply it with. She must have used a great deal of rouge, because at least once during the summer she would send Forbes up to the drugstore with a carton filled with these little empty rouge boxes. He would put them on the counter, saying, in his careful, precise, high-pitched voice, "Mrs. Wingate thought you might be able to use these." My father said he dumped them on the pile of rubbish in back of the store, to be burned, wondering what in the world she thought he would or could use them for. They smelled of perfume, and the reddish powder had discolored them, even on the outside.

Mrs. Wingate grew fatter and fatter, until, finally, getting her in and out of carriages, and then, during a later period, in and out of cars — even cars that were specially built — was impossible unless Forbes was on hand.

Forbes was lean, but he was wiry and tremendously strong. He could get Mrs. Wingate in and out of a carriage or a car without effort; at least he gave the illusion of effortlessness. My father said it was Mrs. Wingate who panted, who frowned, whose flesh quivered, whose forehead was dampened with sweat.

My father always ended his description of this performance by saying, "Remember how he used to have that white woman practically on his back? Yes, sir, practically on his back."

After I heard my father say that, I retained a curious mental picture of Forbes — a lean, wiry black man carrying an enormously fat pink and white woman piggyback. He did not lean over or bend over under the woman's weight; he stood straight, back unbent, so that she kept sliding down, down, down, and as he carried this quivering, soft-fleshed Mrs. Wingate, he was whistling "Has Anybody Seen Miss Dora Dean?"

I don't know that Forbes was actually looking for a reasonable facsimile of Dora Dean, but he found one, and he fell in love with her when he was forty years old. That was in 1900. He was so completely the perfect servant, with no emotional ties of his own and no life of his own, that my family seemed to think it was almost shocking that his attention should have been diverted from his job long enough to let him fall in love.

But it must have been inevitable from the first moment he saw Sarah Trumbull. I have a full-length photograph of her taken before she was married. She might well have been one of those beautiful girls in "The Creole Show." In the photograph, she has a young, innocent face — lovely eyes, and a pointed chin, and a very pretty mouth with a quirk at the corner that suggests a sense of humor. Her hair is slightly frizzy, and it is worn in a high, puffed-out pompadour, which serves as a frame for the small, exquisite face. She is wearing a shirtwaist with big, stiff sleeves, and a tight choker of lace around her throat. This costume makes her waist look tiny and her neck long and graceful.

My mother had been born in Bridgeport, and though she was older than Sarah, she had known her quite well. Sarah was the only child of a Baptist minister, and, according to my mother's rather severe standards, she was a silly, giggling girl with a reputation for being fast. She was frivolous, flirtatious. She liked to play cards, and played pinochle for money. She played the violin very well, and she used to wear a ring with a diamond in it on her little finger, and just before she started to play, she would polish it on her skirt, so that it would catch the light and wink at the audience. She had scandalized the people in her father's church because she played ragtime on the piano at dances, parties, and cakewalks. (I overheard my father say that he had always heard this called "whorehouse music"; he couldn't understand how it got to be "ragtime.")

Anyway, one night in 1900 Forbes had a night off and went

to a dance in New Haven, and there was Sarah Trumbull in a white muslin dress with violet ribbons, playing ragtime on the piano. And there was a cakewalk that night, and Forbes and Sarah were the winners. I found a yellowed clipping about it in one of my mother's scrapbooks — that's how I know what Sarah was wearing.

I have never seen a cakewalk but I have heard it described. About fourteen couples took part, and they walked in time to music — not in a circle but in a square, with the men on the inside. The participants were always beautifully dressed, and they walked with grace and style. It was a strutting kind of walk. The test of their skill lay in the way they pivoted when they turned the corners. The judges stopped the music at intervals and eliminated possibly three couples at a time. The most graceful couple was awarded a beautifully decorated cake, so that they had literally walked to win a cake.

In those days, Sarah Trumbull was tall, slender, and graceful, and John Forbes was equally tall, slender, and graceful. He was probably very solemn and she was probably giggling as they turned the corners in a cakewalk.

A year later, they were married in the Episcopal Church (colored) in Bridgeport. Sarah was a Baptist and her father was a Baptist minister, but she was married in an Episcopal church. If this had been a prize fight, I would say that Mrs. Wingate won the first round on points.

When my family discussed Forbes, they skipped the years after his marriage and went straight from his wedding to Sarah Trumbull in an Episcopal church (colored) to his death, twenty-four years later. Because I knew so little of the intervening years, I pictured him as being as ageless as a highly stylized figure in a marionette show — black, erect, elegantly dressed, effeminate, temperamental as a cat. I had never been able to explain why our cats did the things they did, and since there did not seem to be any reasonable explanation for Forbes' suicide, I attributed to him the unreasonableness of a cat.

The conversations in which my parents conjectured why Forbes killed himself were inconclusive and repetitive. My mother would sigh and say that she really believed Forbes killed himself because Sarah was such a slovenly housekeeper — that he just couldn't bear the dirt and the confusion in which he had to live, because, after all, he was accustomed to the elegance of the Wingate mansion.

My father never quite agreed. He said, "Well, yes, except that he'd been married to Sarah for twenty years or so. Why should he suddenly get upset about dirt after all that time?"

Once, my mother pressed him for his point of view, and he said, "Maybe he was the type that never should have married."

"What do you mean by that?"

"Well, he'd worked for that Mrs. Wingate, and he waited too long to get married, and then he married a young girl. How old was Sarah — twenty, wasn't she? And he was forty at the time, and —"

"Yes, yes," my mother said impatiently. "But what did you mean when you said he was a type that never should have married?"

"Well, if he'd been another type of man, I would have said there was more than met the eye between him and Mrs. Wingate. But he was so ladylike there couldn't have been. Mrs. Wingate thought a lot of him, and he thought a lot of Mrs. Wingate. That's all there was to it — it was just like one of those lifetime friendships between two ladies."

" 'Between two ladies'!" my mother said indignantly. "Why, what a wicked thing to say! Forbes was — Well, I've never seen another man, white or black, with manners like his. He was a perfect gentleman."

"Too perfect," my father said dryly. "That type don't make good husbands."

"But something must have *happened* to make him kill himself. He was thrifty and hard-working and intelligent and honest. Why should he kill himself?"

My father tried to end the conversation. "It isn't good to keep talking about the dead like this, figuring and figuring about why they did something — it's like you were pulling at them, trying to pull them back. After all, how do you know but you might succeed in bringing them back? It's best to let them alone. Let Forbes alone. It isn't for nothing that they have that saying about let them rest in peace."

There was silence for a while. Then my mother said softly, "But I do wish I knew why he killed himself."

My father said, "Sarah told you he said in the letter he was tired of living. I don't believe that. But I guess we have to accept it. There's just one thing I'd like to know."

"What's that?"

"I keep wondering what he was doing in Shacktown. That seems a strange place for a respectable married man like Forbes. That's where all those barefooted foreign women live, and practically every one of those orange-crate houses they live in has a red light in the window. It seems like a strange part of the city for a respectable married man like Forbes to have been visiting."

By the time I was ten, Forbes' death had for me a kind of reality of its own — a theatrical reality. I used to sit on the steps in front of the drugstore, and half close my eyes so that I could block out the church green and the picket fences and the elm trees and the big old houses, and I would pretend that I was looking at a play instead. I set it up in my mind's eye. The play takes place on the wrong side of the railroad tracks, where the land is all cinders, in a section where voluptuous, big-hipped foreign women go barefooted, wrap their heads and shoulders in brilliant red and green shawls, and carry bundles on their heads — that is, those who work. Those who do not work wear hats with so many feathers on them they look as if they had whole turkeys on their heads. The houses in this area are built entirely of packing cases and orange crates. There is the sound of a train in the distance, and a thin, carefully dressed black man, in a neat black suit and polished shoes, walks swiftly onstage and up the slight incline toward the railroad tracks — no path there, no road. It is a winter's night and cold. This is Forbes and he is not wearing an overcoat.

As narrator for an imaginary audience, I used to say, "What is he doing in this part of town in his neat black suit and his starched white shirt? He could not possibly know anyone here in Shacktown, a place built of cinders and packing cases. Bleak. Treeless. No road here. What is he doing here? Where is he going?"

The train whistles, and Forbes walks up the embankment and lies down across the tracks. The train comes roaring into sight and it slices him in two — quickly, neatly. And the curtain comes down as a telephone rings in a drugstore miles away.

This picture of Forbes remained with me, unchanged; I still see him like that. But in the intervening years Sarah changed. My first distinct recollection of her was of a stout middle-aged woman with a querulous voice, which was always lifted in complaint. Her complaint centered on money — the lack of it, the importance of it. But even in middle age there were vestigial remains of the girl who scandalized the religious black folk of Bridgeport by pounding out whorehouse music on the piano, and who looked as though she had just stepped out of the chorus line of "The Creole Show": the wonderful smooth reddish brown skin, the giggle over which she seemed to have no control, and the flirtatious manner of a Gay Nineties beauty. The coyness and the fits of giggling she had as an old woman were relics of these mannerisms.

I got to Bridgeport just at dusk. As I rang the bell of the two-story frame house where Sarah lived, I remembered something. This was the house that Mrs. Wingate had given to Forbes and Sarah as a wedding present. They had lived in it together exactly three weeks, and then Forbes went back to live at the Wingate mansion. Mrs. Wingate had asked him to come back because she might want to go out at night, and how could she get in and out of a car without him? It would be very inconvenient to have to wait for him to come all the way from the other side of town. (The Wingate mansion was at the south end of the city, and the dark brown, two-story taxpayer was at the north end of the city.) Mrs. Wingate had said that Sarah would, of course, stay where she was. She increased Forbes' wages and promised to remember him most generously in her will.

"It was a funny thing," my mother once said. "You know, Sarah used to call Forbes by his first name, John, when he was courting her, and when they were first married. After he went back to live at Mrs. Wingate's, she called him Forbes. All the rest of his life, she called him by his last name, just as though she was talking to Mrs. Wingate's butler."

One of Peter Forbes' gangling boys — Sarah's younger grandson — opened the door, and I stopped thinking about the past. He was a nice-mannered, gentle-looking boy, tall and thin, his face shaped rather like Sarah's in the old photograph — a small-boned face. His skin was the same wonderful reddish brown color. I wondered why he wasn't in school, and immediately asked him.

"I've finished," he said. "I finished last June. I'm eighteen and I'm going in the Army."

I said what most people say when confronted by evidence of the passage of time. "It doesn't seem possible."

He said, "Yeah, that's right," took a deep breath, and said, "Nana's in the bedroom. You'd better come right in."

He seemed to be affected by the same need for haste that had made his father urge me to come see Sarah right away. I did not pause even long enough to take my coat off; I followed him down a dark hall, trying to remember what his real name was. Sarah had brought Peter's children up. Peter had been married to a very nice girl, and they had two boys. The very nice girl left Peter after the second baby was born and never came back. Sarah had given nicknames to the boys; the older was called Boodie, and the younger was Lud. It was Lud who had answered the door. I could not remember anything but the nickname — Lud.

We entered a bedroom at the back of the house. The moment I saw Sarah, I knew that she was dying. She was sitting slumped over in a wheelchair. In the two years since I had seen her, she had become a gaunt old woman with terrible bruised shadows under her eyes and she was so thin that she looked like a skeleton. Her skin, which had been that rich reddish brown, was now overlaid with gray.

Lud said, "Nana, she's here. She's come, Nana."

Sarah opened her eyes and nodded. The eyes that I had remembered as black and penetrating were dull and their color had changed; they were light brown. I bent over and kissed her.

"I'm not so bright today," she said, and the words came out slowly, as though she had to think about using the muscles of her throat, her tongue, her lips — had to think, even, before she breathed. After she finished speaking, she closed her eyes and she looked as though she were already dead.

"She isn't asleep," Lud said. "You just say something to her. She'll answer — won't you, Nana?"

Sarah did not answer. I took off my coat, for the heat in the room was unbearable, and I looked around for a place to put it and laid it on a chair, thinking that the room had not changed. It was exactly as I remembered it, and I had not been in it for twenty years. There was too much furniture, the windows were heavily curtained, there was a figured carpet on the floor, and a brass bed, a very beautiful brass bed; one of the walls was covered with framed photographs.

A white cat darted through the room, and I jumped, startled, remembering another white cat that used to dart through these same rooms — but that was twenty years ago. "That's surely not the same cat, Lud? The one you've always had?"

"We've had this one about three years."

"Oh. But the other cat was white, too, wasn't it? It was deaf and it had never been outside the house — isn't that right? And it had blue eyes."

"So's this one. He doesn't go outside. He's deaf and he's got blue eyes." Lud grinned and his face was suddenly lively and very young. "And he's white," he said, and then laughed out loud. "Nana calls him our white folks."

"What's the cat's name?"

"Willie."

That was the name of the other cat, the one I had known. And Willie, so Sarah Forbes had said (boasted, perhaps?) — Willie did not like men. I wondered if this cat did.

"Is he friendly?"

"No," Lud said.

"Doesn't like men," Sarah Forbes said. Her voice was strong and clear, and it had its old familiar querulousness. The boy and I looked at her in surprise. She seemed about to say something more, and I wondered what it was going to be, for there was a kind of malevolence in her expression.

But Peter Forbes came into the room and she did not say anything. We shook hands and talked about the weather, and I thought how little he had changed during the years I had known him. He is a tall, slender man, middle-aged now, with a shaggy head and a petulant mouth that has deeply etched lines at the corners.

At the sight of Peter, Sarah seemed to grow stronger. She sat up straight. "Wheel me out to the dining room," she ordered.

"Yes, Ma," he said obediently. The wheelchair made no sound. "You come, too," he said to me.

"There's some china . . ." Sarah's voice trailed off, and she was slumping again, almost onto one arm of the wheelchair, her arms, head, and neck absolutely limp. She looked like a discarded rag doll.

We stood in the dining room and looked at her, all three of us. I said, "I'd better go. She's not well enough to be doing this. She hasn't the strength."

"You can't go," Peter said, with a firmness that surprised me. "Ma has some dishes she wants you to have. She's been talking about them for days now. She won't give us a minute's peace until you have them. You've got to stay until she gives them to you." Then he added, very politely and quite winningly, "Please don't go."

So I stayed. The dining room was just as hot as the bedroom. It, too, was filled with furniture — a dining room set, three cabinets filled with china and glassware, a studio couch, and in a bay window, a big aquarium with fish in it.

Willie, the white cat, ran into the room from the hall, clawed his way up the draperies at the bay window and sat crouched on the cornice, staring into the fish tank. His round blue eyes kept following the movements of the fish, back and forth, back and forth.

"Doesn't he try to catch the fish?" I asked.

Lud said, "That's what he wants to do. But he can't get at them. So he just watches them."

"Why, that's terrible," I said. "Can't you —"

Sarah had straightened up again. "Open those doors," she said.

"Yes, Ma." Peter opened one of the china cabinets.

"Get my cane."

"Yes, Ma." He went into the bedroom and came back with a slender Malacca cane. She took it from him in a swift snatching movement, and, holding it and pointing with it, was transformed. She was no longer a hideous old woman dying slowly but an arrogant, commanding figure.

"That," she said, "and that," pointing imperiously to a shelf in the china cabinet where a tall chocolate pot stood, with matching cups and saucers, covered thick with dust.

"Get a carton and some newspapers." She pointed at Lud, and she jabbed him viciously in the stomach with the cane. He jumped, and said, "Oh, oo-ooh!" pain and outrage in his voice.

"Go get the carton," Peter said matter-of-factly.

While we waited for Lud to come back, Sarah seemed to doze. Finally, Peter sat down and motioned to me to sit down. He picked up a newspaper and began to read.

Something about the way Sarah had ordered him around set me to wondering what kind of childhood Peter had had. He must have been about twelve years old when Mrs. Wingate died and left thirty-five thousand dollars to Forbes.

With this money, Forbes took what he called a flyer in real estate; he acquired an equity in six tenement houses. My mother had disapproved. She distrusted the whole idea of mortgages and loans, and she felt that Forbes was gambling with his inheritance; if his tenants were unable to pay the rent, he would be unable to meet the interest on his notes and would lose everything.

During this period, Mother went to see Sarah fairly often and she always came away from these visits quite disturbed. She said that Sarah, who had at one time cared too much about her looks, now did not seem to care at all. The house was dreadful — confused and dusty. She said that Forbes had changed. He was still immaculate, but he was now too thin — bony — and his movements were jerky. He seemed to have a dreadful, almost maniacal urge to keep moving, and he would sit down, stand up, walk about the room, sit down again, get up, walk about again. At first she used to say that he was nervous, and then she amended this and enlarged it by saying he was distraught.

Mrs. Wingate had been dead exactly two years when Forbes committed suicide. Immediately, all of Sarah's friends predicted financial disaster for her. Forbes' money was tied up in heavily mortgaged real estate, and shortly after his death the depression came along, with its eviction notices and foreclosures.

I glanced at Sarah, dozing in the wheelchair, her chin resting on her chest. At twenty, she had been a silly, giggling girl. And yet somewhere under the surface there must have been the makings of a cold, shrewd property owner, a badgering, browbeating fishwife of a woman who could intimidate drunks, evict widows and orphans — a woman capable of using an umbrella or a hatpin as a weapon. She had made regular weekly collections of rent, because she soon learned that if she went around only once a month, the rent money would have gone for food or for liquor or for playing the numbers. Peter went with her when she made her collections. He was tall, thin, and asthmatic, and wore tweed knee pants and long stockings — a ridiculous costume for a boy in his teens.

It was during those years that Sarah perfected her technique of leaning against people, and began to develop a whining voice. She began to get fat. Her behind seemed to swell up, but her legs stayed thin, like pipestems, so that she walked carefully. She was what my father called spindle-shanked.

I suppose she had to whine, to threaten, to cajole, perhaps cry, in order to screw the rent money out of her tenants; at any rate, she succeeded. Years later, she told Mother that she had not lost a single piece of property. She finally sold all of it except the two-story taxpayer where they lived. She said that the bank that held the mortgages and notes had congratulated her; they told her that no real estate operator in Bridgeport had been able to do what she had done — bring all his property through the depression intact.

Sarah straightened up in the wheelchair and pointed with her cane. "That," she said. Peter hesitated. "That" seemed to be some white cups and saucers with no adornment of any kind. Sarah threatened Peter with the cane, and he took them out of the cabinet and put them on the table.

"Perfect," she said to me. "Six of them. All perfect. Belonged to my grandmother. Handed down. They're yours now. You hand them down."

I shook my head. "Wait a minute," I said, slowly and distinctly, in order to be sure she understood. "What about your grandsons? What about Lud and Boodie? These cups should belong to Lud and Boodie."

"They will run with whores," she said coldly. "Just like Peter does. Just like Forbes kept trying to do, only he couldn't. That's what he was after in Shacktown that time, and when he found he couldn't — just wasn't able to — he laid himself down on the railroad track." She paused for a moment. "I cried for three days afterward. For three whole days." She paused again. "I wasn't crying because of what happened to him. I was crying because of what had happened to me. To my whole life. My whole life."

I could not look at Peter. I heard him take a deep breath.

Sarah said, "Those cups are yours. I'm giving them to you so that I'll know where they are. I'll know who owns them. If they should stay here . . ." She shrugged.

Lud came back with the carton and a pile of newspapers and Sarah did not even glance in his direction. She said, "The chocolate cups belonged to a French king. Mrs. Wingate gave them to me for a wedding present when I married her Forbes. I want you to have them so that I'll know who owns them."

We wrapped the pieces of china separately, and put wads of crumpled newspaper in between as we packed the carton. Sarah watched us. Sometimes she half closed her eyes, but she kept looking until we had finished. After that, her head slumped and her breathing changed. It was light, shallow, with pauses in between. I could hear the thumping of her heart way across the room.

I said, "Good-bye, Sarah," and kissed the back of her neck, but she did not answer or move.

It was still snowing when Lud carried the carton out to the car for me, held the door open, and closed it after I got in. I thought he did it with a kind of gracefulness that he couldn't possibly have acquired from Peter; perhaps it was something inherited from Forbes, his grandfather.

Lud said, "Did those cups really belong to one of the kings of France?"

"Maybe. I really don't know. I wish you'd put them back in the house. This whole carton of china is more yours than it is mine. These things belonged to your grandmother and they should stay in your family."

"Oh, no," he said hastily, and he stepped away from the car. "I don't want them. What would I do with them? Besides, Nana's ghost would come back and bug me." He laughed uneasily. "And if Nana's ghost bugged anybody, they'd flip for sure."

When I got home, I washed the chocolate set, and having got rid of the accumulated dust of fifty years, I decided that it could easily have belonged to one of the kings of France. It was of the very old, soft-paste type of porcelain. It had been made in the Sèvres factory and it was exquisitely decorated in the lovely color known as rose pompadour.

I was admiring the shape of the cups when the telephone rang. It was Peter Forbes. He said, "Ma died in her sleep just a few minutes after you left."

The Migraine Workers

PEDRO GONZALES WAS all set to go home for the night. He was sitting in the jeep with the motor running, looking idly around the gas station, telling himself that he'd left enough change for Mike, the man who worked for him, and he'd tied the dog out by the tire shed and there wasn't anything else for him to do before he took off.

He was a huge man, with hand and face darkened by the sun and from the grease and oil embedded in his skin. He knew he was too fat — his doctor and his friends were always telling him so — but he liked the feel of his own flesh, except of course in real hot weather like today around noon when he wished he was so thin he was just bone, no flesh. But now that the sun had gone down he felt fine, just fine.

He thought the station looked good, all of it — from the white one-story building that housed his office and the rest rooms and the salesroom where he sold car accessories, to the vast shed in the back where he stored truck tires and where Mike fed all the stray cats in the neighborhood. Over the years, he and Mike had made it the best-known truck stop between New York and Buffalo; it was located so the driver of a big rig could pull in right off the throughway and refuel with diesel or get a tire changed or pick up a free cup of coffee, open right around the clock, three hundred and sixty-five days a year.

While he sat there a truck came bouncing into the station — an old truck, its motor coughing and sputtering, the body rattling, bluish smoke belching out of the tail pipe. The driver pulled past the pumps and stopped off to one side with brakes squealing. Pedro wondered what the guy was carrying, because the flaps were closed in the back but every once in a while they kind of bulged out, and obviously there was something alive in there and moving around. The license plates were so covered with mud and so dented he couldn't tell what state the truck was registered in. He shook his head in disapproval, because a gypsy outfit like that could be carrying almost anything. They never had their hands on enough money to buy a new rig, had to keep spending it in driblets for gas and oil and minor repairs, and one day the truck would quit on them and they'd go pawing through junkyards trying to find spare parts or to salvage a tire or an old battery. Maybe that's why this one had come bouncing into the station — he was looking for a spare part or a tire that wasn't nailed down.

Pedro cut off the motor of the jeep. He'd wait until the gypsy left; you never knew what kind of trickery an outfit like that was up to. He'd seen many a one who gave a casual-seeming look at the tire shed, but when he or Mike said, "Shag!

Guard!" and the shepherd growled a response deep in his throat, why, the gypsy would take off without a backward glance.

When Mike came out of the building, the driver got out of the truck and walked toward him. He was a black man, of medium height, not fat but fleshy, and he seemed to be asking some kind of favor of Mike because he tilted his head to one side and his manner was apologetic. Mike frowned and pointed at the ramshackle truck, and the black man kept talking and talking and gesturing, and finally Mike shrugged and pointed to the jeep, indicating that he would have to ask the boss. The driver smiled and nodded in Pedro's direction, his eyes gleaming, and Pedro, noting the layer of fat under his skin — skin so sleek it looked as though it had been oiled — thought, Bastard, pure bastard.

Mike came over to the jeep and said, "He wants to know is it all right to use the rest rooms."

"Who? Who wants to use them? Him?"

Before Mike could answer, a big rig pulled in at the diesel pumps, and Pedro said, "Go service them. Let the bastard wait. It won't hurt him."

He watched Mike at the pumps, thinking, We been in this racket close to thirty years now, so it's only to be expected we don't look the same as when we started out. Mike wasn't fat, but he had put on weight; he had kind of thickened in the middle and there was soft flesh around his jowls. Close up you could see gray in his hair and crow's-feet around his eyes.

Then he glanced at the truck again and wondered what the guy carried. Years of running a gas station had made him wary. He'd had encounters with deadbeats, thieves, punks, finks, hoods, even a murderer; everything out on rubber on the road headed for his station because it was the only one that stayed open all the time — holidays and all, day and night. So naturally he wanted to know what this black man was carrying in that broken-down truck. He could have cobras in it or boa constrictors or lions.

In the summer you never knew what would show up. Just yesterday a blonde, riding in a convertible with the top down, had stopped for gas, and when he went up to the car to see what she wanted he saw what he thought was a fur jacket lying on the seat beside her. But it turned out to be an ocelot with a black velvet ribbon around its neck and what looked like a diamond dangling from the ribbon. The beast lunged toward him, snarling, and he jumped back and tripped over his own feet and almost fell down trying to get out of the way; and the woman said, "Ooo-oooh! You looked so funny!" and laughed and laughed and laughed. He picked up a tire iron and threatened her with it, yelling, "Get out of here! Get out of here! You can't horse around here with no lion. Out!" And she drove away, cursing him, and snarling just like the beast that traveled with her.

About an hour later one of the local cops came by and asked him what happened — that's how he knew it was an ocelot and not a lion or a tiger that had lunged at him. He'd told the cop, a young fellow in a brand-new uniform with a cap too big for him — it came down over his ears and made his face look very small — that, sure he threatened the woman with a tire iron, what with the heat and the humidity and all the rat finks running over the bell, honking their horns to hurry you up, saying fill her up, wash the windshield, check the battery, can I charge it, I haven't got the toll for the bridge, I need a dime for the telephone, can I put it on my credit card, what with that and the feel of the oil and the grease on his skin, and the stink of the diesel fuel and the stink from the exhaust from the big trucks in his nose, well, with all that, why, you go up to a car and there is some grinning woman with her skirt up to her thighs and her blond hair straggling down around her shoulders and half over her face, and she laughs because the tiger on the seat with her lunges at the big slob who is working twelve hours a day, and the slob jumps back and almost falls down because his wits have been half scared out of him, why —

"All right," he'd said to the cop, and he kept talking faster and faster and his voice kept getting louder and louder, "all right. Hot as it was, what with the smell of that tiger she had with her and the look on her face when she laughed — why, if she'd stayed long enough, I would have smashed her face in with the tire iron. And if you want to make something out of it, I'll sign a statement and I'll say just that, and I'll put in what I think about all these rich kids who come in here barefoot, all of them with dirty feet, and I'll tell what I think about these women who don't wear anything but little straight pieces of cloth for dresses and have all that dirty hair hanging down their backs and they don't even bother to comb it anymore, and I'll tell you what I think about —"

The cop interrupted him. "It wasn't a tiger. It was an ocelot, and we gave her a summons for transporting an uncaged wild animal around with her. It's okay — I just wanted to hear your side of the story."

Then Mike was back beside the jeep, tapping on the side of the door. He said impatiently, "What'll I tell the man? He wants to know is it all right to use the rest rooms."

"Use the rest rooms? What's he asking that for? What's he carrying in the truck?"

"Well, they're these migraine workers."

"What's that mean?"

"It means these colored people who go from place to place to pick beans and stuff. The driver brings them from down South every year, and he's taking them upstate. He says he don't usually come through here, but he took a wrong turn somewhere."

"Are they in that truck?"

"Yeah."

"Tell him yes."

Mike nodded to the black man to indicate that the boss had approved. Pedro got out of the jeep and walked over to the truck. He was so fat that he walked with a rocking motion. He was wearing enormous dark green pants slung low, way down to his hipbones, and a voluminous dark green shirt with "Pedro's Gas Station" embroidered in red on one of the breast pockets. Both pockets bulged with papers. He wore high-laced leather shoes, bright yellow in color.

The black man opened the flaps of the truck. "Come on," he said. "Git out. Git out. All right. Now, come on, now, line up. Line up, now!"

The truck was filled with black people — men, women, children and nursing babies. They were ragged, dirty, their dark skins covered with sores, and there were burrs and straw in their matted hair.

Pedro looked at them first out of the corner of his eye, stealing glances at them, and then as he became aware that none of them was looking at him, that they kept looking down at the ground, heads down, eyes averted, he frankly stared at them.

"All right. Git in the line."

They kept coming out of the truck, blinking, stumbling, shivering a little, perhaps because of the fresh, cool air. Pedro backed away because they smelled so awful and they looked so awful, and then his curiosity made him go closer.

"Where you from?" he asked.

They did not look at him; they did not reply.

"What language do they speak?"

"Same as us," the driver said.

The last one out was an old black man, bearded, dirtier than the others, his work pants so filled with holes and torn places that he looked like a bundle of rags. After the flaps had swung back in place behind him, Pedro looked inside the truck. There was nowhere to sit except the floor. The stench made him cough, and over it was the yeasty smell of some kind of rotgut liquor. Then he moved away because there was someone lying way back in a corner — a very old woman who peered at him and then drew back in fear.

The driver of the truck was herding the people toward the rest rooms. Pedro beckoned to him and indicated that he wanted to ask him something.

"How come it's got no seats?"

"No room for seats," the driver said, smiling, his eyes gleaming, head tilted to one side. "I hauls crops so as I can pay for the gas, and if there was seats, they'd have to be nailed down and I couldn't git much of the crops in."

Pedro said, frowning, "I never seen such a sight before in my life."

"Well, folks don't usually see 'em," the driver said apologetically, head bobbing up and down in a series of small bows, smiling his ingratiating smile. "We run 'em through at night and don't stop nowhere; nobody sees 'em and nobody gets upset about 'em. But this time the truck broke down and it was morning before I could git it going, and then I took the wrong turn and that's how we come through to your place. Pure accident, boss, pure accident."

Yeah, he thought, and you're pure bastard.

"Are they hungry?"

The driver shrugged. "Well, like us, they can always eat a little. You got anything, you give it to me and I'll see they gits it further up the road where it's dark. That way nobody'll git upset about 'em."

"They'll eat it here," Pedro said. The driver couldn't get it out of their stomachs once it was inside them, and it was a sure thing they'd never see any food if the driver got his hands on it first. Pedro went inside the station and told Mike to get out the loaves of bread the baker had left — it couldn't be sold in the stores as day-old bread because the outfit that made it wouldn't permit it. He had six quarts of milk in the refrigerator, and there was a crate of oranges that had bounced off the back of one of those big coast-to-coast trucks and a crate of evaporated milk and one of those big tinned hams and a case of corned beef.

Anyway, they fed everybody. They sliced up the ham and handed it out. Then he opened tin after tin of corned beef — the stuff was always falling off the back of trucks. The kids drank the fresh milk and they each ate a can of corned beef, wolfed it down, and they ate oranges. Then he and Mike opened cans of evaporated milk and mixed the stuff with water, the whole case of it, and the ragged old man poured it into paper cups and they drank it fast.

He'd never seen people eat with such haste — they put

whole slices of bread in their mouths, stuffing it in, and they did the same thing with the meat. He ran out of paper cups, and the driver said, "They kin use the same ones over again, hand it to the next person," but Pedro sent Mike back into the station for more cups.

They didn't talk while they were eating, and when they got back in the truck they ducked their heads down, bowing as they went past him. The driver was annoyed and he showed it, because he said thanks in a short, sharp way and left out the obsequious ducking of his head and then herded them back into the truck, heckling them with his voice. He gave the kids a push here and a hard shove there, which they ignored, making no protest, and Pedro decided they were so accustomed to being pushed around that they accepted it as a normal part of their lives.

He watched the truck go bouncing out of the station, bluish smoke coming from the tail pipe, and thought that it carried a load of misery, pure misery, and for a long while after it left he couldn't seem to think about anything else. He felt as though he had eaten something that disagreed with him and had been left with a sour taste in his mouth.

By the next day everything was fine, just fine. The sun was out, and it was hot but not humid. The trucks came and went and the drivers drank coffee and the regular customers came in for gas and oil and there weren't any ragged, hungry people who traveled standing up in rattletrap trucks or any blondes in convertibles with what looked like Bengal tigers on the seat beside them.

But the day after that Mike said something was snooping around the tire shed at night, knocking the garbage cans over, and that Shag went wild, barking, jumping up in the air, trying to get loose from the chain that held him. He said he ran out to the tire shed, and though he watched and waited and listened, he didn't see anything; but the dog kept hearing something or smelling something that infuriated him, making his hackles rise.

This happened three nights in a row, and on the fourth night Mike said uneasily, "I don't like it. I don't see nothing — no animal, none of those long-haired rat-fink kids that horse around here sometimes. Nothing. But Shag sees something or smells something that sets him crazy. It's spooky."

"So let the dog loose."

"No," Mike said. "Not me. That ain't right."

"That's what he's for." Until they got the German shepherd there had always been a certain amount of petty thievery. Most gas stations had the same problems — a tire or two missing, a new battery not accounted for, the Coke machine broken open for the change. After somebody pried the coin box right out of the telephone booth, Pedro figured they'd better get a guard dog, because they were open all night and they were sitting ducks for a holdup. So a couple of years ago he had bought Shag. He'd cost almost as much as a good used car, but he'd been worth it, for they hadn't had any kind of trouble since.

He told Mike to move the garbage cans right up behind the building where the office was and to turn out the lights in the back and let the dog out, and then he'd be able to catch whatever it was that was messing around with the cans.

Mike said, "I'll move the cans, but I don't want to let the dog loose."

"All right. All right. I'll come back tonight and I'll let him out."

About midnight he went back to the station and turned out the lights in the back and sat down in a straight wooden chair near the door of the room they used as a kitchen. Shag sat down beside him, leaning against him. The air coming through the screen door was balmy. There was a swamp behind the station, and honeysuckle grew there and he could smell it. He thought the night air was like some dandelion wine he'd had years ago. He could still remember the taste of it, and how at the time he drank it he'd thought the old Italian man who'd made the wine had managed to catch hold of the color of the flower and the warmth from the sun and put them in the bottle, and when he had lifted it to his mouth it was all there on the edges of his lips, on his tongue, trickling down his throat.

He could hear the hum of traffic on the turnpike and he frowned, thinking it sounded like some of the peculiar music they broadcast on those midnight-to-dawn radio programs. He sighed and shifted his weight in the hard chair. It was an uncomfortable place to sit because he was too large for the seat, yet he found himself dozing, his head nodding.

Suddenly he leaned forward and then stood up, because someone or something had lifted the cover of one of the garbage cans. It wasn't a loud noise, just a gentle telltale click of metal against metal.

Shag growled and Pedro eased the screen door open and Shag went hurtling through the air as if he'd been thrown from a catapult. Then there were screams and a man's voice saying, "Ah, down, git down, git down, git away" — a man's voice with a tremor in it.

Pedro turned on the outside lights and he saw a man standing still just beyond the door, with the dog quite close to him. Then the man tried to edge away and the dog took hold of his pants, and then as the man pulled hard, trying to run, Shag hurled his weight against him and the man went down, flat on his back. Shag stood over him, guarding him, his mouth open, the great, ravening jaws not a quarter of an inch from the man's throat.

As Pedro approached he saw that the man on the ground was an old black man. He was too frightened even to cry out; his throat quivered and his breathing made a sound like cloth being torn. Pedro bent over him and got a whiff of him and drew back; this old black man was one of those migraine workers. He was the bearded one who had poured the milk.

Mike came running out of the building. "Who is he?"

"Off the truck. He came off that broken-down truck. He's one of them migraine workers. Let him up, Shag. Let him up."

Mike helped the old man to his feet and then went through his pockets. Nothing on him — not a piece of paper, not a penny, not a cigarette or a shred of tobacco. Nothing.

They stood staring at him in a kind of wonderment and finally Pedro said, more to break the silence than anything else, "What's your name?"

"Folks calls me Ben. Yes, sir. They calls me Ben." It was impossible to imitate his speech, though Pedro found his own lips moving in a vain effort to make himself remember it; it was a soft, slurred kind of sound, difficult to understand.

"Where'd you come from?" Mike asked curiously. "Where's your home?"

"I don't know. I don't rightly know, boss." He said it apologetically.

"Where was the truck going when it left here?"

"I never did hear where driver was taking us, boss."

Pedro looked at him in amazement. He was old, emaciated, dirty, ragged. How in the name of God had he planned to live? He couldn't just eat out of garbage cans. What had made him suddenly leave the truck?

"You been up this way before?" he asked.

"Ever' year."

"How'd you come to leave the truck?"

The old man said that when they left the gas station he'd edged toward the tailgate of the truck, parted the flaps a little, and then waited for the truck to stop at a light or a stop sign. He knew he couldn't wait too long or he'd get lost and never be able to find the fat white man's place, and so finally the truck slowed a little and he jumped off and had to scramble out of the way of an oncoming car.

Mike said, "Why'd you come here?"

The old man wouldn't answer. He avoided looking at them and looked at the dog instead and said he was a mighty good dog, about the best he'd ever seen.

Mike said, "Shag, make friends."

To the old man's delight, Shag sat down and extended one of his big paws. The old man shook hands with him and began talking to him, making a soft, mumbling sound.

Pedro went back into the building to call the police and tell them to come and pick up this smelly old man. He had his hand on the telephone and was about to dial when Mike spoke, almost in his ear. He was startled because he hadn't known Mike had followed him inside.

Mike said, "Who are you calling?"

"The police."

"He ain't done nothing except try to find himself something to eat."

"Well, what am I supposed to do with him?"

"He could stay here. He could sleep in the tire shed."

"With all those cats?"

"Sure."

"And where'd he stay in the winter?"

"He could sleep here in this building."

Pedro shook his head and reached for the telephone again, and Mike's hand closed over his. Mike said, "Don't do that."

"Why not? The cops will find out where he belongs and send him back to wherever it is he came from. How else am I going to find out?"

"He don't belong nowhere. You know that. You saw them migraine workers and that stinking truck and that black bastard who was driving it. Let him stay here."

"No," Pedro said, frowning. "He can't stay here. I got all I can do to look after myself and look after you. I can't take on no old black man. Why'd he come here anyway?"

"You don't know?"

Pedro shook his head. "Of course not. And neither do you."

"Oh, yes I do. It's because you're so fat. That old man knows we got plenty of food all the time, because if we didn't have, you couldn't 'a got so fat, and you wouldn't have been giving food away if there wasn't plenty of it around. Didn't you hear him say if he hadn't jumped off the truck when he did, he couldn't 'a found the *fat* white man's place?" Mike said this fast, almost in one breath, and then he stopped, and when he spoke again he whispered, just as though he were telling a dirty joke he didn't want overheard. "It's because you're so fat. That's why."

"I couldn't care less," Pedro said coldly, but he felt as though he'd been betrayed by his own soft flesh, and it made him feel funny, but all he said was, "All right. All right," and he moved away from the telephone.

Mother Africa

SPRING THAT YEAR arrived in New York City on the tenth of
April, quite early in the morning. Even in midtown Manhattan
the air drifting down between the skyscrapers suggested that
the earth was slowly warming up, coming alive again, after a
long hard snowy winter. The early morning sun actually en-
livened the look of the concrete sidewalks and the brick and
stone of the buildings. It reached into the darkest alleys, the
meanest side streets from the lowest tip of the island to the
upper reaches of Harlem.

In Harlem, a small patch of April sunlight managed to filter
through the dirt-encrusted windows of Emanuel Turner's bedroom. Either because of the sun or because of something in the

air that suggested the arrival of spring, he woke up earlier than usual.

He eyed the small patch of sunlight on his bedroom floor. "I better get going early," he said aloud. "They'll all be cleaning house today."

In the spring when women cleaned house his business increased because they threw away a lot of stuff that he picked up and sold. He was the only black man in the area who dealt in junk and secondhand items. He did a good business. His neighbors called him Rags, Ole Rags, Junk, Ole Junk, Bottles, Ole Bottles. His friends called him Man or Mannie.

His preparations for his business day were simple. He slept in his shirt, a ragged buttonless garment, once blue, now a faded gray. Reaching down toward the foot of the bed, he grabbed his trousers, got out of bed, put them on and fastened them about his waist with a piece of rope.

He ate his breakfast with relish: half a bottle of orange juice, four sausages, three eggs, a pot of coffee, half a pan of corn bread left over from the night before. Having thrust his bare feet into his shoes — a pair of combat boots he'd fished out of a garbage can — he was ready to set out on a careful inspection of the contents of as many refuse cans as he could reach before the arrival of the Department of Sanitation trucks. Glorified name for garbage trucks.

The studs who drove those trucks amused him. He laughed whenever he heard the hellish noise they made early in the morning — slam-bang of metal, done deliberately to wake up the people whose stinking garbage they had to handle. They kidded him but they looked out for him. If he was late they yelled, "Wot were you doin', Mannie, gettin' your beauty sleep? We got here fustest with the mostest," and then, "You want any of this stuff?" And they would help him load a discarded chair or a small sofa on his cart.

Another reason he usually got going early was so he wouldn't be caught in heavy traffic with a loaded cart — a good way to get yourself killed. The cars came in close, some of them did it deliberately, and the stink of the exhaust from the buses and the trucks was enough to choke a man to death.

Outside in the big yard, Man paused long enough to make a swift examination of its contents. He ignored the flickering, ever-moving pattern of light and shadow that the sun cast over the disorder and confusion of the yard as he checked the position of the piles of worn-out tires, the inner tubes and parts of cars, the broken chairs and rickety tables, the heaps of clothing and piles of old bottles that constituted his stock. He could tell instantly if anything was missing. He had trained himself to remember the exact position of certain items in relationship to the ones next to them. That way he knew if somebody had been poking through his stuff. People sometimes took a short cut through his yard over to the next block and some of them helped themselves to things they thought they could use, but it didn't happen very often so he never made a fuss about it. But it always gave him a funny feeling. He didn't know when people did this and he felt as though chairs and tables and parts of cars moved away by themselves when he was asleep.

Having made certain that nothing had been disturbed during the night, he got his pushcart from the rotting shed at the back of the yard and set out on his rounds. He was fond of the pushcart; the handles were worn smooth, polished by his hands. They seemed almost like an extension of his hands and arms. And the balance of it on the wheels was beautiful. The cart wheels made a faint rumbling that he could hear despite the street noises, the roar of traffic, the sound of car horns.

In less than a block he picked up a number of salable items: six shapeless felt hats; ten sweaters — most of them in good condition, one not so good; three almost-new quilts; a huge pile of dusty curtains (he would run them through his washing machine — an old one someone gave him in exchange for a dryer he'd picked up free from a moving man); some mismated rubbers; a pair of hardly-worn-at-all galoshes; several usable lamps; an old lantern; a dozen pretty good plates; and a child's highchair in fair condition.

In appreciation of this abundance of salable merchandise and also in appreciation of the clean, cool, shining morning, he began to utter a singsong cry at regular intervals, pausing now and then to look up at the windows of the private houses and the apartment houses he passed.

He had a big baritone voice and he let it out as he half talked, half sang the words: "I B-u-y, b-u-y, b-u-y! Ole rags, ole bottles, ole sewin' machines!" His voice went up and down, down and up. It cut through, went over, went under, the other sounds in the street — the hum of traffic, monotonous, regular; the low-pitched, high-pitched voices of passersby; the sudden sharp screech of brakes slammed on at the traffic light at the corner. No one ever had an old sewing machine to sell or to give away but he liked the sound of the word and his voice lingered on "machines," caressed it, very nearly exhausted the scale on it, as he placed a bit of old metal on his cart.

As he pushed his cart along the edge of the street, near the curb, men and women waiting at bus stops, drivers of trucks and cars, turned for a second look at him. He was so accustomed to being looked at that he ignored the stares, the lingering speculative glances that followed him as he worked his way on down to the next block, moving quickly.

He knew that people did not stare at him because they were

attracted by his melodious voice. They turned to look because
he was so blatantly, and offensively, unwashed, unshaven, un-
combed. His great bushy beard obscured most of his face.
Winter and summer he wore an old navy watch cap pulled way
down on his head, partially covering his well-shaped forehead.
His skin, what could be seen of it, was dark brown. Wind and
weather had burnished it so that there was a faint reddish tinge
under the brown. His eyes were bright, alert; the expression,
wary. His clothing was as unkempt as his hair and his beard.
The blue jeans hitched about his waist might have seen twenty
years of wear, the fabric was so thin and so overlaid with grease
and dirt; the knees and the seat had been reinforced with large
patches of a dark gray material.

What was worse, he gave off a strong goatish smell. Passersby who walked near him, on the curb side, left his vicinity,
hurriedly crossing the street. Having reached the opposite
curb, they usually stopped and looked back, puzzled, appre-
hensive, unbelieving.

He had reached 116th Street with his pushcart when he saw
a long, shiny, chauffeur-driven car slow down and stop, directly
opposite him. He recognized Joe, his old war buddy, and he
crossed the street to talk to him. Joe chauffeured for some rich
white folks out on Long Island and quite often he stopped in
the junkyard and poked around. He was always looking for
brass-bound headlights from very old cars and occasionally he
found one.

Joe said, "Listen, Mannie, I was coming to see you. My
madam is getting rid of a statue. She told me to find a junk
dealer and she'll send it to him. Free. He can do what he wants
with it — sell parts of it separate for antiques or sell all of it for
scrap metal. Is it okay to send it to you, Mannie? You'll make a
lot of money on it."

"A statue?" he said surprised. "Well, sure. Why not?"
Spring and all the women doing housecleaning, black ones and
white ones. Maybe on Long Island when the white women did
their spring cleaning, they got rid of statues.

He started to move off and then he said, "Wait a minute,
Joe," and he frowned. If you stopped to think about it, it was
odd and there was possibly a trick in it. After all, white-
skinned people still fed on the dark-skinned people of the
world. They were like sharks who had discovered an endless
supply of good warm flesh and swarmed around it, gorging
themselves. They started centuries ago in Africa — the ferocious sharks, the slave traders, came first; and the little sharks,
the missionaries, came next with their crosses and their thievish
Christian ways; they were like pilot fish for a breed of truly
ferocious sharks — the looters who came for the ivory, the gold,
the diamonds, the oil. Thieves all of them. He had always
hoped he'd live long enough to see the roles reversed but in the
meantime, a black man had to protect himself against them in
every possible way.

Joe said, "What's on your mind, Mannie?"

"Tell me — why is this white woman getting rid of this
statue?"

"Her husband tried to move it and he got a heart attack and
died and she blames the statue. So she don't want it around any
more. Is it okay to send it to you, huh?"

"Sure. Send it along. Glad to have it. Tell your madam to
send a paper saying it's mine."

"Aw, Mannie, you been dealing with that metalworks for
years. You don't need no paper —"

"Joe," he said, "the metalworks is white and I'm black. Tell
her to send a paper. And thanks."

He watched the shining car pull off. Then he returned to his inspection of the refuse cans. He had bought and sold junk for so many years that he was no longer surprised by the things that people gave away or threw away, and that other people bought. He doubted that Joe's madam was going to send him a statue, the idea of getting rid of it was probably a whim which would vanish as quickly as it came.

Late that afternoon he was fishing through a refuse can on 120th Street. He had found a bundle of broken toys which he carefully placed in his pushcart. Next he pulled out a lamp shade. He was still examining the lamp shade when a little girl came running toward him, calling, "Mr. Junk, Mr. Junk, hurry, hurry, hurry! They want to know where to put it — her — it. Come quick —"

"You're worse than a jumping jack," he said crossly. "Now stop all that hopping up and down and say it all over agin —"

He frowned, listening, and the little girl repeated the same senseless jumble of words with some new ones added: she's come — it's come — hurry — where to put it — her — it — the men — the truck.

After five minutes of 'it's come, she's come,' he placed the lamp shade in his pushcart and headed toward his house, not because he understood the message, but because it was obvious that he was somehow involved in whatever it was that caused such incoherence, such need for hurry.

When he turned into 123rd Street, pushing his cart in front of him, he saw that the street in front of his house was crowded with people. He heard the hum and buzz of their voices, caught exclamations of surprise. They were obviously looking at something or trying to, for the edges of the crowd billowed out, narrowed, bulged again somewhere else as people tried to elbow their way toward the center and were pushed back.

People in the apartment house across the way were leaning out of the windows, staring down into the street, and there were other people on the rooftops and the fire escapes, all pointing, all talking.

He increased his pace to a trot and the cart wheels rumbled as they turned faster and faster. When he reached the edge of the crowd, voices said, "Here he is." "Here's Old Rubbish." "Hi, Bottles." "The Man's come." "Mr. Junk is here, Mister."

Hands thrust him forward, pushed him forward, until he was standing beside a trailer truck, an incredibly long trailer truck. And there, stretched out full length, lying on her back, her face toward the sky, lay a statue of a woman. In one swift, startled glance, Man Turner took in the dark nakedness of the statue, the arch of the breasts, the curve of the thighs.

He sucked in his breath. He could not understand where this thing had come from, why it was here, what it had to do with him.

"What kind of happy horseshit is this?" he demanded. "Where'd this thing come from?"

"Trail's End. Mrs. Treadway's place. Where do you want her?"

"It ain't for me," he said defensively. "I don't go in for no art stuff. There's a mistake."

The driver of the truck thumbed through a sheaf of papers. "You Emanuel Turner?" he asked.

Man admitted, reluctantly, that he was.

"Then it's for you. From Mrs. Charles Edward Treadway." The truck driver took a good long look at Man Turner. He couldn't seem to look away from Man's pants. Finally he said again, "Where you want her put?"

Man did not answer right away. He was staring at the

statue. He had never seen anything like it before. No wonder the whole street had turned out. It was the nakedest woman he'd ever seen or dreamed of or heard of. A most peculiar thing, really, and the truck driver had said something about a Mrs. Treadway.

"Mrs. Treadway?" he said, out of his confusion. "Is she coming, too?"

"The statoor is from Mrs. Treadway," the driver said slowly, carefully. He looked at Man's pants again and shook his head. "Where you want the statoor put?"

"Why —" Man removed his cap, scratched his head, pulled at his beard.

It don't make sense, he thought. Where did it — she — come from? Then he remembered. Of course. It was from Joe's madam. Joe said she wanted to give a statue away. That was all very well and good but he hadn't bargained for anything like this. No wonder she wanted to give it away. He should have known better than to say yes. It just went to prove how a white woman would trick a black man every time — even one she'd never seen. He scowled, thinking it was always open season on black folks in the USA — one way or another.

"Where you want it?" the driver said impatiently.

Man said, "I gotta think."

But he couldn't think. There was a kind of babbling going on in his mind as he stared down at the statue. He had been born in Mississippi, had been taught how to spell the name of the state in a one-room school, shouting in unison with a lot of other half-starved black kids, and in moments of stress the damn thing popped into his thoughts and he would find himself saying it over and over, in march time, just as he was doing now: "M–I–crooked letter–crooked letter–I–crooked letter–

crooked letter–I–humpbacked letter–humpbacked letter–I." As he grew older he thought of Mississippi as a crooked humpbacked state where there was a year-round open season on black folks, no bag limit, no rules, use any weapon — elephant guns, dynamite. Killum. Killum. Kill who? Kill black folks. Killum. And up North? Here in Harlem? Killum. Play tricks on um. Send um statues of big and buck-naked black women and —

"Hey," said the truck driver. "I got all these other deliveries I gotta make — let's go — let's go —"

Man thought, What will I do with it? Certainly he couldn't sell it. There wasn't any market for stuff like that.

"I guess you better put it — her — back there in the yard," he said, pointing toward the rear of the junkyard.

Four men from the trailer truck pushed the statue along on a dolly. Stepping cautiously through the litter, maneuvering the dolly around ancient plumbing fixtures, parts of cars, broken chairs and tables, piles of rusted iron, they headed toward a small rubbish free space near the back of the yard.

The entire nonworking population of the neighborhood, excited housewives and their equally excited preschool-age children, soft-voiced men and women too old or too sick to work, formed an escort, walking just behind, or to the side, or a little ahead of the statue. They shouted to each other and to the children: "You, sonny, get out of the way!" "Look out for them broken bottles!" "Gramps, that's the second time you tripped me with that cane. Now you go home!"

When they reached the back of the yard, the driver said, "We'd better stand her up. There ain't no place to lay her down flat."

Man signed a receipt for the statue, scrawling his name on

the paper the truck driver held out to him. Then the driver handed him another paper saying, "Here. This proves it's yours."

Once the truckers were gone, the neighbors drifted away, leaving him alone with this terribly naked statue. He walked around it, studying it. It occurred to him that he could have refused to accept it.

Reaching in his pants pocket, he got out a corncob pipe, stuffed it with a coarse dark tobacco, lit it. He puffed on it and was dismayed to find that it had lost its power to soothe him — or else he was too upset to be soothed by anything. He should have told the truckers to dump this dark, naked, metal woman in the Harlem River. He couldn't have a thing like this smack in the middle of his junkyard. Well, not exactly in the middle, sort of to one side, near the back fence, but she might as well be right out in the street. Worse than having a three-ring circus in a place of business.

He got his pushcart and went back to his examination of the contents of the refuse cans, hurrying now because it was getting late. He decided that he would not keep the statue. If she didn't sell right off the bat, and he doubted that she would, for no person in their right mind would buy a thing like that, why he'd sell her as scrap metal to the metalworks, and they could melt her down and he'd be rid of her.

That night, after he finished his supper, he went out in the yard, intending to sort over his day's haul of junk. Instead, he stood idle, staring at the statue. The neighbors were staring, too. And talking as they stared.

"Hey, look at what's in the junkyard."

"I'll move out. I won't have my children livin' next to no such a thing as that."

"That dirty old Bottles oughta be ashamed of himself. That thing's a disgrace to the neighborhood."

"I bet you he's out of his mind. You children stay away from him, you hear?"

"Lookit Old Junk standin' there lookin' her over. He's probably drunk." Another voice said, "That's it. He's drunk and crazy. Drunk and crazy."

"Somebody oughta do somethin'!"

Man Turner listened to them, thinking, They act as though I was deaf. His first impulse was to go to the metalworks right then and there and sell the statue for whatever price he could get. And then a small boy and a small girl leaned out of an upper window of the apartment house next door, pointed at him, and chanted, in unison:

Shame! Shame!
Everbody know your dirty black name!
Shame! Shame!
Everbody know your dirty black name!

He frowned. He'd be darned if he'd sell the statue. He'd keep her. Just for spite. He'd done favors for all these people who were now calling him dirty, crazy, drunken. He'd mended toys for those shrill-voiced kids who were making up rhymes about him. For a price, of course, but he gave good value, did good careful work. He didn't sell broken stuff, always fixed it up first. And he didn't have to.

But then after he went inside his house he kept thinking that that statue was the most terribly alive-looking piece of metal he had ever seen — stark naked and alive. He'd best be rid of it. He'd sell her first thing in the morning.

That was the last thing he thought about before he drifted off to sleep, lulled to sleep by the quiet. For to a city ear the street was quiet; so was the house. All sounds were subdued, far-off. Somewhere in the distance a car passed, its motor making a gentle hum. In the next block a bus snorted to a stop, snorted off again; a policeman's whistle sounded; and three streets away a fire engine roared past. Man Turner's ears were so attuned to these street noises that he no longer really heard them. They were like music in the distance — he knew the sounds were there but he had long since stopped listening to them.

And then this normal, quiet, city night suddenly became abnormal, unquiet. Man Turner woke up, sat up in bed. He heard the wail of the siren on a police car, excited voices, and then gunfire. He got up and looked out of his bedroom window. The yard was filled with light — brilliant shafts of white light that picked up and then lost a running, crouching figure which darted back and forth, now hiding behind the piles of junk, now out in the open with other bulkier figures in pursuit.

Man pulled on his pants, fastening them about his waist with the piece of rope as he went down the stairs and then out into the yard. Halfway down the yard he was pinioned in one of the shafts of light.

"Don't move. Who are you?"

White cop, he thought. Ready to shoot. "I live here," he said truculently. "I own the place. What's going on?"

"Guy with a gun. Gone nuts I guess. He's shootin' up the block."

Instantly Man thought of the statue, the metal woman. And walked toward her, looked up at her. She was okay. Queer thing to do, though. If he was going to sell her in the morning, why should he care what happened to her? Folks who bought metal by the pound didn't lower the price if the metal was scratched or scarred or dented by bullets.

A bullet whistled past his head and he ducked.

"He's gone down the back," someone shouted.

There was the sound of running feet, an assault on the back fence — hard, furious, sudden. The fence went down with a splintering sound as the rotten wood gave way.

One of the policeman paused halfway down the yard. His flashlight illuminated the statue. The light wavered.

"What —" the cop said, "what in hell's name is that?"

Man did not answer. And the cop moved off, reluctantly joining the chase. Man watched him go. Then he did something he could not afterwards account for, did it unconsciously, without thinking. When the spotlight fell on the metal woman he saw that she was dusty, a fine film of gray dust overlaid the metal. Using his hands and his arm as a dustcloth, he wiped the gray film from her feet. He was startled by the result. Her feet gleamed in the darkness of the yard. He stared at them wondering what she would look like if she were dusted all over.

The next morning he got up earlier than usual. When he went out into the yard, he took a pail of warm, soapy water and a long-handled window-washing brush with him. He brushed the dust off the metal woman and he washed her and then he rinsed her off. When he was finished he stared up at her, entranced. The dark naked figure glowed. That was the word for it, he thought: glowed. He felt something stir within him, an emotion that he could not put a name to. It was like seeing something dark and beautiful beyond description for the first time and yet recognizing it, because in the deepest part of your mind you had always known that that kind of dark glowing beauty existed. Mother Africa, he thought. That's what she really is: Mother Africa. He made up his mind right then and there to keep her.

Later in the day he wished he hadn't cleaned the metal woman up. After he returned to the yard with his cart, his first customers arrived — women accompanied by their children. He had always enjoyed their visits for they told him all the news of the neighborhood while they bargained over the price of the toys, the dishes, and pots and pans and used clothing they came to buy. But not today.

They took one look at the metal woman and turned sullen or angry; some of them were so embarrassed that they fell silent and left quickly, without so much as a glance at Man's stock of secondhand items. The children hid behind their mothers' skirts and peered out at the statue, giggled, ducked back, eyed the statue again, and were convulsed with a sly, almost adult, laughter.

Many of the women seemed to be outraged by the nakedness of the metal woman, by the perfection of her figure. They vented their feelings in a heavy-handed assault on the children. They cuffed their offspring about the head, the back, slapped them smartly across the legs, shouting, "You take that and that! You laughin' at that nekkid huzzy!" or "You come along home. I'll learn you to stand around pointin' at a thing like that!" Then they dragged the children away, out of the junkyard, away from the statue, and the children howled, emitting such wails of anguish that the mothers paused and slapped them harder.

Man, standing by, silent, distressed, sucked on his corncob pipe, tugged at his beard, thinking that he had never before experienced so disorderly and unprofitable an afternoon. He had not made a single sale.

When his male customers arrived, the disorder increased. The men always came later in the day; they came in search of bolts and nails and odd pieces of lumber or metal. When they saw the metal woman they roared with laughter, and almost immediately they decided to share the sight of this unusual statue with their friends. They kept leaving the junkyard and returning with other men. By five in the afternoon the metal woman was surrounded by the hangers-on, the touts, the evil ones, the lost ones, from all the bars and poolrooms for blocks around. These shameless strangers hooted at the metal woman, shouted hoarse-voiced greetings to her. They slapped her bare metallic bottom, fingered her legs, passed judgment on her breasts.

Man scowled at them, hating the sight of their fumbling, dirty hands and the sound of their raucous laughter. He circled about them, restlessly, willing them to leave; for it was perfectly obvious that they did not intend to buy anything. But they stayed in the junkyard until darkness obscured the metal woman's curves.

He thought that in a day or two the statue would be forgotten and everything would be just as it had been before. But it wasn't. During the night someone, drunk or sober, male or female, hung a pink brassiere on the metal woman, draping it lewdly across her breasts. It flapped in the wind. The harsh pink of the material was an outrage to the dark beauty of the statue. And Man viewing it, felt harassed.

He never knew from one day to the next what item of discarded clothing would be pinned about her waist or draped around her shoulders. Once he found that an ancient straw hat had been pulled down on her head, a woman's hat, out of shape, the straw cracked and dusty, the brim obscuring the metal woman's face; and an old black coat had been thrown around her shoulders. He used a long pole to remove the hat and coat, thinking, Whoever did this musta been ten feet tall to reach up that high.

That same afternoon one of his roomers moved out. He was a thin, dispirited man who had lived in the house for so many years he seemed as much a part of the place as the broken back steps. Yet he packed his shabby belongings in a battered suitcase and moved out. Before he left, he made it a point to protest to Man. He was loud-voiced and indignant, saying, "You mark what I tell you, nobody'll live in your house. They'll all move out. That metal woman walks at night. Walks around without any clothes on. Comes right in my room. Walks in and out of my windows."

The neighbors listened while the thin man talked. But they were not too impressed because everybody knew the thin man was given to drink; and when a man drinks, heavily, night after night, alone, he is liable to see things, statues and such, walking about in his room.

Man was impressed though. He was losing money because of the metal woman. He decided that if she were placed further back in the yard she wouldn't be so conspicuous. He tried to move her. Though he sweated and strained, pushed and pulled, he couldn't budge her. He'd have to have a derrick she was so heavy. Then he thought if he built a kind of barricade of junk in front of her, people wouldn't be able to see her. In the afternoons, after he finished his rounds, he started piling large objects in front of her. He had forgotten he owned some of it. He soon discovered that it was impossible to pile stuff up high enough to cover her up. The men still patted her bare bottom with their horny hands; and the women frowned and slapped the children and dragged them away.

It occurred to him that he could build a new fence across the

back of the yard, taller than the old broken one. This new
fence would at least protect the metal woman from the people
who lived in back of the junkyard. He spent a few afternoons
building the fence, a tight board fence. He painted it white.
When he finished painting it, he stood off and admired it. The
metal woman looked good in front of the fence. Only she sort
of stood out against it, showed up more. Perhaps he shouldn't
have painted it.

He shook his head, frowning, swinging the paint bucket back
and forth. "Should. Shouldn't," he muttered impatiently. He
never had doubted his own decisions before. "I wonder what's
come over me."

He pondered over this as he fixed his supper in the basement
kitchen of the house. He ate slowly, thinking that he had been
a free man for years now, no worries, no doubts. Now and then
he stopped eating to stare at the grimy walls of the kitchen, to
tug at his beard, as he thought about his way of life. It was a
simple life, uncomplicated, ideal, because it was the kind of life
which meant you slept straight through the night; no lying
awake, twisting and turning, while you thought: If I had done
this or had not done that, things would have been better; no
long lost hours spent regretting a course of action.

He was drinking his second cup of hot strong coffee when he
heard a loud outraged voice, a woman's voice, lifted in complaint, in wrath. He recognized the voice at once. It belonged
to Ginny the Baptist, the bedraggled, faded, young-old woman,
who had occupied a room on the second floor of his house for
the last ten years. She was given to disappearing for days at a
time — some of his tenants said she was in jail, others said she
was working. As long as she paid her rent promptly — and she
always did — he didn't give a hoot nor a holler where she went

or how long she was gone. Sometimes she returned from these absences cold sober, other times she was roaring drunk. But drunk or sober, she always smelt of gin.

He listened to her voice, thinking, this time she's drunk and nasty.

"I'll fix you," she shouted. He heard the sound of blows. Resonant. Repeated. "I'll fix you. Stand there laughin' at me, will you, you loon! You take that and that!"

He got up and looked out of the back door and then hurried out into the yard. Ginny the Baptist was beating the metal woman with the rusted fender of a car, stumbling, rocking forward and then back, nearly falling, but striking the metal woman, hip and thigh, and calling her such names that he shuddered.

He wrenched the fender out of her hand. "Get out of here," he shouted, angrily. He aimed a mighty blow at Ginny's head. She ducked and screamed.

"Get out of my yard," he said. "And get out of my house and don't you ever set foot in it again, you black bitch!"

As he watched her shove her miserable belongings into two paper shopping bags, he scowled ferociously. He had never put a roomer out before and he'd had all kinds — drunken, sober, honest, dishonest, clean, dirty, all kinds. As long as they paid their rent and didn't mess around in his affairs, he was content with them. He never had liked change. Yet here he was, after all these years, putting a roomer out and calling her names and —

Ginny lurched toward the stairs, gripped the banisters with a trembling hand and started down. He walked behind her, ignoring her muttered, "Calling the kettle black —"

No, he thought, as she stumbled out of sight around the cor-

ner, he'd never liked change. But — He went out in the yard
and stared at the metal woman and then examined her to see if
Ginny had damaged her. She was all right, the smooth dark
surface was unmarred. But if he was going to keep her like
this, he'd have to move his junkyard. It was the only way to
keep people — drunken women like Ginny the Baptist, dirty-
handed men, snickering children, and their sullen angry
mothers — away from the metal woman.

He did not like the idea but he started tearing down the ramshackle shed which ran along one side of his property. He
would be losing money, for he rented that rotting shed. People
kept their cars under it and paid for the privilege. Having torn
the shed down, he spent the next two weeks rebuilding it. Then
he moved every piece of junk out of the yard, parts of cars,
discarded bathtubs and sinks, bits of metal, piles of bottles,
broken chairs and tables. He made trip after trip, hauling the
stuff in his handcart, sweating, straining, cursing the necessity
that made him do this.

He housed the junk in the rebuilt shed. And he built another
fence, another tight board fence, completely separating the
place where he sold junk from the place where the metal
woman stood.

The day after he finished the fence he saw a garden bench,
an old-fashioned wooden bench, in the window of a Salvation
Army store. He went in and priced it. The woman in the store
eyed his beard and his ragged clothes and drew a little away
from him. "It's three dollars," she said hesitantly.

"Sold," he said.

He took the bench home on his pushcart and put it out in the
yard. Though he knew there must be customers waiting for

him in the shed that now housed his collection of junk, he sat down on the bench, and puffing his corncob pipe, studied the metal woman. He was pleased. The neighbors would forget about her now for they could no longer see her. Neither could his customers. They, too, would forget her. She could be seen only from the rear windows of his house.

As he sat there looking at her, he tried to think what it was she resembled. He decided that she was like a small clean river seen early on a spring morning. The thought made him feel like singing, and he hummed softly under his breath, as he stared at her defined waistline, the curve of her thighs.

He stopped humming, thinking that if she could be seen only from the rear windows of his house, then — he turned and examined the house. It wasn't, if you tried to view it through her eyes, well, it wasn't much to look at. The house, from the back, appeared to be a brick wall punctuated, at intervals, by a series of hazy, soot-encrusted windows like those in that abandoned warehouse near the Harlem River, you couldn't see through them any more. And the back door sagged on its hinges, the bottom step was broken . . .

Turning away from the house, he shrugged his shoulders. Once you started finding fault with a place, you were bound to spend money on it and once you started doing that, it was a sure thing you'd lie awake nights trying to figure out where the money was coming from and then you were no longer free. He glanced down at the hard-packed earth under his feet, scuffed his feet back and forth. The ground was hard, just like concrete. He thought about the statue that sat in the little park at 124th Street — a man on horseback, nothing special about that statue but it looked good because of the grass around it.

He turned his attention back to the metal woman. If she had

grass around her, she would look like spring itself. It wouldn't cost very much to have grass out here in the yard. Couldn't, not if the city was so free with it in the parks and everybody knew the city was stingy, pinch-penny stingy.

He was humming under his breath again when he went to attend to his customers. As he moved about the rebuilt shed, buying and selling and talking about his stock, he congratulated himself for having moved the junkyard. His business was now, suddenly and miraculously, normal. The shed was crowded with women who had come to buy, and now that they were no longer disturbed and angered by the sight of the metal woman's naked beauty, they were completely amiable. They chatted with each other, examined his stock with care, spoke to their children with affection, and bought toys for them.

While he listened to the brisk soprano chatter of the women, relishing it, part of his mind kept evoking a picture of the metal woman, standing not as she did now on hard bare ground, but as she would look when surrounded by thick green grass. This picture, vivid, recurrent, lingered in his mind. It was a stimulus so powerful that it won out over his aversion to spending money. Because of it, he not only purchased grass seed but he also bought loam and topsoil. He dug up the yard — a slow hard job, added loam and topsoil, raked it smooth. After he scattered the grass seed he watched over it with a fierce protectiveness, chasing the cats and dogs who dug in the now soft earth, shooing away the sparrows that picked the seed out of the ground.

His vigilance was rewarded. By the end of May the yard was covered with a pale green fuzz, which he felt well worth the time and effort and money it had cost him. This pale green fuzz slowly deepened in color, thickened in texture, until by the end of June it had become a lawn — smooth, velvety, like an expensive carpet.

The weather turned suddenly hot. There was no rain. So Man watered the lawn every night. He enjoyed this nightly watering of the lawn. The sight of water gushing from the nozzle of the hose, the slow movement with which he directed and redirected its flow toward a patch of grass which looked hot and thirsty, made him feel cool. During the day while he pushed his cart through streets enveloped in thick dreadful heat, he thought with pleasure of the moment when he would turn the hose on the lawn. But he knew that this pleasure was largely due to the presence of the metal woman, for on the hottest afternoon, she looked cool, impervious to the heat.

This sudden wave of heat caused a restlessness throughout the city. And on a night when the moon was full, the restlessness increased. People could not sleep. They were vaguely dissatisfied, and they quarreled or made love and could not explain why they were moved to do either the one or the other. Babies, who as a rule slept straight through the night, woke up and cried or laughed for no reason at all. A holdup man in the upper reaches of the Bronx watched a likely victim approach, in the moonlight, and let him pass, unmolested.

In Man Turner's neighborhood the moon worked its magic, too. The black cop on the beat, big, young, tough, stared up at the moon for a good half-hour and thought about a girl and decided to propose to her, though up to that moment, he had always sneered at marriage and all it represented.

Toward midnight, the monkey in the yard next to Man Turner's, kept chained there by the man who owned him, began to chatter and jabber; and the sound made the night seem hotter, and, curiously enough, quieter. A lean tomcat, who normally maintained a yowling vigil on Man's back fence, was unaccountably silent as he sat, crouched down on the fence, apparently staring at the moonlight shimmering on the leaves of the ailanthus tree that grew along the fence.

The brilliant white light from the moon that was washing over the city, disturbing the city, seeped into Man's disorderly bedroom. He woke up.

He was quite accustomed to the sound of the Ape, as he called the monkey, but he had never heard him chattering at night. He did not know whether it was the heat or the moonlight or the jabbering of the Ape but he simply could not go back to sleep. He pulled on his disreputable pants, and securing them about his waist with the piece of rope that served him as a belt, he walked, barefooted, out into the yard.

Thus for the first time he saw the metal woman in the moonlight. He stared at her, moving toward her slowly like someone who was sleepwalking. His bare feet were deep in the soft grass, cool in the soft grass. He reached out his hand, tentatively, and touched her. She did not feel like metal at all. Cool, yes. But she seemed to respond, to come alive, to move under the touch of his hand, to leap with life.

He felt like singing. But he had no song, never had heard of any song, suited for such a moment, no melody that could possibly match the feeling of tenderness that suddenly assailed him at the thought that this big dark woman was his. He had Mother Africa right here in his yard.

He sang, "I buy — buy — buy — ole clothes — ole rags — ole sewin' machines!" and it became a paean of praise, sung softly, sweetly, in the moonlight. He went up and down the scale five times on 'ole sewin' machines.'

And then he padded softly back into the house.

First thing the next morning he looked down the length of the grass-covered yard at the metal woman. Flickering sunlight dappled her shapely legs, her outstretched arms, her slender waist. In his mind's eye he saw her as she had looked in the soft light from the moon — so alive that he thought of her as a living, breathing black woman, so beautiful that there were no words to describe her except: Mother Africa.

He began to whistle. He whistled a tune that he made up, on the spur of the moment. He whistled it over and over, thinking that it matched the metal woman, was suited to her. It was a young tune, it had a lilt and a lift to it.

Under the spell of this whistled tune, he walked over and looked at himself in the long, cloudy mirror that hung on the door of his bedroom. He did not know why, but he had expected to find in his own reflection something of the beauty of the tune, something of the beauty of the metal woman. Instead — well, he loathed what he saw. There was nothing in his dirty, ragged, unkempt appearance to suggest that he could create beauty, certainly nothing to suggest that he would ever be able to recognize beauty in anything. He looked like a creature born solely for the creation of ugliness.

He suddenly yearned to be clean.

He took a bath. Before he was clean he took three baths in hot soapy water, rinsing himself off each time in clear water. He scrubbed himself from head to foot. Then he got a pair of scissors and hacked at his hair, at his beard. The result was dreadful. Finally he dressed, hurriedly put on a clean shirt, hitched his disreputable pants about his waist with the piece of rope. Then he went to the barber shop on the corner.

Sam, the barber, looked at Man Turner over the top of the morning paper.

"I ain't got nothin' to sell today, Junk," he said quickly, "nor to give away." He talked fast, hoping that Junk would leave fast because he'd have to air the place out before any customers dropped in and airing out after Junk had been in the shop for five minutes was kind of hard.

Man sat down in the barber chair nearest the window. "Shave and haircut," he said.

Sam the barber groaned. "I always figgered this was goin' to happen to me someday," he said. "My daddy used to say to me when I took up barberin', 'Sam, someday you goin' to get a customer what ain't never had no shave, and never had no hair-cut and then you goin' regret havin' took up barberin' as a way of eatin'. There's easier ways to get food.'" He approached Man with caution, sniffing the air. He sniffed again, incredu-lously. For some reason Junk didn't smell bad anymore; just faintly bad.

"It's them pants," Sam the barber said, under his breath.

Sam set to work. He started with Man's head. He snipped, he clipped, he combed, he brushed. He slowly clipped and snipped his way through the matted underbrush that was Man Turner's hair, again and yet again.

He said bitterly, "Wouldya mind tellin' me how long it's been since you had a haircut and a shave?"

Man smiled. He felt light as air, like a cloud in the sky, like a red balloon floating down a street, moved by the merest pulsa-tion of a breeze. Light as air and clean as a whistle.

"It's been years," he said happily. He bet he could float right out through the door of Sam's shop, out through the door, down the street, through stone walls and brick walls. He smiled again. He had very good teeth, sound, evenly spaced, white. "I've lost track, it's been so many years —"

Twenty-five years, at least, he thought. Could be longer. Time had a way of fooling you. Probably closer to twenty-six years. During the Second World War he had endured months of spit and polish, of schedules, exact, unchanging — summed up for him at least, in those mocking words, "You're in the army now, you son of a bitch — you're in the army now —" Well, anyway, his thoughts had been a refrain, repeated, never varying: If I ever get out of here alive, if I ever get out of here alive, if I ever get out of here alive, so help me God, I'll never shave or comb my hair or —

But he did.

While Man sat there in the barber shop, soothed by the snip-snip-snip of Sam's scissors, he thought about the past. Sam talked as he worked on Man. Man heard some of what he said, missed a lot of what he said. Once he started to get up out of the chair because it seemed to him that he was making a dreadful mistake, losing his beard and his hair, all at once.

Why was he getting a haircut and shave? He really didn't know. That time, so long ago, when he came out of the army, the war over, and the peace already half over, at one and the same time, he hadn't stopped shaving. Oh, no. Because he met Mary Lou Brown on a street in Harlem. Right at the corner of 125th Street and Seventh Avenue, to be exact. He bumped into her. And he knew he couldn't live without Mary Lou Brown.

He convinced Mary Lou Brown she couldn't live without him. After they were married he found out that she believed that cleanliness was next to godliness. She didn't say this, and looking at her a man wouldn't necessarily know it — though he should have suspicioned it because she always looked and smelt as though she had just stepped out of a tub of hot soapy water. Her clothes were like that, too. And her hair. She had a passion for scrubbing and washing and dusting and sweeping.

During those first few months of their marriage, he found out something else about Mary Lou Brown. She firmly believed that many a mickle makes a muckle. She didn't say this either. But she headed him straight toward a job. He worked in a factory where he punched a time clock and every Friday night he handed his pay envelope, unopened, over to Mary. He ate his meals according to a time clock, too; or at least he might as well have, because breakfast was at seven-thirty, sharp; lunch at twelve-thirty; and dinner at six-thirty. These hours never varied. Just like in the army, he knew beforehand what he was going to eat: fish on Fridays, beans on Saturdays, chicken on Sunday, leftovers on Monday and Tuesday, liver every Wednesday, pork chops on Thursdays and start again with fish on Friday. And he loved it, loved his life with Mary Lou.

Sam the barber started in on Man's face — clipping, snipping, brushing. He muttered softly under his breath.

Man ignored Sam, went back to thinking about Mary Lou. She saw to it that he didn't hang around with the boys anymore. He didn't have time. He went to night school, every night, after dinner, to learn more so he could earn more. Which was peculiar if you stopped and thought about it long enough. But he was too happy to object to the rigid schedule he adhered to; because Mary Lou Turner, nee Brown, had the kind of smile and face and body that would keep a man following her halfway around the world, pacing behind her, on a leading string.

Sam the barber said, peering out of the window, "There goes Fishmouth Taylor with his new girl friend. Kind of spindle-shanked, too, just like the last one. He must like 'em that way —"

Man nodded as best he could for Sam was still snipping away at his face. If Fishmouth Taylor had a new girl friend, then surely the first spindle-shanked one would be getting rid of the material evidence of Fishmouth's affection. He made a mental note to stop at 129th Street first thing in the morning, probably find quite an assortment of souvenir cushions and costume jewelry and other items in the rubbish.

His thoughts returned to Mary Lou. And then — Next they were going to have a baby and life was filled with the wonder of it, the miracle of it. But Mary Lou died in childbirth and the baby died, too. He truly believed if they hadn't been black and lived in Harlem, that Mary Lou and the baby might have survived.

He felt as though something inside him had been torn out, literally. For a long time he stayed in the apartment, not able to do anything, not able to think, not even able to curse whatever fate it was that had destroyed his life. His friend Joe looked after him. He and Joe had been friends for years, in the army together and even before that, born in that crooked humpbacked state, and Joe even knew that same way to remember how to spell Mississippi, M–I–crooked letter–I–and the rest of it.

For days after Mary Lou's death he couldn't eat or think or plan. He did not consciously give up his job or stop attending night school. He just stayed inside the apartment, as lifeless as a sick cat. It was painful to think about even now with the cushion of twenty-five years of living in between.

Finally he moved out of the apartment, sold the furniture. To his surprise, he got more for it than it cost. Mary Lou's careful polishing seemed to have increased its value. His friend Joe got him a room in a rooming house, on 123rd Street. It was a big, old house, with high ceilings, tall windows — completely run-down. There was a large yard in the back. His room didn't cost much and soon he got accustomed to the dirt and grime.

He kept brooding over a business, something that wouldn't require much capital, no regular hours. He remembered the furniture he'd sold. People were always searching for and buying household goods. He decided to sell secondhand furniture. Better still, he'd become a junk dealer. All he needed was a pushcart. The big yard would come in handy; he could store stuff in it, sell stuff from it.

After a month's hard work he happened to look at himself in a mirror. He had been hustling so fast he hadn't had time to go to the barber's. He needed a haircut. He hadn't shaved either. His shirt was filthy, so were his hands and his face; his skin seemed to have absorbed the soot and the grime from the junk he'd handled.

He didn't bother to get a haircut or to shave. As his hair and his beard grew longer, he found they were an asset. He looked as though he could not pay much of anything for discarded furniture, clothing, bric-a-brac. People often gave him stuff.

"Hey, Junkman," they said. "Come around to the back. We got some things for you. You can have 'em."

Other folks bought these same discarded items with an eagerness that astonished him. It was a funny world, he often thought, with one half of it willing to pay good hard cash for what the other half threw away.

He spent very little money. When the seat of his pants finally gave way, he simply selected another pair from the stock he kept in the basement and wore those until the knees and seat gave way. He wore no underwear, no socks. If it hadn't been for the concrete sidewalks, he would have gone barefoot. He not only made money but he saved it too. And he was able to buy the shabby old rooming house. He started renting out rooms himself.

As the years slipped away, he slowly came to the conclusion

that he was one of the few really free men, white or black, any-where in the world. Other men were slaves to jobs or automo-biles or houses or women. Time cracked a remorseless whip over their heads, urging them on whenever they faltered, tight-ening the chains about their wrists and ankles. No matter how fast they trotted, it was never quite fast enough for them to make enough money to be free. But *he* was free. It cost him little or nothing to live; he was able to go and come as he pleased, work only if he felt like it.

Sam the barber lathered Man and shaved him. As a matter of fact, he lathered and shaved him three times before he reached what he called rock bottom — that is, Man Turner's skin.

Man slowly became aware that Sam was staring at him, open-mouthed, backing away, peering, coming up close again.

Sam said, "Why, you ain't old at all, Junk." He sounded sur-prised. And then he said, "Nobody'll know you. Not a livin' soul'll know you." Pause. "Say, you know you could disappear and nobody'd know where to find you. They could pass you on the street and they wouldn't know you was you." He handed Man a mirror, murmuring, "Nobody'd know you. Look at your-self, Junk!"

Man accepted the mirror and frowned. He didn't really want to look at himself. No man wants to look head-on at his own face after not having seen it for twenty-five years. He glanced in the mirror and the frown deepened. He'd felt like a red bal-loon floating down the street; well, now, his stomach was turn-ing around inside him and he felt solid, heavy, flesh-blood-and-bone heavy — earthbound.

This was his face? He shivered. It was like seeing your own ghost. Because this face unearthed by Sam the barber was the face of Mary Lou's husband, the face that had endured shock and sorrow. It was a little heavier about the jowls; and it was a — well, it wasn't a bad face, not an evil face. The skin was surprisingly smooth. He had forgotten what the skin on his face looked like. It was an unnatural faded color where the beard had been but the sun would take care of that.

Once again he knew doubt. If he had had his beard trimmed a little, not cut off, it might have been better. Having it cut off made him feel as though he had borrowed a face back, reached back twenty-five years to the days when he was married to Mary Lou and helped himself to that face — and — well, this clean-shaven face was in bondage now. This time there was no Mary Lou to make the bondage desirable.

"Should. Shouldn't," he muttered irritably. Well, he'd done it. His face was bare now, like the top of a bald man's head — billiard-ball bare. And that was that.

"Clean, anyway," he said, as he handed the mirror back to Sam.

Sam brushed Man off, unpinned the cloth from around his neck. He said, "Lissen, Junk, mebbe I shouldn't say so. But — er — now you got yourself all nice and cleaned up, and most of the smell is gone, you oughta get rid of them pants."

"Get rid of my pants?" Man said. He had heard what Sam the barber said, but he had been thinking his own private thoughts, and it was a sad truth but there was damn little connection between what went on inside your head, and what was going on at the same time inside another man's head; and inevitably, when the other man spoke his thoughts aloud, as Sam had just done, you always ended up startled by the complete lack of connection.

"Yeah," Sam said. "Them pants don't smell good. No offense meant but —"

"Oh — uh — well, no offense taken. I kind of wondered —"

Man left the barber shop and went straight home. He selected a new pair of pants from the stock in the basement. Corduroy pants, clean, never worn. They were a pretty good fit, too. He rummaged around until he found a belt.

Then he went upstairs, put on the new pants, and looked at himself in the mirror, that long cloudy mirror that hung in his room. He had to get used to himself before he took the pushcart out. He gestured with his hands, smiled, raised his eyebrows. Then he half talked, half sang his cry, "I buy-buy-buy ole rags, ole bottles, ole sewin' machines!"

He felt like a fool, watching this clean bare-faced stranger who was himself. Even his cry, familiar as it was, sounded strange to his ears. He could not trace the way he'd come, and that made him feel queerer. Why, after all these years, had he cut off his beard, his hair? The back of his neck felt cold. And the new corduroy pants were stiff, unyielding.

The metal woman, he suddenly remembered, was responsible for this change in him. But why? It was the way she looked, just last night, with the moon shining on her. It seemed a long time ago, not last night. When he lost his beard he must have lost all sense of the passing of time.

He went out in the yard to confront the metal woman, in the hope that she would make him feel better. But she didn't. He frowned as he looked at her. She was only a statue, made of some dark metal. Yet he resented her as deeply as though she had been a live woman who had tricked him into cutting off his beard.

Turning away from her, he got his pushcart and set out on his rounds of the refuse cans. He was late. And the pickings were few and far between. The sanitation trucks had beaten him to the best places; other junkmen had gone through the rest of the stuff.

It was an effort to push the cart. He found himself suddenly and violently aware of the passing of time. He kept wondering whether he had done the best possible thing with his life, whether perhaps he'd missed his original destiny. It may have been marked down somewhere and he had ignored it, and now would never reach it. This troubling thought gave him a gnawing sense of guilt, as though he had betrayed the man whose face he now bore.

His afternoon customers did not lift his spirits. Sam the barber was right. Nobody knew him. His oldest customers prowled under the shed, seeking bargains, eyed him, ignored him. Having decided on their purchase, they approached him, saying, "Where's Ole Bottles? You bought him out?"

It was a mixing-up business and obviously a dreadful mistake on his part. Children, who the day before had leaned against him, their bodies warm, and pressed close as they watched him mend their broken toys, now stared at him distrustfully, as though suddenly confronted by a stranger who had not yet declared whether he was friend or foe. What was more disconcerting, many of the sensitive little ones recognized his voice, and stared up at his face, his mouth, in an awful unwinking appraisal. He suspected that they thought he had swallowed Ole Bottles and, as a result, was now speaking with Ole Bottles' voice.

He had never committed any serious crimes against the law or against the state. He did not have any major breaches of the moral code on his conscience. But when he found himself surrounded by a group of children, all staring at him with fixed gaze, he turned away from them, and began a fidgety nervous appraisal of his life. He almost convinced himself that somewhere in his past he had committed a dark and treacherous deed which these children had ferreted out.

Turning on the children, he shouted roughly, "Go home! All of you go home!" He spoke with Ole Bottles' voice, and the children backed away from him, edged toward the door of the shed, still staring, whispering, "It's him," "It ain't him," " 'Tis, too."

As he watched them leave, he felt ashamed because he had sent them away and yet he was glad to be rid of them. He wanted to be alone so that he could straighten out his thoughts. He went towards the back of the yard to look at the metal woman again.

"Oh, goddamn," he said aloud.

While he was out on his rounds, someone had put a long dress on the metal woman — it was a gaudy print, purple and red and orange and blue. The sleeves of the dress had been pulled over the outstretched arms and it had been buttoned all the way from the neck to the hem. A bright red bandana had been wrapped tightly around her head and tied in place.

Reaching up he gave the dress a violent jerk and it tore and he was able to pull it off.

"Oh, goddamn," he said again, this time under his breath. The dress that he held in his hands was made of cheap cotton. White missionaries had put dresses just like this on African women, covering them from neck to ankles, even the arms, and Africa a tropical country. They had them wear bandanas and head rags, so that even their hair was concealed. They made Africans ashamed of their good strong black bodies. The white missionaries came first and brought all that cheap bright cotton with them. The other white folks came in behind them, white thieves who stole the gold and the ivory and the diamonds and the oil, stole a whole continent and used this same kind of cheap bright cloth as bait. It irritated him that a lot of the young dudes hanging around on the street corners wore loose shirts made of gaudy cotton cloth, and called them dashikis, thought they were African, but the truth of the matter was that white missionaries had brought that stuff into Africa to keep the black folks moral, cover them up.

He couldn't reach the bandana. Whoever tied it around the metal woman's head must have stood on something. He got a stepladder out of the basement, and standing on the fourth step from the bottom, he was able to untie the tight knots.

He started to turn away and then realizing that he was, for the first time, face to face with the metal woman, he took a head-on look at her.

"Jesus Christ!" he said. He had forgotten he was standing on a ladder, stepped back and away from the statue into space, and fell crashing to the ground.

He lay still, too shocked to move. It had never occurred to him that this alive-looking statue was of a white woman. There wasn't any question about it — tell by the hair, the straight sharp nose, the thin-lipped mouth. He'd been so busy looking at her breasts and her thighs, he hadn't paid any attention to her face. Besides, bronze darkened with age and just on the basis of the darkness of the metal, he had thought this was a statue of a shapely black woman. Mother Africa.

His thoughts blurred. Mother Africa, he murmured. Thought it was Mother Africa. Got a shave and a haircut, a shave and a haircut, me from the humpbacked crooked state, thought she was Mother Africa.

He got up slowly, painfully. He tried to run as he went toward the house and couldn't, could only limp. He had hurt his leg and his back and from the way it felt, he must have wrenched his shoulder.

Once inside he went straight to the telephone in the hall. He called the Harlem Metalworks. He'd done business with them for years. He said he had a large bronze statue. About ten feet. He was selling her for scrap. Yes, he had all the papers on her.

"Come right away," he shouted. "Hurry."

The Bones of Louella Brown

OLD PEABODY AND YOUNG WHIFFLE, partners in the firm of
Whiffle and Peabody, Incorporated, read with mild interest the
first article about Bedford Abbey which appeared in the Boston
papers. But each day thereafter the papers printed one or two
items about this fabulous project. And as they learned more
about it, Old Peabody and Young Whiffle became quite excited.

For Bedford Abbey was a private chapel, a chapel which
would be used solely for the weddings and funerals of the Bedford family — the most distinguished family in Massachusetts.

What was more important, the Abbey was to become the
final resting-place for all the Bedfords who had passed on to

greater glory and been buried in the family plot in Yew Tree Cemetery. These long-dead Bedfords were to be exhumed and reburied in the crypt under the marble floor of the chapel. Thus Bedford Abbey would be officially opened with the most costly and the most elaborate funeral service ever held in Boston.

As work on the Abbey progressed, Young Whiffle (who was seventy-five) and Old Peabody (who was seventy-nine) frowned and fumed while they searched the morning papers for some indication of the date of this service.

Whiffle and Peabody were well aware that they owned the oldest and the most exclusive undertaking firm in the city; and having handled the funerals of most of the Bedfords, they felt that, in all logic, this stupendous funeral ceremony should be managed by their firm. But they were uneasy. For Governor Bedford (he was still called Governor though it had been some thirty years since he held office) was unpredictable. And most unfortunately, the choice of undertakers would be left to the Governor, for the Abbey was his brain-child.

A month dragged by, during which Young Whiffle and Old Peabody set an all-time record for nervous tension. They snapped at each other, and nibbled their fingernails, and cleared their throats, with the most appalling regularity.

It was well into June before the Governor's secretary finally telephoned. He informed Old Peabody, who quivered with delight, that Governor Bedford had named Whiffle and Peabody as the undertakers for the service which would be held at the Abbey on the twenty-first of June.

When the Bedford exhumation order was received, Old Peabody produced an exhumation order for the late Louella Brown. It had occurred to him that this business of exhuming the Bedfords offered an excellent opportunity for exhuming Louella, with very little additional expense. Thus he could rectify a truly terrible error in judgment made by his father, years ago.

"We can pick 'em all up at once," Old Peabody said, handing the Brown exhumation order to Young Whiffle. "I want to move Louella Brown out of Yew Tree Cemetery. We can put her in one of the less well-known burying places on the outskirts of the city. That's where she should have been put in the first place. But we will, of course, check up on her as usual."

"Who was Louella Brown?" asked Young Whiffle.

"Oh, she was once our laundress. Nobody of importance," Old Peabody said carelessly. Though as he said it he wondered why he remembered Louella with such vividness.

Later in the week, the remains of all the deceased Bedfords, and of the late Louella Brown, arrived at the handsome establishment of Whiffle and Peabody. Though Young Whiffle and Old Peabody were well along in years, their research methods were completely modern. Whenever possible they checked on the condition of their former clients and kept exact records of their findings.

The presence of so many former clients at one time — a large number of Bedfords and Louella Brown — necessitated the calling in of Stuart Reynolds. He was a Harvard medical student who did large-scale research jobs for the firm, did them well, and displayed a most satisfying enthusiasm for his work.

It was near closing time when Reynolds arrived at the imposing brick structure which housed Whiffle and Peabody, Incorporated.

Old Peabody handed Reynolds a sheaf of papers and tried to explain about Louella Brown, as tactfully as possible.

"She used to be our laundress," he said. "My mother was very fond of Louella, and insisted that she be buried in Yew Tree Cemetery." His father had consented — grudgingly, yes, but his father should never have agreed to it. It had taken the careful discriminatory practices of generations of Peabodys, undertakers like himself, to make Yew Tree Cemetery what it was today — the final home of Boston's wealthiest and most aristocratic families. Louella's grave had been at the very tip edge of the cemetery in 1902, in a very undesirable place. But just last month he had noticed, with dismay, that due to the enlargement of the cemetery, over the years, she now lay in one of the choicest spots — in the exact center.

Before Old Peabody spoke again he was a little disconcerted, for he suddenly saw Louella Brown with an amazing sharpness. It was just as though she had entered the room — a quick-moving little woman, brown of skin and black of hair, and with very erect posture.

He hesitated a moment and then he said, "She was — uh — uh — a colored woman. But in spite of that, we will do the usual research."

"Colored?" said Young Whiffle sharply. "Did you say 'colored'? You mean a black woman? And buried in Yew Tree Cemetery?" His voice rose in pitch.

"Yes," Old Peabody said. He lifted his shaggy eyebrows at Young Whiffle as an indication that he was not to discuss the matter further. "Now, Reynolds, be sure and lock up when you leave."

Reynolds accepted the papers from Old Peabody and said, "Yes, sir. I'll lock up." And in his haste to get at the job he left the room so fast that he stumbled over his own feet and very nearly fell. He hurried because he was making a private study of bone structure in the Caucasian female as against the bone structure in the female of the darker race, and Louella Brown was an unexpected research plum.

Old Peabody winced as the door slammed. "The terrible enthusiasm of the young," he said to Young Whiffle.

"He comes cheap," Young Whiffle said gravely. "And he's polite enough."

They considered Reynolds in silence for a moment.

"Yes, of course," Old Peabody said. "You're quite right. He is an invaluable young man and his wages are adequate for his services." He hoped Young Whiffle noticed how neatly he had avoided repeating the phrase "he comes cheap."

"'Adequate,'" murmured Young Whiffle. "Yes, yes, 'adequate.' Certainly. And invaluable." He was still murmuring both words as he accompanied Old Peabody out of the building.

Fortunately for their peace of mind, neither Young Whiffle nor Old Peabody knew what went on in their workroom that night. Though they found out the next morning to their very great regret.

It so happened that the nearest approach to royalty in the Bedford family had been the Countess of Castro (nee Elizabeth Bedford). Though neither Old Peabody nor Young Whiffle knew it, the countess and Louella Brown had resembled each other in many ways. They both had thick glossy black hair. Neither woman had any children. They had both died in 1902, when in their early seventies, and been buried in Yew Tree Cemetery within two weeks of each other.

Stuart Reynolds did not know this either, or he would not have worked in so orderly a fashion. As it was, once he entered the big underground workroom of Whiffle and Peabody, he began taking notes on the condition of each Bedford, and then carefully answered the questions on the blanks provided by Old Peabody.

He finished all the lesser Bedfords, then turned his attention to the countess.

When he opened the coffin of the countess, he gave a little murmur of pleasure. "A very neat set of bones," he said. "A small woman, about seventy. How interesting! All of her own teeth, no repairs."

Having checked the countess, he set to work on Louella Brown. As he studied Louella's bones he said, "Why how extremely interesting!" For here was another small-boned woman, about seventy, who had all of her own teeth. As far as he could determine from a hasty examination, there was no way of telling the countess from Louella.

"But the hair! How stupid of me. I can tell them apart by the hair. The colored woman's will be —" But it wasn't. Both women had the same type of hair.

He placed the skeleton of the Countess of Castro on a long table, and right next to it he drew up another long table, and placed on it the skeleton of the late Louella Brown. He measured both of them.

"Why, it's sensational!" he said aloud. And as he talked to himself he grew more and more excited. "It's a front page story. I bet they never even knew each other and yet they were the same height, had the same bone structure. One white, one black, and they meet here at Whiffle and Peabody after all these years — the laundress and the countess. It's more than front page news, why, it's the biggest story of the year —"

Without a second's thought Reynolds ran upstairs to Old Peabody's office and called the *Boston Record*. He talked to the night city editor. The man sounded bored, but he listened.

Finally he said, "You got the bones of both these ladies out on tables, and you say they're just alike. Okay, be right over —"

Thus two photographers and the night city editor of the *Boston Record* invaded the sacred premises of Whiffle and Peabody, Incorporated. The night city editor was a tall, lank individual, and very hard to please. He no sooner asked Reynolds to pose in one position than he had him moved, in front of the tables, behind them, at the foot, at the head. Then he wanted the tables moved. The photographers cursed audibly as they dragged the tables back and forth, turned them around, sideways, lengthways. And still the night city editor wasn't satisfied.

Reynolds shifted position so often that he might have been on a merry-go-round. He registered surprise, amazement, pleasure. Each time the night city editor objected.

It was midnight before the newspapermen said, "Okay, boys, this is it." The photographers took their pictures quickly and then started picking up their equipment.

The newspaperman watched the photographers for a moment, then he strolled over to Reynolds and said, "Now —uh — sonny, which one of these ladies is the countess?"

Reynolds started to point at one of the tables, stopped, and let out a frightened exclamation. "Why —" His mouth stayed open. "Why — I don't know!" His voice was suddenly frantic. "You've mixed them up! You've moved them around so many times I can't tell which is which — nobody could tell —"

The night city editor smiled sweetly and started for the door.

Reynolds followed him, clutched at his coat sleeve. "You've got to help me. You can't go now," he said. "Who moved the tables first? Which one of you —" The photographers stared and then started to grin. The night city editor smiled again. His smile was even sweeter than before.

"I wouldn't know, sonny," he said. He gently disengaged Reynolds' hand from his coat sleeve. "I really wouldn't know —"

It was, of course, a front page story. But not the kind that Reynolds had anticipated. There were photographs of that marble masterpiece, Bedford Abbey, and the caption under it asked the question that was later to seize the imagination of the whole country: "Who will be buried under the marble floor of Bedford Abbey on the twenty-first of June — the white countess or the black laundress?"

There were photographs of Reynolds, standing near the long tables, pointing at the bones of both ladies. He was quoted as saying: "You've moved them around so many times I can't tell which is which — nobody could tell —"

When Governor Bedford read the *Boston Record,* he promptly called Whiffle and Peabody on the telephone and cursed them with such violence that Young Whiffle and Old Peabody grew visibly older and grayer as they listened to him.

Shortly after the Governor's call, Stuart Reynolds came to offer an explanation to Whiffle and Peabody. Old Peabody turned his back and refused to speak to, or look at, Reynolds. Young Whiffle did the talking. His eyes were so icy cold, his face so frozen, that he seemed to emit a freezing vapor as he spoke.

Toward the end of his speech, Young Whiffle was breathing hard. "The house," he said, "the honor of this house, years of working, of building a reputation, all destroyed. We're ruined, ruined —" he choked on the word. "Ah," he said, waving his hands, "Get out, get out, get out, before I kill you —"

The next day the Associated Press picked up the story of this dreadful mix-up and wired it throughout the country. It was a particularly dull period for news, between wars so to speak, and every paper in the United States carried the story on its front page.

In three days' time Louella Brown and Elizabeth, Countess of Castro, were as famous as movie stars. Crowds gathered outside the mansion in which Governor Bedford lived; still larger and noisier crowds milled in the street in front of the offices of Whiffle and Peabody.

As the twenty-first of June approached, people in New York and London and Paris and Moscow asked each other the same question: Who would be buried in Bedford Abbey, the countess or the laundress?

Meanwhile Young Whiffle and Old Peabody talked, desperately seeking something, anything, to save the reputation of Boston's oldest and most expensive undertaking establishment. Their talk went around and around in circles.

"Nobody knows which set of bones belongs to Louella and which to the countess. Why do you keep saying that it's Louella Brown who will be buried in the Abbey?" snapped Old Peabody.

"Because the public likes the idea," Young Whiffle snapped back. "A hundred years from now they'll say it's the black laundress who lies in the crypt at Bedford Abbey. And that we put her there. We're ruined — ruined — ruined —" he muttered. "A black washerwoman!" he said, wringing his hands. "If only she had been white —"

"She might have been Irish," said Old Peabody coldly. He was annoyed to find how very clearly he could see Louella. With each passing day her presence became sharper, more strongly felt. "And a Catholic. That would have been equally as bad. No, it would have been worse. Because the Catholics would have insisted on a mass, in Bedford Abbey, of all places!

Or she might have been a foreigner — a — a — Russian. Or, God forbid, a Jew!"

"Nonsense," said Young Whiffle pettishly. "A black washer-woman is infinitely worse than anything you've mentioned. People are saying it's some kind of trick, that we're proving there's no difference between the races. Oh, we're ruined — ruined — ruined —" Young Whiffle moaned.

As a last resort, Old Peabody and Young Whiffle went to see Stuart Reynolds. They found him in the shabby rooming house where he lived.

"You did this to us," Old Peabody said to Reynolds. "Now you figure out a way, an acceptable way, to determine which of those women is which or I'll —"

"We will wait while you think," said Young Whiffle, looking out of the window.

"I *have* thought," Reynolds said wildly. "I've thought until I'm nearly crazy."

"Think some more," snapped Old Peabody, glaring.

Peabody and Whiffle seated themselves on opposite sides of the small room. Young Whiffle glared out of the window and Old Peabody glared at Reynolds. And Reynolds couldn't decide which was worse.

"You knew her, knew Louella, I mean," said Reynolds. "Can't you just say, this one's Louella Brown, pick either one, because, the body, I mean, Whiffle and Peabody, they, she was embalmed there —"

"Don't be a fool!" said Young Whiffle, his eyes on the windowsill, glaring at the windowsill, annihilating the windowsill. "Whiffle and Peabody would be ruined by such a statement, more ruined than they are at present."

"How?" demanded Reynolds. Ordinarily he wouldn't have

argued but being shut up in the room with this pair of bony-fingered old men had turned him desperate. "Why? After all, who could dispute it? You could get the embalmer, Mr. Ludastone, to say he remembered the neck bone, or the position of the foot —" His voice grew louder. "If you identify the black woman first, nobody'll question it —"

"Lower your voice," said Old Peabody.

Young Whiffle stood up and pounded on the dusty window-sill. "Because black people, bodies, I mean the black dead —"

He took a deep breath. Old Peabody said, "Now relax, Mr. Whiffle, relax. Remember your blood pressure."

"There's such a thing as a color line," shrieked Young Whiffle. "You braying idiot, you, we're not supposed to handle colored bodies, the colored dead, I mean the dead colored people, in our establishment. We'd never live down a statement like that. We're fortunate that so far no one has asked how the corpse of Louella Brown, a colored laundress, got on the premises in 1902. Louella was a special case but they'd say that we —"

"But she's already there!" Reynolds shouted. "You've got a colored body or bones, I mean, there now. She *was* embalmed there. She *was* buried in Yew Tree Cemetery. Nobody's said anything about it."

Old Peabody held up his hand for silence. "Wait," he said. "There is a bare chance —" He thought for a moment. He found that his thinking was quite confused, he felt he ought to object to Reynolds' suggestion but he didn't know why. Vivid images of Louella Brown, wearing a dark dress with white collars and cuffs, added to his confusion.

Finally he said, "We'll do it, Mr. Whiffle. It's the only way. And we'll explain it with dignity. Speak of Louella's long service, true she did laundry for others, too, but we won't mention that, talk about her cheerfulness and devotion, emphasize the devotion, burying her in Yew Tree Cemetery was a kind of reward for service, payment of a debt of gratitude, remember that phrase, 'debt of gratitude.' And call in —" he swallowed hard, "the press. Especially that animal from the *Boston Record*, who wrote the story up the first time. We might serve some of the old brandy and cigars. Then Mr. Ludastone can make his statement. About the position of the foot, he remembers it —" He paused and glared at Reynolds. "And as for you! You needn't think we'll ever permit you inside our doors again, dead or alive."

Gray-haired, gray-skinned Clarence Ludastone, head embalmer for Whiffle and Peabody, dutifully identified one set of bones as being those of the late Louella Brown. Thus the identity of the countess was firmly established. Half the newspapermen in the country were present at the time. They partook generously of Old Peabody's best brandy and enthusiastically smoked his finest cigars. The last individual to leave was the weary gentleman who represented the *Boston Record*.

He leaned against the doorway as he spoke to Old Peabody. "Wonderful yarn," he said. "Never heard a better one. Congratulations —" And he drifted down the hall.

Because of all the stories about Louella Brown and the Countess of Castro, most of the residents of Boston turned out to watch the funeral cortege of the Bedfords on the twenty-first of June. The ceremony that took place at Bedford Abbey was broadcast over a national hook-up, and the news services wired it around the world, complete with pictures.

Young Whiffle and Old Peabody agreed that the publicity accorded the occasion was disgraceful. But their satisfaction over the successful ending of what had been an extremely embarrassing situation was immense. They had great difficulty preserving the solemn mien required of them during the funeral service.

Young Whiffle and Old Peabody both suffered slight heart attacks when they saw the next morning's edition of the *Boston Record.* For there on the front page was a photograph of Mr. Ludastone, and over it in bold, black type were the words "child embalmer." The article which accompanied the picture, said, in part:

> Who is buried in the crypt at Bedford Abbey? The countess, or Louella the laundress? We ask because Mr. Clarence Ludastone, the suave gentleman who is head embalmer for Whiffle and Peabody, could not possibly identify the bones of Louella Brown, despite his look of great age. Mr. Ludastone, according to his birth certificate (which is reproduced on this page) was only two years old at the time of Louella's death. This reporter has questioned many of Boston's oldest residents but he has, as yet, been unable to locate anyone who remembers a time when Whiffle and Peabody employed a two-year-old child as embalmer . . .

Eighty-year-old Governor Bedford very nearly had apoplexy when he saw the *Boston Record.* He hastily called a press conference. He said that he would personally, publicly (in front of the press), identify the countess, if it was the countess. He remembered her well, for he had been only thirty-five when she died. He would know instantly if it were she.

Two days later the Governor stalked down the center aisle of that marble gem — Bedford Abbey. He was followed by a veritable hive of newsmen and photographers. Old Peabody and Young Whiffle were waiting for them just inside the crypt.

The Governor peered at the interior of the opened casket and drew back. He forgot the eager-eared newsmen, who surrounded him, pressed against him. When he spoke he reverted to the simple speech of his early ancestors.

"Why they be nothing but bones here!" he said. "Nothing but bones! Nobody could tell who this be."

He turned his head, unable to take a second look. He, too, someday, not too far off, how did a man buy immortality, he didn't want to die, bones rattling inside a casket — ah, no! He reached for his pocket handkerchief, and Young Whiffle thrust a freshly laundered one into his hand.

Governor Bedford wiped his face, his forehead. But not me, he thought. I'm alive. I can't die. It won't happen to me. And inside his head a voice kept saying over and over, like the ticking of a clock: It will. It can. It will. It can. It will.

"You were saying, Governor," prompted the tall thin newsman from the *Boston Record*.

"I don't know!" Governor Bedford shouted angrily. "I don't know! Nobody could tell which be the black laundress and which the white countess from looking at their bones."

"Governor, Governor," protested Old Peabody. "Governor, ah — calm yourself, great strain —" And leaning forward, he hissed in the Governor's reddening ear, "Remember the press, don't say that, don't make a statement, don't commit yourself —"

"Stop spitting in my ear!" roared the Governor. "Get away! And take your blasted handkerchief with you." He thrust Young Whiffle's handkerchief inside Old Peabody's coat, up near the shoulder. "It stinks, it stinks of death." Then he strode out of Bedford Abbey, muttering under his breath as he went.

The Governor's statement went around the world, in direct quotes. So did the photographs of him, peering inside the casket, his mouth open, his eyes staring. There were still other photographs that showed him charging down the center aisle of

Bedford Abbey, head down, shoulders thrust forward, even the back of his neck somehow indicative of his fury. Cartoonists showed him, in retreat, words issuing from his shoulder blades, "Nobody could tell who this be — the black laundress or the white countess —"

Sermons were preached about the Governor's statement, editorials were written about it, and Congressmen made long-winded speeches over the radio. The Mississippi legislature threatened to declare war on the sovereign State of Massachusetts because Governor Bedford's remarks were an unforgiveable insult to believers in white supremacy.

Many radio listeners became completely confused and, believing that both ladies were still alive, sent presents to them, sometimes addressed in care of Governor Bedford, and sometimes addressed in care of Whiffle and Peabody.

Whiffle and Peabody kept the shades drawn in their establishment. They scuttled through the streets each morning, hats pulled low over their eyes, en route to their offices. They would have preferred to stay at home (with the shades drawn) but they agreed it was better to act as though nothing had happened. So they spent ten hours a day on the premises as was their custom, though there was absolutely no business.

Young Whiffle paced the floor, hours at a time, wringing his hands, and muttering, "A black washerwoman! We're ruined — ruined — ruined —!"

Old Peabody found himself wishing that Young Whiffle would not speak of Louella with such contempt. In spite of himself he kept dreaming about her. In the dream, she came quite close to him, a small, brown woman with merry eyes. And after one quick look at him, she put her hands on her hips, threw her head back and laughed and laughed.

He was quite unaccustomed to being laughed at, even in a

dream; and the memory of Louella's laughter lingered with him for hours after he woke up. He could not forget the smallest detail of her appearance: how her shoulders shook as she laughed, and that her teeth were very white and evenly spaced.

He thought to avoid this recurrent visitation by sitting up all night, by drinking hot milk, by taking lukewarm baths. Then he tried the exact opposite — he went to bed early, drank cold milk, took scalding hot baths. To no avail. Louella Brown still visited him, each and every night.

Thus it came about that one morning when Young Whiffle began his ritual muttering: "A black washerwoman — we're ruined — ruined — ruined —" Old Peabody shouted: "Will you stop that caterwauling? One would think the Loch Ness monster lay in the crypt at Bedford Abbey." He could see Louella Brown standing in front of him, laughing, laughing. And he said, "Louella Brown was a neatly built little woman, a fine woman, full of laughter. I remember her well. She was a gentlewoman. Her bones will do no injury to the Governor's damned funeral chapel."

It was a week before Young Whiffle actually heard what Old Peabody was saying, though Peabody made this same outrageous statement, over and over again.

When Young Whiffle finally heard it, there was a quarrel, a violent quarrel, caused by the bones of Louella Brown — that quick-moving, merry little woman.

By the end of the day, the partnership was dissolved, and the ancient and exclusive firm of Whiffle and Peabody, Incorporated, went out of business.

Old Peabody retired; after all, there was no firm he could consider associating with. Young Whiffle retired, too, but he moved all the way to California, and changed his name to

Smith, in the hope that no man would ever discover he had once been a member of that blackguardly firm of Whiffle and Peabody, Incorporated.

Despite his retirement, Old Peabody found that Louella Brown still haunted his dreams. What was worse, she took to appearing before him during his waking moments. After a month of this, he went to see Governor Bedford. He had to wait an hour before the Governor came downstairs, walking slowly, leaning on a cane.

Old Peabody wasted no time being courteous. He went straight to the reason for his visit. "I have come," he said stiffly, "to suggest to you that you put the names of both those women on the marble slab in Bedford Abbey."

"Never," said the Governor. "Never, never, never!"

He is afraid to die, Old Peabody thought, eying the Governor. You can always tell by the look on their faces. He shrugged his shoulders. "Every man dies alone, Governor," he said brutally. "And so it is always best to be at peace with this world and any other world that follows it, when one dies."

Old Peabody waited a moment. The Governor's hands were shaking. Fear or palsy, he wondered. Fear, he decided. Fear beyond the question of a doubt.

"Louella Brown visits me every night and frequently during the day," Peabody said softly. "I am certain that unless you follow my suggestion, she will also visit you." A muscle in the Governor's face started to twitch. Peabody said, "When your bones finally lie in the crypt in your marble chapel, I doubt that you want to hear the sound of Louella's laughter ringing in your ears — till doomsday."

"Get out!" said the Governor, shuddering. "You're crazy as a loon."

"No," Old Peabody said firmly. "Between us, all of us, we have managed to summon Louella's spirit." And he proceeded to tell the Governor how every night, in his dreams, and sometimes during the day when he was awake, Louella came to stand beside him, and look up at him and laugh. He told it very well, so well in fact that for a moment he thought he saw Louella standing in the room, right near Governor Bedford's left shoulder.

The Governor turned, looked over his shoulder. And then he said, slowly and reluctantly, and with the uneasy feeling that he could already hear Louella's laughter, "All right." He paused, took a deep unsteady breath. "What do you suggest I put on the marble slab in the crypt?"

After much discussion, and much writing, and much tearing up of what had been written, they achieved a satisfactory epitaph. If you ever go to Boston and visit Bedford Abbey you will see for yourself how Old Peabody propitiated the bones of the late Louella Brown. For after these words were carved on the marble slab, Louella ceased to haunt Old Peabody:

HERE LIES
ELIZABETH, COUNTESS OF CASTRO
OR
LOUELLA BROWN, GENTLEWOMAN
1830–1902
REBURIED IN BEDFORD ABBEY JUNE 21, 1947

"They both wore the breastplate of faith and love;
And for a helmet, the hope of salvation."

Olaf and His Girl Friend

THIS IS OLAF'S STORY. I don't pretend to know all of it. I saw parts of it that happened on the dock in Bridgetown, Barbados, just at the beginning of the war. And I saw the ending of the story in New York. The rest of it I had to piece together from the things that Olaf's friends told me. As a result, I think I'm the only person who actually knows why a beautiful young dancer disappeared very suddenly from the New York night-club where she sang calypso songs and danced the conga and the beguine. She was beginning to make the place famous. Then she vanished.

It's only if you know Olaf's story that you can understand her disappearance. He was a great big black guy who worked on the dock in Bridgetown. Some two hundred and twenty pounds of muscle and six feet of height. I liked to watch him. When the sun shone on him it caught highlights in his skin, so that he looked like an ebony man. I soon discovered that there was a slender native girl who found him even more interesting to watch than I did. I only wanted to paint him against the green water of Carlisle Bay. She wanted to marry him.

Her name was Belle Rose. She had that sinuous kind of grace that suggests the born dancer. When she walked she swayed a little as though she were keeping time to a rumba that played somewhere inside her head.

She used to show up at noontime, two or three days a week. She'd sit by him while he ate his lunch, talking and laughing. His great laugh would boom out the length of the dock and the other dock hands would grin because they couldn't help it.

"Olaf's girl's here," they'd say.

She couldn't have been more than seventeen years old. The dock boys used to look at her out of the corner of their eyes and flash their white teeth at her but it seemed to be pretty well accepted that she was Olaf's girl.

It was nearly a month before things started going wrong. One day I heard a lot of noise at one end of the dock. I welcomed the interruption, for I'd been trying to paint the bay and I simply could not capture that incredible green on canvas. So I left my easel to investigate.

Olaf's girl was standing sort of huddled up. All the laughter gone out of her. She was holding her face as though it hurt. A short, stumpy, dark brown woman was facing Olaf a little way off from the girl.

The woman was neatly dressed even to the inevitable umbrella that the upper class island women carry and she looked for all the world like a bantam rooster. She had one hand on her hip and with the other hand she was gesticulating with the raised umbrella while she berated Olaf in a high, shrill voice.

"I tell you I won't have you seeing her. She's too good for your kind. Belle Rose will marry a teacher," she shook the umbrella under his very nose.

He looked like an abashed Great Dane. But he stood his ground.

"I do no harm. I love her. I want to marry her."

And that set the old girl off again. "Marry her? You?" she choked on the words. "You think you'll marry her? I'll have you locked up. I'll —" she was overcome with sheer rage.

"I'm honest. I love her. I think she's beautiful. I wouldn't harm her," he pleaded.

She shook her head violently and went off muttering that Belle Rose's father had been a schoolteacher and Belle Rose wasn't going to marry any dockhand. Her umbrella was still quivering as she hurried away holding the girl firmly by the arm.

She turned around when she was half the length of the dock. "Besides, you're a coward. Everybody knows you're scared of the water. Belle Rose will never marry a coward."

Olaf followed them. I don't know how that particular episode ended. But I was curious about him and questioned the dockhands. They told me his father had been a sailor and his grandfather before him. Olaf should have been a sailor but his mother brought him up to be afraid of the water. It seems his father went down with a ship during a violent storm.

Shortly after I learned about Olaf's fear of the sea, he slipped on the dock and went head first into the bay. He managed to stay afloat until the boys fished him out but he was obviously half dead from fright. It was a week before he came back to work.

"You all right, mahn?" the boys asked.

Olaf nodded and kept any feelings he had about it to himself.

It was only because he loved Belle Rose that he came back to work. I overheard them talking about it. They were sitting on the edge of the dock. It seemed to me they were the most paintable pair I'd ever seen. He was stripped to the waist because he'd been working. His wide, cream-colored straw hat and faded blue dungarees were a perfect foil for the starched white of her dress and the brilliant red of the turban wound so deftly around her head.

"And we'll have a house not too near the sea," she said in a very soft voice.

"Yes. Not too near the sea," was his answer. "It'll be just near enough to watch the sun on the water in the bay."

"Olaf, you don't like this job. Do you?" she asked.

"Only for you. I like it for you. It means we can get married soon. That's why I came back to work."

I walked away and I asked the boys what had happened to Olaf's girl friend's aunt. Had she decided they could get married after all? The boys looked sheepish.

"They will have big wedding. Olaf goes every Sunday now to call on Belle Rose. All dressed up in scissors-tail coat. With stiff collar. Olaf takes the aunt plantains every Sunday. I don't think she change her mind. Olaf just too big. And she got no man to deal with him," was the answer.

The boys were right in one respect. The marriage banns were posted. But it wasn't to be the big church wedding Belle Rose's aunt had set her heart on. Olaf threatened to elope unless it was a small wedding. And Auntie gave in gracefully. I wondered about that. She seemed a domineering kind of old girl to agree to a small wedding when she wanted a large one. The more I thought about it the queerer it seemed that she should have consented to any kind of wedding.

The dock crew quits about five o'clock in Bridgetown. The day I discovered that the girl's aunt had no intentions of allowing any kind of marriage, a big American merchant ship had been loaded with fruit. She was due to sail at seven o'clock. On that particular day Belle Rose's aunt sent Olaf on an errand that took him halfway across the island.

I went down to watch the passengers clamber aboard the launch. There were a great many women at the dock. They were seeing a couple of passengers off. You could hear their good-byes and messages halfway across the bay.

I stared in amazement. It was Belle Rose and her aunt who were going away. The aunt all officious and confidential at the same time. Ordering Belle Rose to do this and did she have that and where was the small bag. She was fairly bursting with importance.

"My boy in New York sent me the money. The passage fare for both of us," she explained loudly for the benefit of a latecomer.

"Belle Rose, do you think you'll like it?" asked one of the younger women.

The aunt didn't give the girl time to answer. "Of course she will," she said firmly. "She's never been off the island. She wants to see the world a bit. Don't you, dear?"

Belle Rose nodded. "Yes, I do. But I wish I could have said good-bye to Olaf. And I did want to stay near him." Her voice was wistful.

"You can write to him. You'll see him soon. After all, he can come and see you, you know," and with that she hurried the girl into the steamer's launch. She leaned over to whisper to an older woman, "You know, it aren't as though he were fit for her," and then turned her attention back to the girl and their bags.

I stood on the dock watching the ship until it was out of sight, thinking that the old woman had tricked the girl. She knew that New York was a long ways from Barbados yet she had given Belle Rose the impression that they were going somewhere close by and that Olaf would be dropping in to see them fairly often. She'd said, "You'll see him soon."

I kept wishing that I could turn the ship around and bring it back to the bay. For if ever a man loved a woman that man was Olaf and the woman was Belle Rose. He stopped laughing after he discovered the girl was gone. He got very quiet. It wasn't that he brooded or was sullen. He was just quiet and he worked with a grim determination.

When he got letters from her he seemed to come alive again. And I could tell whenever he'd received one. Then the letters stopped coming. I asked him about it. "Have you heard from your girl?"

"No. Not lately. I don't understand it," he said.

A whole year crept around. A year that brought the war a little closer to us. A year in which his letters kept coming back marked "Moved. Left no address." A year in which the native women came down to the dock to look coyly at Olaf. They walked past him and flirted with him. He ignored them.

I found out later that Belle Rose never received the letters that he wrote her. Auntie saw to that. Finally she intercepted the letters that Belle Rose wrote to him. And then, of course, they moved and Auntie gave the post office no forwarding address.

One day out of a clear sky, Olaf signed up on a ship. Olaf who was so afraid of the sea that when he looked out over the bay his eyes would go dead and blank. Olaf who worked with one eye on the sky when the storms came up suddenly. He signed on one of those gray, raffish-looking ships that were forever limping into port and disgorging crews of unshaven, desperate-looking men. Olaf, who hated the sea, signed on a merchant ship.

It was a long time before I found out how it happened. It seems that he got a message. These days people talk about tho underground of the little people in the conquered countries of Europe. But there's always been an underground that could send a message halfway around the world.

It happened in Olaf's case. The message traveled in the mouths of ship's stewards and messboys. It took a good six months for Olaf to get it.

The first boat with the message on it left New York and went to Liverpool. And then to northern Africa. She bummed halfway around the world — sneaking from one port to another carrying guns and men and God knows what. And Olaf's message. And everywhere she went the message was transferred to other ships and other men.

The steward on a boat that lumbered back and forth across the Atlantic helped relay it — "tell Olaf . . ." The message went to India and the messmen on an English ship learned about it.

Finally it got to Olaf. It was a little excitable man with just two hours' leave who delivered it to him on the dock.

"Belle Rose is dancing in New York in a place that is not good. Not by 'alf. Elmer and Franklin and Stoner sent back word to you. They work in that same place. She dances. And it is not a good dance."

The word had come such a long way and had been such a long time getting to its destination that the little man was breathless from the sheer weight of it. He'd learned it from two sailors in an infamous house on the edge of the waterfront in Liverpool. His beard fairly quivered with the excitement of it.

"Did you hear me, Olaf?" he asked sharply, as though his voice would bring a reaction. "It is not a good dance."

Olaf stared out at the sea. It was a long time before he spoke. "I heard. Yes," he said slowly. "I heard. I will take care of it."

And he walked off the dock and signed up on the same ship that had brought the little man with the message. Just like that. The man who was afraid of the sea signed up on a ship.

I learned afterward that he worked in the ship's galley — washing dishes and helping with the cooking. He was very quiet. His quietness permeated the stuffy bunk rooms. It made the men uneasy even when they were shooting craps, or singing, or just talking.

He was always in his bunk when he wasn't working. He lay there staring up at the ceiling with an unwinking gaze.

"S'matter with the big guy?" the mate asked nervously. "Guys like that bring bad luck."

"Just quiet," was the usual apologetic answer of the little man who was responsible for Olaf's being aboard.

Olaf hadn't even bothered to find out what port they were heading for. When they docked on a cold, wet night he asked a question for the first time. "New York?"

"This England, mahn," was the answer. "Liverpool."

But they headed for New York on the return trip. If Olaf thought about the danger of the queer, crazy voyage, he didn't show it. He was on deck hours before the boat docked, peering into the dark. He would start his search now. At once. In a few minutes.

He asked a black man on the dock, "You know a girl named Belle Rose?"

The man shook his head. "Bud, there's a lot of women here. All kinds of people. You won't find no woman that way. What she look like?" And then he added, "Where does she live?"

"Like — like —" Olaf fumbled for words, his throat working, "like the sun. She's so high." He indicated a spot on his chest. "She's warm like the sun —" His voice broke. "I don't know where she lives."

The man stared at him. "What's your name? Where you from?"

"The Islands. Barbados. To the south. My name is Olaf," and then his voice grew soft as he said again, "Her name is Belle Rose." He seemed to linger over her name.

"Naw," the man returned to his work, "you won't find her, bud, just knowin' her name."

They were in port just two hours and they were gone again. But the underground had the message, "Olaf from Barbados is looking for Belle Rose."

The dock worker told a friend, and the story went into the kitchens and the freight elevators of great hotels. Doormen knew it and cooks and waiters. It traveled all the way from the waterfront to Harlem. People who'd never heard of Belle Rose knew that a man named Olaf was looking for her.

The cook in a nightclub told three West Indian drummers who were part of the floor show. Elmer, Franklin, and Stoner looked at each other and gesticulated despairingly when they heard it. A message started back to Olaf. It took a long time. Olaf saw the edge of Africa and a port in Australia and Liverpool again before the message reached him.

His silence had grown ominous, portentous. The men never

spoke to him. They left him alone — completely alone. They shivered a little when they looked at him.

One of the crew picked the message up in Liverpool and brought it to him. "The name of the place where Belle Rose dances is the Conga."

Olaf went to the mate when he heard it and asked when they'd dock in New York again. The mate stared at him, "I don't know. I never know where we're goin' until we're under way. You got some reason for wantin' to go to New York?"

"Yes. I have to find a girl there," Olaf looked past the man as he spoke.

"You? A girl?" The mate couldn't conceal his amazement. "I didn't know you were interested in girls."

But Olaf had turned away to watch the ship being loaded. They left Liverpool that same night. It was a bad voyage. Stormy and cold. With high seas.

They docked in New York early on a cold bitter morning. They were paid off for the Atlantic voyage and given two days shore leave. The crew disappeared like magic. Only Olaf was left behind.

He asked a policeman on the dock, "Where do black people live in this place?" He gestured toward the city.

"You better take a taxi, boy. Tell the driver you want the YMCA on One Hundred Thirty-fifth Street between Lenox and Seventh Avenues. In Harlem."

The man wrote it down for him on the back of an envelope. Olaf looked at the paper frequently while the cab crawled through a city that looked half dead. It was shrouded in gray. It was cold. There were no lights in the buildings and few people on the streets. They snaked their way between tall buildings, over cobblestoned streets, along miles of a highway

that ran for a while along the edge of the river. It was getting
lighter and he became aware that all the people on the streets
through which they were passing were dark.

He relaxed a little. He was getting near the end of his long
journey. "All this place — is all this place New York?" He indicated the sidewalk.

The driver studied him in the mirror and nodded, "Yeah. All
of it's New York. Where you from?"

"Barbados," Olaf said simply. He was wondering what could
have happened to Belle Rose in this place. And where would
he find her?

It was the first thing he asked the man behind the wicket
when he paid for his room at the 'Y.'

"I wouldn't know anybody with a name like that," the man
said coldly.

"Where is the place called the Conga?" Olaf asked.

"I never heard of it," the man shoved a receipt towards him.
"Take the elevator to the fifth floor. Your room is number five
sixty-three. Next, please."

But the elevator man had heard about the Conga. He told
Olaf how to get there. Even told him that eleven o'clock at
night was the best time to visit it.

Olaf sat in his room — waiting. He was like a man who had
been running in a cross-country race and realizes suddenly that
the finish line is just a little ways ahead because he can see it.

At eleven o'clock he was in a taxi, on his way to the Conga.
The taxi went swiftly.

It was the expression in his eyes that made the doorman at
the place try to stop him from going in. He tried to block his
way and Olaf brushed him aside, lightly, effortlessly, as though
he'd been a fly.

Once inside he was a little confused. There was smoke, and the lights were dim. People were laughing and talking, their voices blurred and loud from liquor. He walked to a table right at the edge of the space used for dancing. A protesting waiter hurried toward him, pointed at the reserved sign on the table. Olaf looked at him and put the sign on the floor. The waiter backed away and didn't return.

I recognized him when he sat down. He folded his arms on the table and sat there perfectly indifferent to the looks and the whispered conversations around him.

I used to go up to the Conga rather often. Barney, the guy who runs it, was a friend of mine. He told me a long time ago that all the dance lovers in town were flocking into his place because of a young West Indian girl who did some extraordinary dancing. Barney knew I'd lived in the Islands and he thought I'd be interested.

I was more than interested, for the girl, of course, was Belle Rose. After the first visit I went there every night because I figured that sooner or later Olaf would show up. I wanted to be there when he arrived. Luck was with me. As I said before, I saw him when he came in and sat down.

He'd completely lost that friendly look he'd had. He was a dangerous man. It was in his eyes, in the way he carried his head. It was in his tightly closed mouth. A mouth that looked as though laughter were a stranger that had never passed that way. All of the humor had gone out of him. He was like an elastic band that had been stretched too far.

The lights went down and the three West Indian drummers came in — Elmer and Franklin and Stoner. They filed in carrying the drums that they played. Drums made of hollowed logs with hide stretched across them. They sat astride them.

I couldn't swear to it that they'd actually seen Olaf. After all, if you play in one of those places long enough, I imagine you get to know the tricks of lighting and you can see everybody in the place. And yet I don't know. Maybe they had some kind of umpteenth sense. Perhaps they felt some difference in the atmosphere.

When they started to drum it was — well, different. The tempo was faster and there was something subtly alarming about it. It ran through the audience. Men tapped ashes off their cigarettes — and there wasn't any ash there. Women shivered from a draft that didn't exist. The waiters moved ashtrays and bottles for no reason at all. The headwaiter kept shooting his shirt cuffs and fingering around the edge of his collar.

Belle Rose came on suddenly. One moment she wasn't there. And the next moment she was bowing to the audience. I wonder if I can make you see her. Half of New York used to go to that dinky little club just to watch her dance. She was a deep reddish brown color and very slender. Her eyes were magnificent. They were black and very large with a curious lack of expression. There's an old obeah woman in Barbados with those same strange eyes.

I think I said that Barney Jones was a showman. He'd gotten her up so that she looked like some gorgeous tropical bird — all life and color and motion.

She was barefooted. There was a gold anklet around one ankle and a high gold collar around her neck that almost touched her ear lobes. The dress she wore was made of calico and it had a bustle in the back so that every time she moved the red calico flirted with her audience. She had on what looked to be yards of ruffled petticoats. They were starched so stiffly that

the dress stood out and the white ruffling showed from underneath the dress. A towering red turban covered her hair completely. There were flowers and fruit and wheat stuck in the
turban.

She sang a calypso number first. Something about marrying
a woman uglier than you. The nightclub was very quiet.
Somebody knocked over a glass and giggled in a high, hysteri-
cal fashion. There was a queer stillness afterward.

I looked at Olaf. He wasn't moving at all. He was staring at
Belle Rose. His hands were flat on the table. He looked as
though he might spring at any moment. The reflection from
the spotlight shone on the beads of sweat on his forehead.

And I thought of that other time when I used to see him,
laughing on the dock at Bridgetown with the sun shining on
him. Now he was in a nightclub in a cold, alien city watching
the girl he had intended to marry.

The applause that greeted that first number of hers was terrific. She bowed and said, "I weel now do for you the obeah
woman."

Olaf stiffened. His eyes narrowed. The drums started again.
And this time I tell you they talked as plainly as though they
were alive. Human. They talked danger. They talked hate.
They snarled and they sent a chill down my spine. The back of
my neck felt cold and I found I was clutching my glass so
tightly that my hand hurt.

Belle Rose crouched and walked forward and started singing. It was an incantation to some far-off evil gods. It didn't
belong in New York. It didn't belong in any nightclub that has
ever existed anywhere under the sun.

"Ah, you get your man," and then the drums. Boom. Boom.
"Ah, you want a lover." Boom. Boom. Boom-de-de-boom.
"Ah, I see the speer-et." And the drums again. Louder.

And she walked toward Olaf. She was standing directly in front of him. Hands outstretched. Eyes half-shut. Swaying. She stopped singing and the drums kept up their message — their repeated, nerve-racking message. The faces of the drummers were perfectly expressionless. Only their eyes were alive — glittering. Eyes that seemed to have a separate life from their faces.

Belle Rose went on dancing. It's a dance I've never seen done before in a nightclub. It was the devil dance — a dance that's used to exorcise an evil spirit. I don't know exactly what effect it had on Olaf. I could only conjecture. I knew he'd been on boats and ships for months trying to reach New York. The drummers told me.

He'd been tasting the salt air of the sea. Seeing nothing but water. Gone to sleep at night hearing it slap against the ship. Listened to it cascade over the decks when the seas were high. Living with it morning, noon, and night. Even in port it was always there, moving against the sides of the ship.

And he hated the sea. He was afraid of it. He must have gone through hell during those months. Always that craven gnawing fear in the pit of his stomach. Always surrounded by the sea that he loathed.

And then he sees Belle Rose. She's completely unaware of him and more beautiful than ever. With artificial red on her lips and a caste mark between her eyes.

I said Barney was a showman. I suppose he thought it made the girl more exotic. As a final touch he'd had a caste mark painted on her forehead. It was done with something shiny. It may only have been a bit of tinsel — but it caught the light and glowed every time she moved.

I heard Olaf growl deep in his throat when he saw it. He'd been completely silent before. He stood up. All muscle. All brawn. All dangerous, lonely, desperate strength. He walked over the railing that separated the customers from the dance floor. Just stepped over it as though it wasn't there. And confronted her. He had a knife in his hand. I could swear, now, to this day, that he meant to kill her.

She kept right on dancing. She moved nearer to him. I say again that he meant to kill her. And I say, too, that she knew it. And she reached back into that ancient, complicated African past that belongs to all of us and invoked all the gods she knew or that she'd ever heard of.

The drums had stopped. Everything had stopped. There wasn't so much as a glass clinking or the sound of a cork pulled. It seemed to me that I had stopped breathing, and that no one in the place was breathing. She began to sing in a high, shrill voice. I couldn't understand any of the words. It was the same kind of chant that a witch doctor uses when he casts a spell; the same one that the conjure women use and the obeah women.

Her voice stopped suddenly. They must have stared at each other for all of five minutes. The knife slipped out of his hand. Clinked on the floor. Suddenly he reached out and grabbed her and shook her like a dog would shake a kitten. She didn't say anything. Neither did he. And then she was in his arms and he was kissing her and putting his very heart into it.

They walked hand in hand the length of the room and out through the street door. A sigh ran around the tables.

I think Barney, the guy who owns the joint, came to first. He ran after them. And I followed him. When I reached the street he was standing at the curb raving, frothing at the mouth as he watched his biggest drawing card disappear up the street in a taxi. I could just see the red taillight turn the corner.

"That black baboon," Barney fumed. "Where in the hell did he come from?"

I started laughing and that seemed to infuriate him even more. Finally I said, "Barbados. Where Belle Rose came from. It took a long time for him to find her but I'll guarantee New York will never see her again."

I was right. She disappeared. With Olaf. I worried Elmer and Franklin and Stoner until I finally heard that they were back in Bridgetown.

You can have your choice as to why Olaf didn't kill her that night in the Conga. I like to think that when he got that close to her he remembered that he loved her and that he'd gone through hell to find her. And all he wanted was to hold her tight in his arms. After all, she was very beautiful.

On the other hand, though Belle Rose's father may have been a schoolteacher, her grandmother was an obeah woman.

Like a Winding Sheet

He had planned to get up before Mae did and surprise her by fixing breakfast. Instead he went back to sleep and she got out of bed so quietly he didn't know she wasn't there beside him until he woke up and heard the queer soft gurgle of water running out of the sink in the bathroom.

He knew he ought to get up but instead he put his arms across his forehead to shut the afternoon sunlight out of his eyes, pulled his legs up close to his body, testing them to see if the ache was still in them.

Mae had finished in the bathroom. He could tell because she never closed the door when she was in there and now the sweet smell of talcum powder was drifting down the hall and into the bedroom. Then he heard her coming down the hall.

"Hi, babe," she said affectionately.

"Hum," he grunted, and moved his arms away from his head, opened one eye.

"It's a nice morning."

"Yeah." He rolled over and the sheet twisted around him, outlining his thighs, his chest. "You mean afternoon, don't ya?"

Mae looked at the twisted sheet and giggled. "Looks like a winding sheet," she said. "A shroud —" Laughter tangled with her words and she had to pause for a moment before she could continue. "You look like a huckleberry — in a winding sheet —"

"That's no way to talk. Early in the day like this," he protested.

He looked at his arms silhouetted against the white of the sheets. They were inky black by contrast and he had to smile in spite of himself and he lay there smiling and savoring the sweet sound of Mae's giggling.

"Early?" She pointed a finger at the alarm clock on the table near the bed and giggled again. "It's almost four o'clock. And if you don't spring up out of there, you're going to be late again."

"What do you mean 'again'?"

"Twice last week. Three times the week before. And once the week before and —"

"I can't get used to sleeping in the daytime," he said fretfully. He pushed his legs out from under the covers experimentally. Some of the ache had gone out of them but they weren't really rested yet. "It's too light for good sleeping. And all that standing beats the hell out of my legs."

"After two years you oughta be used to it," Mae said.

He watched her as she fixed her hair, powdered her face, slipped into a pair of blue denim overalls. She moved quickly and yet she didn't seem to hurry.

"You look like you'd had plenty of sleep," he said lazily. He had to get up but he kept putting the moment off, not wanting to move, yet he didn't dare let his legs go completely limp because if he did he'd go back to sleep. It was getting later and later but the thought of putting his weight on his legs kept him lying there.

When he finally got up he had to hurry, and he gulped his breakfast so fast that he wondered if his stomach could possibly use food thrown at it at such a rate of speed. He was still wondering about it as he and Mae were putting their coats on in the hall.

Mae paused to look at the calendar. "It's the thirteenth," she said. Then a faint excitement in her voice, "Why, it's Friday the thirteenth." She had one arm in her coat sleeve and she held it there while she stared at the calendar. "I oughta stay home," she said. "I shouldn't go outa the house."

"Aw, don't be a fool," he said. "Today's payday. And payday is a good luck day everywhere, any way you look at it." And as she stood hesitating he said, "Aw, come on."

And he was late for work again because they spent fifteen minutes arguing before he could convince her she ought to go to work just the same. He had to talk persuasively, urging her gently, and it took time. But he couldn't bring himself to talk to her roughly or threaten to strike her like a lot of men might have done. He wasn't made that way.

So when he reached the plant he was late and he had to wait to punch the time clock because the day-shift workers were streaming out in long lines, in groups and bunches that impeded his progress.

Even now just starting his workday his legs ached. He had to force himself to struggle past the outgoing workers, punch the time clock, and get the little cart he pushed around all night, because he kept toying with the idea of going home and getting back in bed.

He pushed the cart out on the concrete floor, thinking that if this was his plant he'd make a lot of changes in it. There were too many standing-up jobs for one thing. He'd figure out some way most of 'em could be done sitting down and he'd put a lot more benches around. And this job he had — this job that forced him to walk ten hours a night, pushing this little cart, well, he'd turn it into a sitting-down job. One of those little trucks they used around railroad stations would be good for a job like this. Guys sat on a seat and the thing moved easily, taking up little room and turning in hardly any space at all, like on a dime.

He pushed the cart near the foreman. He never could remember to refer to her as the forelady even in his mind. It was funny to have a white woman for a boss in a plant like this one.

She was sore about something. He could tell by the way her face was red and her eyes were half-shut until they were slits. Probably been out late and didn't get enough sleep. He avoided looking at her and hurried a little, head down, as he passed her though he couldn't resist stealing a glance at her out of the corner of his eyes. He saw the edge of the light-colored slacks she wore and the tip end of a big tan shoe.

"Hey, Johnson!" the woman said.

The machines had started full blast. The whirr and the

grinding made the building shake, made it impossible to hear conversations. The men and women at the machines talked to each other but looking at them from just a little distance away, they appeared to be simply moving their lips because you couldn't hear what they were saying. Yet the woman's voice cut across the machine sounds — harsh, angry.

He turned his head slowly. "Good evenin', Mrs. Scott," he said, and waited.

"You're late again."

"That's right. My legs were bothering me."

The woman's face grew redder, angrier looking. "Half this shift comes in late," she said. "And you're the worst one of all. You're always late. Whatsa matter with ya?"

"It's my legs," he said. "Somehow they don't ever get rested. I don't seem to get used to sleeping days. And I just can't get started."

"Excuses. You guys always got excuses," her anger grew and spread. "Every guy comes in here late always has an excuse. His wife's sick or his grandmother died or somebody in the family had to go to the hospital," she paused, drew a deep breath. "And the niggers is the worse. I don't care what's wrong with your legs. You get in here on time. I'm sick of you niggers —"

"You got the right to get mad," he interrupted softly. "You got the right to cuss me four ways to Sunday but I ain't letting nobody call me a nigger."

He stepped closer to her. His fists were doubled. His lips were drawn back in a thin narrow line. A vein in his forehead stood out swollen, thick.

And the woman backed away from him, not hurriedly but slowly — two, three steps back.

"Aw, forget it," she said. "I didn't mean nothing by it. It slipped out. It was an accident." The red of her face deepened until the small blood vessels in her cheeks were purple. "Go on and get to work," she urged. And she took three more slow backward steps.

He stood motionless for a moment and then turned away from the sight of the red lipstick on her mouth that made him remember that the foreman was a woman. And he couldn't bring himself to hit a woman. He felt a curious tingling in his fingers and he looked down at his hands. They were clenched tight, hard, ready to smash some of those small purple veins in her face.

He pushed the cart ahead of him, walking slowly. When he turned his head, she was staring in his direction, mopping her forehead with a dark blue handkerchief. Their eyes met and then they both looked away.

He didn't glance in her direction again but moved past the long work benches, carefully collecting the finished parts, going slowly and steadily up and down, back and forth the length of the building, and as he walked he forced himself to swallow his anger, get rid of it.

And he succeeded so that he was able to think about what had happened without getting upset about it. An hour went by but the tension stayed in his hands. They were clenched and knotted on the handles of the cart as though ready to aim a blow.

And he thought he should have hit her anyway, smacked her hard in the face, felt the soft flesh of her face give under the hardness of his hands. He tried to make his hands relax by offering them a description of what it would have been like to strike her because he had the queer feeling that his hands were

not exactly a part of him anymore — they had developed a separate life of their own over which he had no control. So he
dwelt on the pleasure his hands would have felt — both of
them cracking at her, first one and then the other. If he had
done that his hands would have felt good now — relaxed,
rested.

And he decided that even if he'd lost his job for it, he should
have let her have it and it would have been a long time, maybe
the rest of her life, before she called anybody else a nigger.

The only trouble was he couldn't hit a woman. A woman
couldn't hit back the same way a man did. But it would have
been a deeply satisfying thing to have cracked her narrow lips
wide open with just one blow, beautifully timed and with all
his weight in back of it. That way he would have gotten rid of
all the energy and tension his anger had created in him. He
kept remembering how his heart had started pumping blood so
fast he had felt it tingle even in the tips of his fingers.

With the approach of night, fatigue nibbled at him. The corners of his mouth drooped, the frown between his eyes deepened, his shoulders sagged; but his hands stayed tight and
tense. As the hours dragged by he noticed that the women
workers had started to snap and snarl at each other. He
couldn't hear what they said because of the sound of machines
but he could see the quick lip movements that sent words tum-
bling from the sides of their mouths. They gestured irritably
with their hands and scowled as their mouths moved.

Their violent jerky motions told him that it was getting close
on to quitting time but somehow he felt that the night still
stretched ahead of him, composed of endless hours of steady
walking on his aching legs. When the whistle finally blew he
went on pushing the cart, unable to believe that it had sounded.
The whirring of the machines died away to a murmur and he

knew then that he'd really heard the whistle. He stood still for a moment, filled with a relief that made him sigh.

Then he moved briskly, putting the cart in the storeroom, hurrying to take his place in the line forming before the paymaster. That was another thing he'd change, he thought. He'd have the pay envelopes handed to the people right at their benches so there wouldn't be ten or fifteen minutes lost waiting for the pay. He always got home about fifteen minutes late on payday. They did it better in the plant where Mae worked, brought the money right to them at their benches.

He stuck his pay envelope in his pants' pocket and followed the line of workers heading for the subway in a slow-moving stream. He glanced up at the sky. It was a nice night, the sky looked packed full to running over with stars. And he thought if he and Mae would go right to bed when they got home from work they'd catch a few hours of darkness for sleeping. But they never did. They fooled around — cooking and eating and listening to the radio and he always stayed in a big chair in the living room and went almost but not quite to sleep and when they finally got to bed it was five or six in the morning and daylight was already seeping around the edges of the sky.

He walked slowly, putting off the moment when he would have to plunge into the crowd hurrying toward the subway. It was a long ride to Harlem and tonight the thought of it appalled him. He paused outside an all-night restaurant to kill time, so that some of the first rush of workers would be gone when he reached the subway.

The lights in the restaurant were brilliant, enticing. There was life and motion inside. And as he looked through the window he thought that everything within range of his eyes gleamed — the long imitation marble counter, the tall stools, the white porcelain-topped tables and especially the big metal coffee urn right near the window. Steam issued from its top and a gas flame flickered under it — a lively, dancing, blue flame.

A lot of the workers from his shift — men and women — were lining up near the coffee urn. He watched them walk to the porcelain-topped tables carrying steaming cups of coffee and he saw that just the smell of the coffee lessened the fatigue lines in their faces. After the first sip their faces softened, they smiled, they began to talk and laugh.

On a sudden impulse he shoved the door open and joined the line in front of the coffee urn. The line moved slowly. And as he stood there the smell of the coffee, the sound of the laughter and of the voices, helped dull the sharp ache in his legs.

He didn't pay any attention to the white girl who was serving the coffee at the urn. He kept looking at the cups in the hands of the men who had been ahead of him. Each time a man stepped out of the line with one of the thick white cups the fragrant steam got in his nostrils. He saw that they walked carefully so as not to spill a single drop. There was a froth of bubbles at the top of each cup and he thought about how he would let the bubbles break against his lips before he actually took a big deep swallow.

Then it was his turn. "A cup of coffee," he said, just as he had heard the others say.

The white girl looked past him, put her hands up to her head and gently lifted her hair away from the back of her neck, tossing her head back a little. "No more coffee for a while," she said.

He wasn't certain he'd heard her correctly and he said, "What?" blankly.

"No more coffee for a while," she repeated.

There was silence behind him and then uneasy movement.

He thought someone would say something, ask why or protest, but there was only silence and then a faint shuffling sound as though the men standing behind him had simultaneously shifted their weight from one foot to the other.

He looked at the girl without saying anything. He felt his hands begin to tingle and the tingling went all the way down to his finger tips so that he glanced down at them. They were clenched tight, hard, into fists. Then he looked at the girl again. What he wanted to do was hit her so hard that the scarlet lipstick on her mouth would smear and spread over her nose, her chin, out toward her cheeks, so hard that she would never toss her head again and refuse a man a cup of coffee because he was black.

He estimated the distance across the counter and reached forward, balancing his weight on the balls of his feet, ready to let the blow go. And then his hands fell back down to his sides because he forced himself to lower them, to unclench them and make them dangle loose. The effort took his breath away because his hands fought against him. But he couldn't hit her. He couldn't even now bring himself to hit a woman, not even this one, who had refused him a cup of coffee with a toss of her head. He kept seeing the gesture with which she had lifted the length of her blond hair from the back of her neck as expressive of her contempt for him.

When he went out the door he didn't look back. If he had he would have seen the flickering blue flame under the shiny coffee urn being extinguished. The line of men who had stood behind him lingered a moment to watch the people drinking coffee at the tables and then they left just as he had without having had the coffee they wanted so badly. The girl behind the counter poured water in the urn and swabbed it out and as she waited for the water to run out, she lifted her hair gently from the back of her neck and tossed her head before she began making a fresh lot of coffee.

But he had walked away without a backward look, his head down, his hands in his pockets, raging at himself and whatever it was inside of him that had forced him to stand quiet and still when he wanted to strike out.

The subway was crowded and he had to stand. He tried grasping an overhead strap and his hands were too tense to grip it. So he moved near the train door and stood there swaying back and forth with the rocking of the train. The roar of the train beat inside his head, making it ache and throb, and the pain in his legs clawed up into his groin so that he seemed to be bursting with pain and he told himself that it was due to all that anger-born energy that had piled up in him and not been used and so it had spread through him like a poison — from his feet and legs all the way up to his head.

Mae was in the house before he was. He knew she was home before he put the key in the door of the apartment. The radio was going. She had it tuned up loud and she was singing along with it.

"Hello, babe," she called out, as soon as he opened the door.

He tried to say 'hello' and it came out half grunt and half sigh.

"You sure sound cheerful," she said.

She was in the bedroom and he went and leaned against the doorjamb. The denim overalls she wore to work were carefully draped over the back of a chair by the bed. She was standing in front of the dresser, tying the sash of a yellow housecoat around her waist and chewing gum vigorously as she admired her reflection in the mirror over the dresser.

"Whatsa matter?" she said. "You get bawled out by the boss or somep'n?"

"Just tired," he said slowly. "For God's sake, do you have to crack that gum like that?"

"You don't have to lissen to me," she said complacently. She patted a curl in place near the side of her head and then lifted her hair away from the back of her neck, ducking her head forward and then back.

He winced away from the gesture. "What you got to be always fooling with your hair for?" he protested.

"Say, what's the matter with you anyway?" She turned away from the mirror to face him, put her hands on her hips. "You ain't been in the house two minutes and you're picking on me."

He didn't answer her because her eyes were angry and he didn't want to quarrel with her. They'd been married too long and got along too well and so he walked all the way into the room and sat down in the chair by the bed and stretched his legs out in front of him, putting his weight on the heels of his shoes, leaning way back in the chair, not saying anything.

"Lissen," she said sharply. "I've got to wear those overalls again tomorrow. "You're going to get them all wrinkled up leaning against them like that."

He didn't move. He was too tired and his legs were throbbing now that he had sat down. Besides the overalls were already wrinkled and dirty, he thought. They couldn't help but be for she'd worn them all week. He leaned farther back in the chair.

"Come on, get up," she ordered.

"Oh, what the hell," he said wearily, and got up from the chair. "I'd just as soon live in a subway. There'd be just as much place to sit down."

He saw that her sense of humor was struggling with her anger. But her sense of humor won because she giggled.

"Aw, come on and eat," she said. There was a coaxing note in her voice. "You're nothing but an old hungry nigger trying to act tough and —" she paused to giggle and then continued, "You —"

He had always found her giggling pleasant and deliberately said things that might amuse her and then waited, listening for the delicate sound to emerge from her throat. This time he didn't even hear the giggle. He didn't let her finish what she was saying. She was standing close to him and that funny tingling started in his finger tips, went fast up his arms and sent his fist shooting straight for her face.

There was the smacking sound of soft flesh being struck by a hard object and it wasn't until she screamed that he realized he had hit her in the mouth — so hard that the dark red lipstick had blurred and spread over her full lips, reaching up toward the tip of her nose, down toward her chin, out toward her cheeks.

The knowledge that he had struck her seeped through him slowly and he was appalled but he couldn't drag his hands away from her face. He kept striking her and he thought with horror that something inside him was holding him, binding him to this act, wrapping and twisting about him so that he had to continue it. He had lost all control over his hands. And he groped for a phrase, a word, something to describe what this thing was like that was happening to him and he thought it was like being enmeshed in a winding sheet — that was it — like a winding sheet. And even as the thought formed in his mind, his hands reached for her face again and yet again.

The Witness

IT HAD BEEN SNOWING for twenty-four hours, and as soon as it stopped, the town plows began clearing the roads and sprinkling them with a mixture of sand and salt. By nightfall the main roads were what the roadmaster called clean as a whistle. But the little winding side roads and the store parking lots and the private walkways lay under a thick blanket of snow.

Because of the deep snow, Charles Woodruff parked his station wagon, brand-new, expensive, in the road in front of the Congregational church rather than risk getting stuck in the lot behind the church. He was early for the minister's class so he sat still, deliberately savoring the new-car smell of the station wagon. He found himself sniffing audibly and thought the sound rather a greedy one and so got out of the car and stood on the snow-covered walk, studying the church. A full moon lay low on the horizon. It gave a wonderful luminous quality to the snow, to the church, and to the branches of the great elms dark against the winter sky.

He ducked his head down because the wind was coming in gusts straight from the north, blowing the snow so it swirled around him, stinging his face. It was so cold that his toes felt as though they were freezing and he began to stamp his feet. Fortunately his coat insulated his body against the cold. He hadn't really planned to buy a new coat but during the Christmas vacation he had been in New York City and he had gone into one of those thickly carpeted, faintly perfumed, crystal-chandeliered stores that sell men's clothing and he had seen the coat hanging on a rack — a dark gray cashmere coat, lined with nutria and adorned by a collar of black Persian lamb. A tall, thin salesman who smelled of heather saw him looking at the coat and said: "Try it on, sir — it's toast-warm, cloud-light, guaranteed to make you feel like a prince — do try it on, here let me hold your coat, sir." The man's voice sounded as though he were purring and he kept brushing against Woodruff like a cat, and managed to sell him the coat, a narrow-brimmed felt hat, and a pair of fur-lined gloves.

If Addie had been alive and learned he had paid five hundred dollars for an overcoat, she would have argued with him fiercely, nostrils flaring, thin arched eyebrows lifted. Standing there alone in the snow, in front of the church, he permitted himself a small indulgence. He pretended Addie was standing beside him. He spoke to her, aloud: "You always said I had to dress more elegantly than my students so they would respect my clothes even if they didn't respect my learning. You said —"

He stopped abruptly, thinking he must look like a lunatic, standing in the snow, stamping his feet and talking to himself. If he kept it up long enough, someone would call the state police and a bulletin about him would go clattering out over the teletype: "Attention all cruisers, attention all cruisers, a black man, repeat, a black man is standing in front of the Congregational church in Wheeling, New York; description follows, description follows, thinnish, tallish black man, clipped moustache, expensive (extravagantly expensive, outrageously expensive, unjustifiably expensive) overcoat, felt hat like a Homburg, eyeglasses glittering in the moonlight, feet stamping in the moonlight, mouth muttering in the moonlight. Light of the moon we danced. Glimpses of the moon revisited . . ."

There was no one in sight, no cars passing. It was so still it would be easy to believe that the entire population of the town had died and lay buried under the snow and that he was the sole survivor, and that would be ironic because he did not really belong in this all-white community.

The thought of his alien presence here evoked an image of Addie — dark-skinned, intense, beautiful. He was sixty-five when she died. He had just retired as professor of English at Virginia College for Negroes. He had spent all of his working life there. He had planned to write a grammar to be used in first-year English classes, to perfect his herb garden, catalogue his library, tidy up his files, and organize his clippings — a wealth of material in those clippings. But without Addie these projects seemed inconsequential — like the busy work that grade school teachers devise to keep children out of mischief. When he was offered a job teaching in a high school in a small town in New York, he accepted it quickly.

Everybody was integrating and so this little frozen Northern town was integrating, too. Someone probably asked why there were no black teachers in the school system and the school board and the Superintendent of Schools said they were searching for 'one' — and the search yielded that brand-new black widower, Charles Woodruff (nigger in the woodpile, he thought, and then, why that word, a word he despised and never used so why did it pop up like that, does a full moon really affect the human mind) and he was eager to escape from his old environment and so for the past year he had taught English to academic seniors in Wheeling High School.

No problems. No hoodlums. All of his students were being herded toward college like so many cattle. He referred to them (mentally) as the Willing Workers of America. He thought that what was being done to them was a crime against nature. They were hard-working, courteous, pathetic. He introduced a new textbook, discarded a huge anthology that was filled with mutilated poetry, mutilated essays, mutilated short stories. His students liked him and told him so. Other members of the faculty said he was lucky but just wait until another year — the freshmen and the sophomores were "a bunch of hoodlums" — "a whole new ball game —"

Because of his success with his English classes, Dr. Shipley, the Congregational minister, had asked him if he would assist (Shipley used words like "assist" instead of "help") him with a class of delinquent boys — the class met on Sunday nights. Woodruff felt he should make some kind of contribution to the life of this small town which had treated him with genuine friendliness so he had said yes.

But when he first saw those seven boys assembled in the minister's study, he knew that he could neither help nor assist the minister with them — they were beyond his reach, beyond the minister's reach. They sat silent, motionless, their shoulders hunched as though against some chill they found in the air of that small book-lined room. Their eyelids were like shutters drawn over their eyes. Their long hair covered their foreheads, obscuring their eyebrows, reaching to the collars of their jackets. Their legs, stretched out straight in front of them, were encased in pants that fit as tightly as the leotards of a ballet dancer.

He kept looking at them, studying them. Suddenly, as though at a signal, they all looked at him. This collective stare was so hostile that he felt himself stiffen and sweat broke out on his forehead. He assumed that the same thing had happened to Dr. Shipley because Shipley's eyeglasses kept fogging up, though the room was not overly warm.

Shipley had talked for an hour. He began to get hoarse. Though he paused now and then to ask a question and waited hopefully for a reply, there was none. The boys sat mute and motionless.

After they left, filing out, one behind the other, Woodruff had asked Shipley about them — who they were and why they attended this class in religion.

Shipley said, "They come here under duress. The Juvenile Court requires their attendance at this class."

"How old are they?"

"About sixteen. Very bright. Still in high school. They're all sophomores — that's why you don't know them. Rambler, the tall thin boy, the ringleader, has an IQ in the genius bracket. As a matter of fact, if they weren't so bright, they'd be in reform school. This class is part of an effort to — well — to turn them into God-fearing responsible young citizens."

"Are their families poor?"

"No, indeed. The parents of these boys are — well, they're the backbone of the great middle class in this town."

After the third meeting of the class where the same hostile

silence prevailed, Woodruff said, "Dr. Shipley, do you think we are accomplishing anything?" He had said "we" though he was well aware that these new young outlaws spawned by the white middle class were, praise God, Shipley's problem — the white man's problem. This cripplingly tight shoe was usually on the black man's foot. He found it rather pleasant to have the position reversed.

Shipley ran his fingers through his hair. It was very short hair, stiff-looking, crew-cut.

"I don't know," he said frowning. "I really don't know. They don't even respond to a greeting or a direct question. It is a terribly frustrating business, an exhausting business. When the class is over, I feel as though I had spent the entire evening lying prone under the unrelieved weight of all their bodies."

Woodruff, standing outside the church, stamping his feet, jumped and then winced because he heard a sound like a gunshot. It was born on the wind so that it seemed close at hand. He stood still, listening. Then he started moving quickly toward the religious education building which housed the minister's study.

He recognized the sound — it was made by the car the boys drove. It had no muffler and the snorting, back-firing sounds made by the spent motor were like a series of gunshots. He wanted to be out of sight when the boys drove up in their rusted car. Their lithe young bodies were a shocking contrast to the abused and ancient vehicle in which they traveled. The age of the car, its dreadful condition, was like a snarled message aimed at the adult world: All we've got is the crumbs, the leftovers, whatever the fat cats don't want and can't use; the turnpikes and the throughways and the seventy-mile-an-hour speedways are filled with long, low, shiny cars built for speed, driven by bald-headed, big-bellied rat finks and we're left with the junk, the worn-out beat-up chassis, the thin tires, the brakes that don't hold, the transmission that's shot to hell. He had seen them push the car out of the parking lot behind the church. It wouldn't go in reverse.

Bent over, peering down, picking his way through the deep snow lest he stumble and fall, Woodruff tried to hurry and the explosive sound of that terrible engine kept getting closer and closer. He envisioned himself as a black beetle in a fur-collared coat silhouetted against the snow trying to scuttle out of danger. Danger: Why should he think he was in danger? Perhaps some sixth sense was trying to warn him and his beetle's antenna (did beetles have antennae, did they have five senses and some of them an additional sense, extrasensory —) picked it up — by the pricking of my thumbs, something wicked this way comes.

Once inside the building he drew a deep breath. He greeted Dr. Shipley, hung his hat and coat on the brass hat rack, and then sat down beside Shipley behind the old fumed oak desk. He braced himself for the entrance of the boys.

There was the sound of the front door opening followed by the click-clack sound of their heavy boots, in the hall. Suddenly they were all there in the minister's study. They brought cold air in with them. They sat down with their jackets on — great quilted dark jackets that had been designed for European ski slopes. At the first meeting of the class, Dr. Shipley had suggested they remove their jackets and they simply sat and stared at him until he fidgeted and looked away obviously embarrassed. He never again made a suggestion that was direct and personal.

Woodruff glanced at the boys and then directed his gaze away from them, thinking, if a bit of gilt braid and a touch of velvet were added to their clothing, they could pass for the seven dark bastard sons of some old and evil twelfth-century king. Of course they weren't all dark. Three of them were blond, two had brown hair, one had red hair, only one had black hair. All of them were white. But there was about them an aura of something so evil, so dark, so suggestive of the far reaches of the night, of the black horror of nightmares, that he shivered deep inside himself whenever he saw them. Though he thought of them as being black, this was not the blackness of human flesh, warm, soft to the touch, it was the blackness and the coldness of the hole from which D. H. Lawrence's snake emerged.

The hour was almost up when to Woodward's surprise, Rambler, the tall boy, the one who drove the ramshackle car, the one Shipley said was the leader of the group, began asking questions about cannibalism. His voice was husky, low in pitch, and he almost whispered when he spoke. Woodruff found himself leaning forward in an effort to hear what the boy was saying. Dr. Shipley leaned forward, too.

Rambler said, "Is it a crime to eat human flesh?"

Dr. Shipley said, surprised, "Yes. It's cannibalism. It is a sin and it is also a crime." He spoke slowly, gently, as though he were wooing a timid, wild animal that had ventured out of the woods and would turn tail and scamper back if he spoke in his normal voice.

"Well, if the cats who go for this human flesh bit don't think it's a sin and if they eat it because they haven't any other food, it isn't a sin for them, is it?" The boy spoke quickly, not pausing for breath, running his words together.

"There are many practices and acts that are acceptable to non-Christians which are sinful. Christians condemn such acts no matter what the circumstances."

Woodruff thought uncomfortably, why does Shipley have to sound so pompous, so righteous, so from-off-the-top-of-Olympus? The boys were all staring at him, bright-eyed, mouths slightly open, long hair obscuring their foreheads. Then Rambler said, in his husky whispering voice, "What about you, Doc?"

Dr. Shipley said, "Me?" and repeated it, his voice losing its coaxing tone, rising in pitch, increasing in volume. "Me? What do you mean?"

"Well, man, you're eatin' human flesh, ain't you?"

Woodruff had no idea what the boy was talking about. But Dr. Shipley was looking down at his own hands with a curious self-conscious expression and Woodruff saw that Shipley's nails were bitten all the way down to the quick.

The boy said, "It's self-cannibalism, ain't it, Doc?"

Shipley put his hands on the desk, braced himself, preparatory to standing up. His thin, bony face had reddened. Before he could move, or speak, the boys stood up and began to file out of the room. Rambler leaned over and ran his hand through the minister's short-cut, bristly hair and said, "Don't sweat it, Doc."

Woodruff usually stayed a half-hour or more after the class ended. Dr. Shipley liked to talk and Woodruff listened to him patiently, though he thought Shipley had a second-rate mind and rambled when he talked. But Shipley sat with his head bowed, a pose not conducive to conversation and Woodruff left almost immediately after the boys, carrying in his mind's eye a picture of all those straight, narrow backs with the pants so tight they were like elastic bandages on their thighs, and the oversized bulky jackets and the long, frowsy hair. He thought they looked like paper dolls, cut all at once, exactly alike with a few swift slashes of scissors wielded by a skilled hand. Addie could do that — take paper and fold it and go snip, snip, snip with the scissors and she'd have a string of paper dolls, all fat, or all thin, or all bent over, or all wearing top hats, or all bearded Santas or all Cheshire cats. She had taught arts and crafts in the teacher-training courses for elementary-school teachers at Virginia College and so was skilled in the use of crayon and scissors.

He walked toward his car, head down, picking his way through the snow and then he stopped, surprised. The boys were standing in the road. They had surrounded a girl. He didn't think she was a high school girl though she was young. She had long blond hair that spilled over the quilted black jacket she was wearing. At first he couldn't tell what the boys were doing but as he got closer to them, he saw that they were moving toward their ancient car and forcing the girl to move with them though she was resisting. They were talking to each other and to her, their voices companionable, half-playful.

"So we all got one in the oven."

"So it's all right if it's all of us."

The girl said, "No."

"Aw, come on, Nellie, hurry up."

"It's colder'n hell, Nellie. Move!"

They kept pushing her toward the car and she turned on them and said, "Quit it."

"Aw, get in."

One of them gave her a hard shove, sent her closer to the car and she screamed and Rambler clapped his hand over her mouth and she must have bitten his hand because he snatched it away and then she screamed again because he slapped her and then two of them picked her up and threw her on the front seat and one of them stayed there, holding her.

Woodruff thought, There are seven of them, young, strong, satanic. He ought to go home where it was quiet and safe, mind his own business — black man's business; leave this white man's problem for a white man, leave it alone, not his, don't interfere, go home to the bungalow he rented — ridiculous type of architecture in this cold climate, developed for India, a hot climate, and that open porch business —

He said, "What are you doing?" He spoke with the voice of authority, the male schoolteacher's voice and thought, Wait, slow down, cool it, you're a black man speaking with a white man's voice.

They turned and stared at him; as they turned, they all assumed what he called the stance of the new young outlaw: the shoulders hunched, the hands in the pockets. In the moonlight he thought they looked as though they belonged in a frieze around a building — the hunched-shoulder posture repeated again and again, made permanent in stone. Classic.

"What are you doing?" he said again, voice louder, deeper.

"We're standin' here."

"You can see us, can't you?"

"Why did you force that girl into your car?"

"You're dreamin'."

"I saw what happened. And that boy is holding her in there."

"You been readin' too much."

They kept moving in, closing in on him. Even on this cold, windy night he could smell them and he loathed the smell — cigarettes, clothes washed in detergents and not rinsed enough and dried in automatic driers. They all smelled like that these days, even those pathetic college-bound drudges, the Willing Workers of America, stank so that he was always airing out his classroom. He rarely ever encountered the fresh clean smell of clothes that had been washed in soap and water, rinsed in boiling water, dried in the sun — a smell that he associated with new-mown hay and flower gardens and — Addie.

There was a subtle change in the tone of the voice of the next speaker. It was more contemptuous and louder.

"What girl, ho-daddy, what girl?"

One of them suddenly reached out and knocked his hat off his head, another one snatched his glasses off and threw them in the road and there was the tinkling sound of glass shattering. It made him shudder. He was half-blind without his glasses, peering about, uncertain of the shape of objects — like the woman in the Thurber cartoon, oh, yes, of course, three balloons and an H or three cats and a dog — only it was one of those scrambled alphabet charts.

They unbuttoned his overcoat, went through the pockets of his pants, of his jacket. One of them took his wallet, another took his car keys, picked up his hat, and then was actually behind the wheel of his station wagon and was moving off in it.

He shouted, "My car. Damn you, you're stealing my car —" his brand-new station wagon; he kept it immaculate, swept it out every morning, washed the windows. He tried to break out of that confining circle of boys and they simply pushed him back toward their car.

"Don't sweat it, man. You goin' ride with us and this little chick-chick."

"You goin' be our pro-tec-shun, ho-daddy. You goin' be our protec-shun."

They took his coat off and put it around him backward without putting his arms in the sleeves and then buttoned it up. The expensive coat was just like a strait jacket — it pinioned his arms to his sides. He tried to work his way out of it by flexing his muscles, hoping that the buttons would pop off or a seam would give, and thought, enraged, They must have stitched the goddamn coat to last for a thousand years and put the goddamn buttons on the same way. The fur collar pressed against his throat, choking him.

Woodruff was forced into the back seat, two boys on each side of him. They were sitting half on him and half on each other. The one holding his wallet examined its contents. He whistled. "Hey!" he said, "Ho-daddy's got one hundred and forty-four bucks. We got us a rich ho-daddy —"

Rambler held out his hand and the boy handed the money over without a protest, not even a sigh. Then Rambler got into the front seat behind the wheel. The girl was quiet only because the boy beside her had his hand around her throat and from the way he was holding his arm, Woodruff knew he was exerting a certain amount of pressure.

"Give the man a hat," Rambler said.

One of the boys felt around until he found a cap. They were so close to each other that each of his movements slightly disrupted their seating arrangement. When the boy shifted his weight, the rest of them were forced to shift theirs.

"Here you go," the boy said. He pulled a black wool cap down on Woodruff's head, over his eyes, over his nose.

He couldn't see anything. He couldn't breathe through his nose. He had to breathe through his mouth or suffocate. The freezing cold air actually hurt the inside of his mouth. The overcoat immobilized him and the steady pressure of the fur collar against his windpipe was beginning to interfere with his normal rate of breathing. He knew that his whole circulatory system would gradually begin to slow down. He frowned, thinking what a simple and easily executed method of rendering a person helpless — just an overcoat and a knit cap. Then he thought, alarmed, If they should leave me out in the woods like this, I would be dead by morning. What do they want of me anyway?

He cleared his throat preparatory to questioning them but Rambler started the car and he could not make himself heard above the sound of the engine. He thought the noise would shatter his eardrums and he wondered how these boys could bear it — the terrible cannon fire sound of the engine and the rattling of the doors and the windows. Then they were off and it was like riding in a jeep — only worse because the seat was broken and they were jounced up out of the seat and then back down into a hollowed-out place, all of them on top of each other. He tried to keep track of the turns the car made but he couldn't, there were too many of them. He assumed that whenever they stopped it was because of a traffic light or a stop sign.

It seemed to him they had ridden for miles and miles when the car began to jounce up and down more violently than ever and he decided they had turned onto a rough, rutted road. Suddenly they stopped. The car doors were opened and the boys pushed him out of the car. He couldn't keep his balance and he stumbled and fell flat on his face in the snow and they all laughed. They had to haul him to his feet for his movements were so constricted by the overcoat that he couldn't get up without help.

The cap had worked up a little so that he could breathe more freely and he could see anything that was in his immediate vicinity. Either they did not notice that the cap had been pushed out of place or they didn't care. As they guided him along he saw that they were in a cemetery that was filled with very old tombstones. They were approaching a small building and his station wagon was parked to one side. The boy who had driven it opened the door of the building and Woodruff saw that it was lighted inside by a big bulb that dangled from the ceiling. There were shovels and rakes inside and a grease-encrusted riding mower, bags of grass seed, and a bundle of material that looked like the artificial grass used around new graves.

Rambler said, "Put the witness here."

They stood him against the back wall, facing the wall.

"He's here and yet he ain't here."

"Ho-daddy's here — and yet — he ain't here."

"He's our witness."

And then Rambler's voice again, "If he moves, ice him with a shovel."

The girl screamed and then the sound was muffled, only a kind of far-off moaning sound coming through something. They must have gagged her. All the sounds were muffled — it was like trying to see something in a fog or hear something when other sounds overlay the one thing you're listening for. What had they brought him here for? They would go away and leave him with the girl but the girl would know that he hadn't —

How would she know? They had probably blindfolded her, too. What were they doing? He could see shadows on the wall. Sometimes they moved, sometimes they were still, and then the shadows moved again and then there would be laughter. Silence after that and then thuds, thumps, silence again. Terrible sounds behind him. He started to turn around and someone poked him in the back, sharply, with the handle of a shovel or a rake. He began to sweat despite the terrible cold.

He tried to relax by breathing deeply and he began to feel as though he were going to faint. His hands and feet were numb. His head ached. He had strained so to hear what was going on behind him that he was afraid he had impaired his own hearing.

When Rambler said, "Come on, ho-daddy, it's your turn," he was beginning to lose all feeling in his arms and legs.

Someone unbuttoned his coat, plucked the cap off his head. He let his breath out in a long drawn-out sigh. He doubted that he could have survived much longer with that pressure on his throat. The boys looked at him curiously. They threw his coat on the hard-packed dirt floor and tossed the cap on top of it. He thought that the black knit cap they'd used, like a sailor's watch cap, was as effective a blindfold as could be found — providing, of course, the person couldn't use his hands to remove it.

The girl was lying on the floor, half-naked. They had put some burlap bags under her. She looked as though she were dead.

They pushed him toward her saying, "It's your turn."

He balked, refusing to move.

"You don't want none?"

They laughed. "Ho-daddy don't want none."

They pushed him closer to the girl and someone grabbed one of his hands and placed it on the girl's thigh, on her breasts, and then they laughed again. They handed him his coat, pulled the cap down on his head.

"Let's go, ho-daddy. Let's go."

Before he could put his coat back on they hustled him outdoors. One of them threw his empty wallet at him and another aimed his car keys straight at his head. The metal stung as it hit his cheek. Before he could catch them the keys disappeared in the snow. The boys went back inside the building and emerged carrying the girl, half-naked, head hanging down limply the way the head of a corpse would dangle.

"The girl —" Woodruff said.

"You're our witness, ho-daddy. You're our big fat witness."

They propped the girl up in the back seat of their car. "You're the only witness we got," they repeated it, laughing. "Take good care of yourself."

"She'll freeze to death like that," he protested.

"Not Nellie."

"She likes it."

"Come on, man, let's go, let's go, let's go," Rambler said impatiently.

Woodruff's arms and hands were so numb that he had trouble getting his coat on. He had to take his gloves off and poke around in the snow with his bare hands before he could retrieve his wallet and the car keys. The pain in his hands was as sharp and intense as if they had been burned.

Getting into his car he began to shake with fury. Once he got out of this wretched cemetery he would call the state police. Young animals. He had called them outlaws; they weren't outlaws, they were animals. In his haste he dropped the keys and had to feel around on the floor of the car for them.

When he finally got the car started he was shivering and shaking and his stomach was quivering so that he didn't dare try to drive. He turned on the heater and watched the tiny taillight on Rambler's car disappear — an old car and the taillight was like the end of a pencil glowing red in the dark. The loud explosive sound of the engine gradually receded. When he could no longer hear it, he flicked on the light in his car and looked at his watch. It was quarter past three. Wouldn't the parents of those godforsaken boys wonder where they were at that hour? Perhaps they didn't care — perhaps they were afraid of them — just as he was.

Though he wanted to get home as quickly as possible, so he could get warm, so he could think, he had to drive slowly, peering out at the narrow rutted road because he was half blind without his glasses. When he reached the cemetery gates he stopped, not knowing whether to turn right or left for he had no idea where he was. He took a chance and turned right and followed the macadam road, still going slowly, saw a church on a hill and recognized it as the Congregational church in Brooksville, the next town, and knew he was about five miles from home.

By the time he reached his own driveway, sweat was pouring from his body just like water coming out of a showerhead — even his eyelashes were wet; it ran down his ears, dripped off his nose, his lips, even the palms of his hands.

In the house he turned on the lights, in the living room, in the hall, in his bedroom. He went to his desk, opened a drawer and fished out an old pair of glasses. He had had them for years. They looked rather like Peter Cooper's glasses — he'd seen them once in the Cooper Union Museum in New York — small-lensed, with narrow, silvery-looking frames. They evoked an image of a careful scholarly man. When he had started wearing glasses, he had selected frames like Peter Cooper's. Addie had made him stop wearing them. She said they gave him the look of another era, made it easy for his students to caricature him — the tall, slender figure, slightly stooped, the steel-rimmed glasses. She said that his dark, gentle eyes looked as though they were trapped behind those little glasses.

Having put on the glasses, he went to the telephone and

stood with one hand resting on it, sweating again, trembling again. He turned away, took off his overcoat and hung it on a hanger and placed it in the hall closet.

He began to pace up and down the living room — a pleasant spacious room, simply furnished. It had a southern exposure and there were big windows on that side of the room. The windows faced a meadow. The thought crossed his mind, lightly, like the silken delicate strand of a cobweb, that he would have to leave here and he brushed it away — not quite away, a trace remained.

He wasn't going to call the police. Chicken. That was the word his students used. Fink was another one. He was going to chicken out. He was going to fink out.

Why wasn't he going to call the police? Well, what would he tell them? That he'd been robbed? Well, that was true. That he'd been kidnapped? Well, that was true, too, but it seemed like a harsh way of putting it. He'd have to think about that one. That he'd been witness to a rape? He wasn't even certain that they had raped the girl. No? Who was he trying to kid? Himself? Himself.

So why wasn't he going to the police? He hadn't touched the girl. But those horrible little hoods, toads rather, why toads, toe of frog ingredient of witches' brew, poisonous substance in the skin — bufotenine, a hallucinogen found in the skin of the frog, of the toad. Those horrible toadlike hoods would say he had touched her. Well, he had. Hadn't he? They had made sure of that. Would the police believe him? The school board? The PTA? "Where there's smoke there must be fire." "I'm not going to let my daughter stay in his class."

He started shivering again and made himself a cup of tea and sat down on the window seat in the living room to drink it and then got up and turned off the lights and looked out at the snow. The moonlight was so bright that he could see wisps of tall grass in the meadow — yellow against the snow. Immediately he thought of the long blond hair of that starvation-thin young girl. Bleached hair? Perhaps. It didn't lessen the outrage. She was dressed just like the boys — big quilted jacket, skin-tight pants, even her hair worn like theirs, obscuring the forehead, the sides of the face.

There was a sudden movement outside the window and he frowned and leaned forward, wondering what was moving about at this hour. He saw a pair of rabbits, leaping, running, literally playing games with each other. He had never before seen such free joyous movement, not even children at play exhibited it. There was always something unrelaxed about the eyes of children, about the way they held their mouths, wrinkled their foreheads — they looked as though they had been cornered and were impelled to defend themselves or that they were impelled to pursue some object that forever eluded them.

Watching this joyous heel-kicking play of the rabbits, he found himself thinking, I cannot continue to live in the same small town with that girl and those seven boys. The boys knew, before he did, that he wasn't going to report this — this incident — these crimes. They were bright enough to know that he would quickly realize how neatly they had boxed him in and thus would keep quiet. If he dared enter a complaint against them they would accuse him of raping the girl, would say they found him in the cemetery with her. Whose story would be believed? "Where there's smoke there's fire."

Right after that he started packing. He put his clothes into a foot locker. He stacked his books on the floor of the station wagon. He was surprised to find among the books a medical textbook that had belonged to John — Addie's brother.

He sat down and read all the material on angina pectoris. At eight o'clock he called the school and said he wasn't feeling well (which was true) and that he would not be in. Then he called the office of the local doctor and made an appointment for that afternoon.

When he talked to the doctor he described the violent pain in his chest that went from the shoulder down to his finger tips on the left side, causing a squeezing, crushing sensation that left him feeling faint, dizzy.

The doctor, a fat man in an old tweed jacket and a limp white shirt, said after he examined him, "Angina. You'll have to take three or four months off until we can get this thing under control."

"I will resign immediately."

"Oh, no. That isn't necessary. Besides I've been told you're the best English teacher we've ever had. It would be a great pity to lose you."

"No," Woodruff said, "it is better to resign." Come back here and look at that violated little girl? Come back here? Ever?

He scarcely listened to the detailed instructions he was to follow, did not even glance at the three prescriptions he was handed, for he was eager to be on his way. He composed a letter of resignation in his mind. When he went back to the bungalow he wrote it quickly and then put it on the front seat of the station wagon to be mailed en route.

Then he went back into the house and stayed there just long enough to call his landlord. He said he'd had a heart attack and was going back to Virginia to convalesce, that he had turned the thermostat down to sixty-five and he would return the house keys by mail. The landlord said, My goodness, you just paid a month in advance, I'll mail you a refund, what's your new address, so sorry, ideal tenant.

Woodruff hung up the receiver and said, "Peace be with you, brother —" There was already an echo in the room though it wasn't empty — all he'd removed were his books and his clothes.

He put on his elegant overcoat. When he got back to Virginia, he would give the coat away, his pleasure in it destroyed now for he would always remember the horrid feel of the collar tight across his throat, even the feel of the fabric under his finger tips would evoke an image of the cemetery, the tool shed, and the girl.

He drove down the road rather slowly. There were curves in the road and he couldn't go fast, besides he liked to look at this landscape. It was high rolling land. Snow lay over it — blue-white where there were shadows cast by the birch trees and the hemlocks, yellow-white and sparkling in the great meadow where he had watched the heel-kicking freedom of the rabbits at play.

At the entrance to the highway he brought the car to a halt. As he sat there waiting for an opportunity to get into the stream of traffic, he heard close at hand the loud explosive sound of an engine — a familiar sound. He was so alarmed that he momentarily experienced all the symptoms of a heart attack, the sudden terrible inability to breathe and the feeling that something was squeezing his chest, kneading it so that pain ran through him as though it were following the course of his circulatory system.

He knew from the sound that the car turning off the highway, entering the same road that he was now leaving, was Rambler's car. In the sunlight, silhouetted against the snow, it looked like a junkyard on wheels, fenders dented, sides dented, chassis rusted. All the boys were in the car. Rambler was driving. The thin blond girl was in the front seat — a terrible bruise under one eye. For a fraction of a second Woodruff looked straight into Rambler's eyes, just visible under the long, untidy hair. The expression was cold, impersonal, analytical.

After he got on the highway, he kept looking in the rearview mirror. There was no sign of pursuit. Evidently Rambler had not noticed that the car was loaded for flight — books and cartons on the seats, foot locker on the floor, all this was out of his range of vision. He wondered what they were doing. Wrecking the interior of the bungalow? No. They were probably waiting for him to return so they could blackmail him. Blackmail a black male.

On the turnpike he kept going faster and faster — eighty-five miles an hour, ninety, ninety-five, one hundred. He felt exhilarated by this tremendous speed. It was clearing his mind, heartening him, taking him out of himself.

He began to rationalize about what had happened. He decided that Rambler and his friends didn't give a damn that he Woodruff, was a black man. They couldn't care less. They were very bright boys, bright enough to recognize him for what he was: a black man in his sixties, conditioned all his life by the knowledge that "White woman taboo for you" (as one of his African students used to say). The moment he attempted to intervene there in front of the church, they decided to take him with them. They knew he wasn't going to the police about any matter which involved sex and a white girl, especially where there was the certainty that all seven of them would accuse him of having relations with the girl. They had used his presence in that tool shed to give an extra exquisite fillip to their dreadful game.

He turned on the radio and waited impatiently for music,

any kind of music, thinking it would distract him. He got one of those stations that play what he called thump-and-blare music. A husky-voiced woman was shouting a song — not singing, shouting:

> I'm gonna turn on the big beat
> I'm gonna turn up the high heat
> For my ho-daddy, ho-daddy,
> For my ho-daddy, ho-daddy.

He flipped the switch, cutting off the sound and he gradually diminished the speed of the car, slowing, slowing, slowing. "We got us a rich ho-daddy." That's what one of the boys had said there in front of the church when he plucked the money out of Woodruff's wallet. A rich ho-daddy? A black ho-daddy. A witness. Another poor scared black bastard who was a witness.

Solo
on the
Drums

THE ORCHESTRA HAD A WEEK'S engagement at the Randlert Theater at Broadway and Forty-second Street. IIis name was picked out in lights on the marquee. The name of the orchestra and then his name underneath by itself.

There had been a time when he would have been excited by it. And stopped to let his mind and his eyes linger over it lovingly. Kid Jones. The name — his name — up there in lights that danced and winked in the brassy sunlight. And at night his name glittered up there on the marquee as though it had been sprinkled with diamonds. The people who pushed their way through the crowded street looked up at it and recognized it and smiled.

He used to eat it up. But not today. Not after what had happened this morning. He just looked at the sign with his name on it. There it was. Then he noticed that the sun had come out, and he shrugged and went on inside the theater to put on one of the cream-colored suits and get his music together.

After he had finished changing his clothes, he glanced in the long mirror in his dressing room. He hadn't changed any. Same face. No fatter and no thinner. No gray hair. Nothing. He frowned. Because he felt that the things that were eating him up inside ought to show. But they didn't.

When it was time to go out on the stage, he took his place behind the drums, not talking, just sitting there. The orchestra started playing softly. He made a mental note of the fact that the boys were working together as smoothly as though each one had been oiled.

The long gray curtains parted. One moment they were closed. And then they were open. Silently. Almost like magic. The high-powered spots flooded the stage with light. He could see specks of dust gliding down the wide beams of light. Under the bands of light the great space out front was all shadow. Faces slowly emerged out of it — disembodied heads and shoulders that slanted up and back, almost to the roof.

He hit the drums lightly. Regularly. A soft, barely discernible rhythm. A background. A repeated emphasis for the horns and the piano. The man with the trumpet stood up and the first notes came out sweet and clear and high.

Kid Jones kept up the drum accompaniment. Slow. Careful. Soft. And he felt his left eyebrow lift itself and start to twitch as the man played the trumpet. It happened whenever he heard the trumpet. The notes crept up, higher, higher, higher.

So high that his stomach sucked in against itself. Then a little lower and stronger. A sound sustained. The rhythm of it beating against his ears until he was filled with it and sighing with it.

He wanted to cover his ears with his hands because he kept hearing a voice that whispered the same thing over and over again. The voice was trapped somewhere under the roof — caught and held there by the trumpet. "I'm leaving I'm leaving I'm leaving."

The sound took him straight back to the rain, the rain that had come with the morning. He could see the beginning of the day — raw and cold. He was at home. But he was warm because he was close to her, holding her in his arms. The rain and the wind cried softly outside the window.

And now — well, he felt as though he were floating up and up and up on that long blue note of the trumpet. He half closed his eyes and rode up on it. It had stopped being music. It was that whispering voice, making him shiver. Hating it and not being able to do anything about it. "I'm leaving it's the guy who plays the piano I'm in love with him and I'm leaving now today." Rain in the streets. Heat gone. Food gone. Everything gone because a woman's gone. It's everything you ever wanted, he thought. It's everything you never got. Everything you ever had, everything you ever lost. It's all there in the trumpet — pain and hate and trouble and peace and quiet and love.

The last note stayed up in the ceiling. Hanging on and on. The man with the trumpet had stopped playing but Kid Jones could still hear that last note. In his ears. In his mind.

The spotlight shifted and landed on Kid Jones — the man behind the drums. The long beam of white light struck the top of his head and turned him into a pattern of light and shadow. Because of the cream-colored suit and shirt, his body seemed to be encased in light. But there was a shadow over his face so that his features blended and disappeared. His hairline receded so far back that he looked like a man with a face that never ended. A man with a high, long face and dark, dark skin.

He caressed the drums with the brushes in his hands. They responded with a whisper of sound. The rhythm came over but it had to be listened for. It stayed that way for a long time. Low, insidious, repeated. Then he made the big bass drum growl and pick up the same rhythm.

The Marquis of Brund, pianist with the band, turned to the piano. The drums and the piano talked the same rhythm. The piano high. A little more insistent than the drums. The Marquis was turned sideways on the piano bench. His left foot tapped out the rhythm. His cream-colored suit sharply outlined the bulkiness of his body against the dark gleam of the piano. The drummer and the pianist were silhouetted in two separate brilliant shafts of light. The drums slowly dominated the piano.

The rhythm changed. It was faster. Kid Jones looked out over the crowded theater as he hit the drums. He began to feel as though he were the drums and the drums were he.

The theater throbbed with the excitement of the drums. A man, sitting near the front, shivered and his head jerked to the rhythm. A sailor put his arm around the girl sitting beside him, took his hand and held her face still and pressed his mouth close over hers. Close. Close. Close. Until their faces seemed to melt together. Her hat fell off and neither of them moved. His hand dug deep into her shoulder and still they didn't move.

A kid sneaked in through a side door and slid into an aisle seat. His mouth was wide open and he clutched his cap with both hands, tight and hard against his chest as he listened.

The drummer forgot he was in the theater. There was only him and the drums and they were far away. Long gone. He was holding Lulu, Helen, Susie, Mamie close in his arms. And all of them — all those girls blended into that one girl who was his wife. The one who said, "I'm leaving." She had said it over and over again, this morning, while rain dripped down the windowpanes.

When he hit the drums again it was with the thought that he was fighting with the piano player. He was choking the Marquis of Brund. He was putting a knife in clean between his ribs. He was slitting his throat with a long straight blade. Take my woman. Take your life.

The drums leaped with the fury that was in him. The men in the band turned their heads toward him — a faint astonishment showed in their faces.

He ignored them. The drums took him away from them, took him back, and back, and back, in time and space. He built up an illusion. He was sending out the news. Grandma died. The foreigner in the litter has an old disease and will not recover. The man from across the big water is sleeping with the chief's daughter. Kill. Kill. Kill. The war goes well with the men with the bad smell and the loud laugh. It goes badly with the chiefs with the round heads and the peacock's walk.

It is cool in the deep track in the forest. Cool and quiet. The trees talk softly. They speak of the dance tonight. The young girl from across the lake will be there. Her waist is slender and her thighs are rounded. Then the words he wanted to forget were all around Kid Jones again. "I'm leaving I'm leaving I'm leaving."

He couldn't help himself. He stopped hitting the drums and stared at the Marquis of Brund — a long malevolent look, filled with hate.

There was a restless, uneasy movement in the theater. He remembered where he was. He started playing again. The horn played a phrase. Soft and short. The drums answered. The horn said the same thing all over again. The drums repeated it. The next time it was more intricate. The phrase was turned around, it went back and forth and up and down. And the drums said it over, exactly the same.

He knew a moment of panic. This was where he had to solo again and he wasn't sure he could do it. He touched the drums lightly. They quivered and answered him.

And then it was almost as though the drums were talking about his own life. The woman in Chicago who hated him. The girl with the round, soft body who had been his wife and who had walked out on him, this morning, in the rain. The old woman who was his mother, the same woman who lived in Chicago, and who hated him because he looked like his father, his father who had seduced her and left her, years ago.

He forgot the theater, forgot everything but the drums. He was welded to the drums, sucked inside them. All of him. His pulse beat. His heart beat. He had become part of the drums. They had become part of him.

He made the big drum rumble and reverberate. He went a little mad on the big drum. Again and again he filled the theater with a sound like thunder. The sound seemed to come not from the drums but from deep inside himself; it was a sound that was being wrenched out of him — a violent, raging, roar-

ing sound. As it issued from him he thought, This is the story of
my love, this is the story of my hate, this is all there is left of
me. And the sound echoed and reechoed far up under the roof
of the theater.

When he finally stopped playing, he was trembling; his body
was wet with sweat. He was surprised to see that the drums
were sitting there in front of him. He hadn't become part of
them. He was still himself. Kid Jones. Master of the drums.
Greatest drummer in the world. Selling himself a little piece at
a time. Every afternoon. Twice every evening. Only this time
he had topped all his other performances. This time, playing
like this after what had happened in the morning, he had sold
all of himself — not just a little piece.

Someone kicked his foot. "Bow, you ape. Whassamatter
with you?"

He bowed from the waist and the spotlight slid away from
him, down his pants legs. The light landed on the Marquis of
Brund, the piano player. The Marquis' skin glistened like a
piece of black seaweed. Then the light was back on Kid Jones.

He felt hot and he thought, I stink of sweat. The talcum he
had dabbed on his face after he shaved felt like a constricting
layer of cement. A thin layer, but definitely cement. No air
could get through to his skin. He reached for his handkerchief
and felt the powder and the sweat mix as he mopped his face.

Then he bowed again. And again. Like a — like one of those
things you pull the string and it jerks, goes through the motion
of dancing. Pull it again and it kicks. Yeah, he thought, you
were hot all right. The go-go gals ate you up and you haven't
anyplace to go. Since this morning you haven't had anyplace to
go. "I'm leaving it's the guy who plays the piano I'm in love

with the Marquis of Brund he plays such sweet piano I'm leaving leaving leaving —"

He stared at the Marquis of Brund for a long moment. Then he stood up and bowed again. And again.

The Necessary Knocking on the Door

ALICE KNIGHT WOKE UP just a few hours after she had fallen asleep. She sat up in bed, leaning her weight on one elbow, listening, and wondering what had awakened her.

There was no sound anywhere — either in this room or, as far as she could determine, in any other part of the building. She examined the room with care, thinking that a jar of cold cream or, perhaps, a book might have fallen from the small table near the bed. Thus she became aware of the moonlight — pale, cold light that filtered through the small-paned windows, making grotesque patterns on the floor, the walls, the ceiling.

Perhaps a window shade had flapped. But there was no wind

— the sheer curtains, the dark green shades were motionless in the cold, still mountain air. Or, she thought, the floor may have creaked as old floors do at night — the wood protesting against age, making a sound sharp enough to penetrate and disturb your sleep. Why would it creak once and not again? Or someone might have come up the stairs and stumbled. But there were no footsteps in the hall outside.

It was, she decided, much more logical to believe that she had been dreaming and that some phase of her dream had alarmed her. She lay down, pulled the blankets over her shoulders, closed her eyes.

Almost immediately afterward she sat up. Because there *was* a sound — a low, agonized moan. It was followed by heavy, strangled breathing — breathing that gasped and halted and seemed to come almost to a stop before it started again. Then the moan — low, long, drawn out.

She reached for her dressing gown, shoved her feet into her slippers. Opening the door of her room, she went out into the hall. The long corridor was washed with moonlight. The pale, cold light shimmered on the paneled walls. And looking at it, she thought the moon must have fingered its way throughout the building, superimposing an uncanny stillness as it traveled, so that now there was layer after layer of stillness in which no one coughed, or sighed, or turned over in bed.

She bent her head to one side, listening. The low subdued moaning had started again. It was coming from a room which was directly across the hall. She walked toward it, lifted her hand to knock on the door. Then she saw the name on the neat sign which was placed in a corner of the door panel: "Mrs. Taylor." The firm handwriting of the House Secretary stood out sharply black on the small white card.

She had forgotten that this was Mrs. Taylor's room. Her

hand came away from the door. The sound of the uneven breathing, the low faltering moans, made her lift her hand again. But she did not knock. She stood, with her hand raised, staring at the card; and as she looked at it, she shivered.

The woman is sick, she thought. Even if she's sick, she would reject an offer of assistance from you. The sight of you would make her worse. But I have to knock on her door, find out what is wrong. How can I? It is too much to ask of anyone.

She wished there were a brilliant light in the hall — the hard yellow light from an unshaded electric bulb. In the pale moonlight the reality of this moment was lessening, fading, dying away. The outlines of the hall were blurred by the shimmering light; it even seemed to soften the sound of Mrs. Taylor's uneven breathing. She kept her eyes on the small white card, trying to focus her thoughts on it; but in its place she saw the images of all the things that prevented her from knocking at the door — saw them and hated them.

For months she had looked forward to attending this conference — the Annual August Conference on Christianity in the Modern World — held at Rest House, high up in the Berkshires. She had found herself thinking of the week she would spend here as being an oasis in the desert of the years she had lived in Washington — years of suffocating heat that started in June and did not end until October; years of trying to teach grammar to indifferent high school students; years of taking repeated insults that were an integral part of life in the capital.

When she had arrived at Rest House, the brisk mountain air and the fresh green of the countryside had made Washington's hot crowded streets take on the remoteness of a half-remembered dream.

And now — well, this was the second time she had found herself wishing she had stayed at home, in spite of the heat and the lethargy that she knew hung over Washington, in spite of the brilliant Conference speakers.

If she had stayed at home, she would not now be standing shivering, in front of a closed door, afraid to make a perfectly normal, human gesture toward another woman who appeared to be in distress. She would not have been forced to transform her face into a mask of stillness as she had done at breakfast yesterday morning. Why didn't I go home then? she wondered.

As she stood there in the hall, her eyes on the small white card, she relived that moment when she had first seen Mrs. Taylor. It was in the dining room and there were bowls of white phlox on the windowsills and a long T-shaped table extended down the center of the room. The room was filled with women, all of them white. There was only one vacant seat — on her left. She heard the murmur of conversation, heard her own voice joining the other voices discussing minority groups in Europe. As she talked she unconsciously relaxed, basking in the warm-hearted acceptance of the other delegates.

While her head was turned, a woman had slipped into the seat next to her. She had followed a sudden impulse, an impulse born of her deep satisfaction with Rest House, with the Conference itself, with the friendly atmosphere of the dining room, and had tried to draw the newcomer into the conversation.

And so she had said, not hesitantly, not delicately feeling her way, but boldly, with eagerness in her voice, with expectancy in her manner, "My! But this is good coffee!"

The woman looked at her once and then stood up. Alice got a blurred impression of white hair, of contemptuous eyes. Then the woman made a violent thrusting motion with her hands, and the silver rattled, the plates clinked against the water glasses, all up and down the table.

The woman said, "I've never eaten with a nigger and I'm too old to begin now."

She left the dining room, walking swiftly. And Alice saw that she was still holding one of the small green breakfast napkins in her hand.

There was a long, uneasy silence. Remembering it, Alice tried also to remember exactly how she had felt. Hot? Cold? Both at once? One right after the other? Breath constricted? Yes. But why? From embarrassment? From hate? From anger? Perhaps all three.

She had forced every muscle in her body into immobility. And as she sat there so quietly, so calmly, the awful silence increased, widening, spreading. Then from all sides of the room came a babble of conversation — bright, quick talk hastily assembled to fill up the hollow place made by the silence.

Her vision became strangely distorted. For at that moment she saw everything multiplied. The big dining room seemed to be filled with frenzied movement. All about her hundreds of women's heads were nodding and shaking; thousands of hands jerked in an erratic and purposeless pointing and beckoning.

As she watched the moving heads, the gesturing hands, she made her face expressionless, holding it as still as the silence, thinking: They are hurrying to build a bridge across the gaping silence. Each one of them is approaching with a straw to help build the bridge. They are carrying their straws between their teeth; hurrying, hurrying, hurrying, as they come to build the bridge. Why do I mind? Why should a word, a two-syllable word, make me hate them? Not just that one white-haired white woman, but all of these others, too. What earthly difference does one word make?

Yes, she should have gone home right after breakfast yesterday. The determination to stay on until the Conference ended was a kind of defiance, a challenge hurled at the white-haired woman. If she had left right after breakfast the other delegates would have known why. They would have said she was abnormally sensitive. They would have pitied her. She could not bear their pity — that was why she had stayed.

She looked down at her hands. She was clenching and unclenching them. Their convulsive movement was as jerky as the sound of Mrs. Taylor's breathing. The comparison made her realize where she was and what she had to do.

When she extended her hand toward the door again, she was panting as though she had been running. This time her knuckles brushed against it before she stepped back.

You are a coward, she told herself. You are afraid that if you knock on her door, go in her room, she will spit the word "nigger" at you. And though you would be prepared to hear it, you cannot bear it. The sound of that word as it emerges from her lips turns you into an animal, an outcast, an obscene crawling thing. But you *can* bear it. It is only a word. For a moment you would know that dreadful feeling of nausea, and for another moment, you would know that frightening feeling of being suffocated by hate. That would be all.

Instead of knocking on the door she moved farther away from it. Suddenly she stopped moving and eyed the hall, not seeing it, but held motionless by a recollection more vivid than the reality of the present moment.

The evening before, they had gone into the big dining room for dinner. She had chosen a seat in a far corner, behind a great jar of delphiniums. The spiked blossoms had formed an effective screen.

When she saw the white-haired woman enter the room and sit down near the door, she asked a question of her tablemate.

The girl answered quickly, saying, "Why that's Mrs. Gib Taylor. She comes all the way from Mississippi. She's been a member of this Conference for years. I think her room is on the same floor with yours."

At the close of the evening session, Alice studied the names on the doors of the bedrooms opposite her own, wondering if — Yes, Mrs. Taylor's room was directly across the hall. The sight of the name on that small white card had made her feel as though she were behind a screen, twisting and turning her neck in an effort to see what everyone else saw.

She thrust the memory away from her, closed her eyes and then opened them quickly. The hall was still there, and the moonlight, and the door. It was all too real. I must offer to help her, she thought. But if I go into her room she will accuse me of breaking in while she slept, of planning to rifle her belongings, of intending to steal her jewelry.

She had once overheard Mrs. Taylor say, "You can never tell what *they* are liable to do."

But I can walk down the hall and find someone else. They will knock on her door. She paused in front of another door. What would she say if the occupant of this room should ask her why she had not gone into Mrs. Taylor's room?

She searched for words, whispering them softly under her breath: "Mrs. Taylor, Mrs. Gib Taylor, is sick. I don't want to rap on her door because I am afraid she will call me a name. She would not call you a name, the name that she uses for me, so will you rap? Will you begin the knocking, the necessary knocking at Mrs. Taylor's door?"

Why am I standing here mumbling to myself like this? she thought. Her lips formed the words again: "Mrs. Taylor, Mrs. Gib Taylor is sick."

Whomever she talked to would, very logically, ask, "What's the matter with her?"

"I don't know. I haven't been in her room."

"Why?"

And there you had it. There wasn't any way to explain that or anything else. She walked toward her own room. Once inside she closed the door softly, and leaned against it.

When she got back into bed, she lay huddled under the covers, staring at the strange pattern the moonlight was making on the walls and on the ceiling, hearing, and straining to hear, the faint thickened sound of Mrs. Taylor's breathing.

Finally she fell asleep. It was a troubled, uneasy sleep in which she dreamed that the moonlight had taken on the form and shape of an octopus; and the tentacled moonlight, the small white card on Mrs. Taylor's door, and the fountain in the patio outside her window pursued her down an endless hill. And as she ran from them, stumbling, panting, she heard the octopus-moonlight calling to her: "Yours is the greater crime. A crime. A very great crime. It was a crime. And we were the witnesses."

When she woke up she was infinitely weary. Then she saw that the sun was streaming through the casement windows, filling the room with a dancing, sparkling light that set the panes of glass, the draperies, even the furniture to glowing. The sight of the strong clear light made her feel as though a great weight had been lifted out of her arms.

There ought to be a special kind of greeting for a morning like this, she thought. Some gesture of welcome, like an old-fashioned curtsy to the sun, to the day itself.

She almost smiled. Then she remembered her vain effort to force herself to knock on Mrs. Taylor's door and the impulse to smile disappeared.

I must have been half-asleep last night, drowsing and dreaming, while I stood outside that woman's door. There couldn't have been anything really seriously wrong. Perhaps a cold in her head. And at night the sound of labored breathing is sinister, any sound is sinister at that hour. You magnified it out of all proportion — just as you do anything else.

And then she thought: There is always a perfectly normal, easily understood explanation for everything. Unfortunately one does not always have a sun-flooded morning to help one arrive at such an explanation.

Then she frowned because she heard a kind of hustle and bustle outside her door — quick footsteps, loud, alarmed voices. Rest House was always quiet at this hour in the morning. The only sound should have been the high sweet tones of the chapel bells. Curiosity made her get out of bed, open her door, and look out into the hall.

A maid, who was coming up the hall, greeted her with the quick eagerness of one who bears news. "Good morning, miss. Did you hear about last night?"

Alice shook her head. Remembering the moans, the hoarse breathing that had come from the room across the hall, she asked sharply, "What happened?"

"Oh!" the maid said. "That nice Mis' Taylor died in the night. Doctor say if anybody'd known about her havin' a heart attack they coulda saved her."

In Darkness and Confusion

WILLIAM JONES TOOK a sip of coffee and then put his cup down on the kitchen table. It didn't taste right and he was annoyed because he always looked forward to eating breakfast. He usually got out of bed as soon as he woke up and hurried into the kitchen. Then he would take a long time heating the corn bread left over from dinner the night before, letting the coffee brew until it was strong and clear, frying bacon, and scrambling eggs. He would eat very slowly — savoring the early-morning quiet and the just-rightness of the food he'd fixed.

There was no question about early morning being the best part of the day, he thought. But this Saturday morning in July it was too hot in the apartment. There were too many nagging worries that kept drifting through his mind. In the heat he couldn't think clearly — so that all of them pressed in against him, weighed him down.

He pushed his plate away from him. The eggs had cooked too long; much as he liked corn bread, it tasted like sand this morning — grainy and coarse inside his throat. He couldn't help wondering if it scratched the inside of his stomach in the same way.

Pink was moving around in the bedroom. He cocked his head on one side, listening to her. He could tell exactly what she was doing, as though he were in there with her. The soft heavy sound of her stockinged feet as she walked over to the dresser. The dresser drawer being pulled out. That meant she was getting a clean slip. Then the thud of her two hundred pounds landing in the rocker by the window. She was sitting down to comb her hair. Untwisting the small braids she'd made the night before. She would unwind them one by one, putting the hairpins in her mouth as she went along. Now she was brushing it, for he could hear the creak of the rocker; she was rocking back and forth, humming under her breath as she brushed.

He decided that as soon as she came into the kitchen he would go back to the bedroom, get dressed, and go to work. For his mind was already on the mailbox. He didn't feel like talking to Pink. There simply had to be a letter from Sam today. There had to be.

He was thinking about it so hard that he didn't hear Pink walk toward the kitchen.

When he looked up she was standing in the doorway. She was a short, enormously fat woman. The only garment she had on was a bright pink slip that magnified the size of her body. The skin on her arms and shoulders and chest was startlingly black against the pink material. In spite of the brisk brushing she had given her hair, it stood up stiffly all over her head in short wiry lengths, as though she wore a turban of some rough dark gray material.

He got up from the table quickly when he saw her. "Hot, ain't it?" he said, and patted her arm as he went past her toward the bedroom.

She looked at the food on his plate. "You didn't want no breakfast?" she asked.

"Too hot," he said over his shoulder.

He closed the bedroom door behind him gently. If she saw the door was shut, she'd know that he was kind of low in his mind this morning and that he didn't feel like talking. At first he moved about with energy — getting a clean work shirt, giving his shoes a hasty brushing, hunting for a pair of clean socks. Then he stood still in the middle of the room, holding his dark work pants in his hand while he listened to the rush and roar of water running in the bathtub.

Annie May was up and taking a bath. And he wondered if that meant she was going to work. Days when she went to work she used a hot comb on her hair before she ate her breakfast, so that before he left the house in the morning it was filled with the smell of hot irons sizzling against hair grease.

He frowned. Something had to be done about Annie May. Here she was only eighteen years old and staying out practically all night long. He hadn't said anything to Pink about it, but Annie May crept into the house at three and four and five in the morning. He would hear her key go in the latch and then the telltale click as the lock drew back. She would shut the door very softly and turn the bolt. She'd stand there awhile, waiting to see if they woke up. Then she'd take her shoes off and pad down the hall in her stockinged feet.

When she turned the light on in the bathroom, he could see the clock on the dresser. This morning it had been four-thirty when she came in. Pink, lying beside him, went on peacefully snoring. He was glad that she didn't wake up easy. It would only worry her to know that Annie May was carrying on like that.

Annie May put her hands on her hips and threw her head back and laughed whenever he tried to tell her she had to come home earlier. The smoky smell of the hot irons started seeping into the bedroom and he finished dressing quickly.

He stopped in the kitchen on his way out. "Got to get to the store early today," he explained. He was sure Pink knew he was hurrying downstairs to look in the mailbox. But she nodded and held her face up for his kiss. When he brushed his lips against her forehead he saw that her face was wet with perspiration. He thought, With all that weight she must feel the heat something awful.

Annie May nodded at him without speaking. She was hastily swallowing a cup of coffee. Her dark thin hands made a pattern against the thick white cup she was holding. She had pulled her hair out so straight with the hot combs that, he thought, it was like a shiny skullcap fitted tight to her head. He was surprised to see that her lips were heavily coated with lipstick. When she was going to work she didn't use any, and he wondered why she was up so early if she wasn't working. He could see the red outline of her mouth on the cup.

He hadn't intended to say anything. It was the sight of the lipstick on the cup that forced the words out. "You ain't workin' today?"

"No," she said lazily. "Think I'll go shopping." She winked at Pink and it infuriated him.

"How do you expect to keep a job when you don't show up half the time?" he asked.

"I can always get another one." She lifted the coffee cup to her mouth with both hands and her eyes laughed at him over the rim of the cup.

"What time did you come home last night?" he asked abruptly.

She stared out of the window at the blank brick wall that faced the kitchen. "I dunno," she said finally. "It wasn't late."

He didn't know what to say. Probably she was out dancing somewhere. Or maybe she wasn't. He was fairly certain that she wasn't. Yet he couldn't let Pink know what he was thinking. He shifted his feet uneasily and watched Annie May swallow the coffee. She was drinking it fast.

"You know you ain't too big to get your butt whipped," he said finally.

She looked at him out of the corner of her eyes. And he saw a deep smoldering sullenness in her face that startled him. He was conscious that Pink was watching both of them with a growing apprehension.

Then Annie May giggled. "You and who else?" she said lightly. Pink roared with laughter. And Annie May laughed with her.

He banged the kitchen door hard as he went out. Striding down the outside hall, he could still hear them laughing. And even though he knew Pink's laughter was due to relief because nothing unpleasant had happened, he was angry. Lately every time Annie May looked at him there was open, jeering laughter in her eyes, as though she dared him to say anything to her. Almost as though she thought he was a fool for working so hard.

She had been a nice little girl when she first came to live with them six years ago. He groped in his mind for words to describe what he thought Annie May had become. A Jezebel, he decided grimly. That was it.

And he didn't want Pink to know what Annie May was really like. Because Annie May's mother, Lottie, had been Pink's sister. And when Lottie died, Pink took Annie May. Right away she started finding excuses for anything she did that was wrong. If he scolded Annie May he had to listen to a sharp lecture from Pink. It always started off the same way: "Don't care what she done, William. You ain't goin' to lay a finger on her. She ain't got no father and mother except us . . ."

The quick spurt of anger and irritation at Annie May had sent him hurrying down the first flight of stairs. But he slowed his pace on the next flight because the hallways were so dark that he knew if he wasn't careful he'd walk over a step. As he trudged down the long flights of stairs he began to think about Pink. And the hot irritation in him disappeared as it usually did when he thought about her. She was so fat she couldn't keep on climbing all these steep stairs. They would have to find another place to live — on a first floor where it would be easier for her. They'd lived on this top floor for years, and all the time Pink kept getting heavier and heavier. Every time she went to the clinic the doctor said the stairs were bad for her. So they'd start looking for another apartment and then because the top floors cost less, why, they stayed where they were. And —

Then he stopped thinking about Pink because he had reached the first floor. He walked over to the mailboxes and took a deep breath. Today there'd be a letter. He knew it. There had to be. It had been too long a time since they had had a letter from Sam. The last ones that came he'd said the same thing. Over and over. Like a refrain. "Ma, I can't stand this much longer." And then the letters just stopped.

As he stood there, looking at the mailbox, half-afraid to open it for fear there would be no letter, he thought back to the night Sam graduated from high school. It was a warm June night. He and Pink got all dressed up in their best clothes. And he kept thinking, Me and Pink have got as far as we can go. But Sam — he made up his mind Sam wasn't going to earn his living with a mop and a broom. He was going to earn it wearing a starched white collar and a shine on his shoes and a crease in his pants.

After he finished high school Sam got a job redcapping at Grand Central. He started saving his money because he was going to go to Lincoln — a college in Pennsylvania. It seemed like it was no time at all before he was twenty-one. And in the army. Pink cried when he left. Her huge body shook with her sobbing. He remembered that he had only felt queer and lost. There was this war and all the young men were being drafted. But why Sam — why did he have to go?

It was always in the back of his mind. Next thing Sam was in a camp in Georgia. He and Pink never talked about his being in Georgia. The closest they ever came to it was one night when she said, "I hope he gets used to it quick down there. Bein' born right here in New York there's lots he won't understand."

Then Sam's letters stopped coming. He'd come home from work and say to Pink casually, "Sam write today?" She'd shake her head without saying anything.

The days crawled past. And finally she burst out. "What you keep askin' for? You think I wouldn't tell you?" And she started crying.

He put his arm around her and patted her shoulder. She leaned hard against him. "Oh, Lord," she said. "He's my baby. What they done to him?"

Her crying like that tore him in little pieces. His mind kept going around in circles. Around and around. He couldn't think what to do. Finally one night after work he sat down at the kitchen table and wrote Sam a letter. He had written very few letters in his life because Pink had always done it for him. And now standing in front of the mailbox he could even remember the feel of the pencil in his hand; how the paper looked — blank and challenging — lying there in front of him; that the kitchen clock was ticking and it kept getting louder and louder. It was hot that night, too, and he held the pencil so tight that the inside of his hand was covered with sweat.

He had sat and thought a long time. Then he wrote: "Is you all right? Your Pa." It was the best he could do. He licked the envelope and addressed it with the feeling that Sam would understand.

He fumbled for his key ring, found the mailbox key and opened the box quickly. It was empty. Even though he could see it was empty he felt around inside it. Then he closed the box and walked toward the street door.

The brilliant sunlight outside made him blink after the darkness of the hall. Even now, so early in the morning, it was hot in the street. And he thought it was going to be a hard day to get through, what with the heat and its being Saturday and all. Lately he couldn't seem to think about anything but Sam. Even at the drugstore where he worked as a porter, he would catch himself leaning on the broom or pausing in his mopping to wonder what had happened to him.

The man who owned the store would say to him sharply,

"Boy, what the hell's the matter with you? Can't you keep your mind on what you're doing?" And he would go on washing windows, or mopping the floor or sweeping the sidewalk. But his thoughts, somehow, no matter what he was doing, drifted back to Sam.

As he walked toward the drugstore he looked at the houses on both sides of the street. He knew this street as he knew the creases in the old felt hat he wore the year round. No matter how you looked at it, it wasn't a good street to live on. It was a long cross-town street. Almost half of it on one side consisted of the backs of the three theaters on 125th Street — a long blank wall of gray brick. There were few trees on the street. Even these were a source of danger, for at night shadowy, vague shapes emerged from the street's darkness, lurking near the trees, dodging behind them. He had never been accosted by any of those disembodied figures, but the very stealth of their movements revealed a dishonest intent that frightened him. So when he came home at night he walked an extra block or more in order to go through 125th Street and enter the street from Eighth Avenue.

Early in the morning like this, the street slept. Window shades were drawn down tight against the morning sun. The few people he passed were walking briskly on their way to work. But in those houses where the people still slept, the window shades would go up about noon, and radios would blast music all up and down the street. The bold-eyed women who lived in these houses would lounge in the open windows and call to each other back and forth across the street.

Sometimes when he was on his way home to lunch they would call out to him as he went past, "Come on in, Poppa!" And he would stare straight ahead and start walking faster.

When Sam turned sixteen it seemed to him the street was

unbearable. After lunch he and Sam went through this block together — Sam to school and he on his way back to the drugstore. He'd seen Sam stare at the lounging women in the windows. His face was expressionless, but his eyes were curious.

"I catch you goin' near one of them women and I'll beat you up and down the block," he'd said grimly.

Sam didn't answer him. Instead he looked down at him with a strangely adult look, for even at sixteen Sam had been a good five inches taller than he. After that when they passed through the block, Sam looked straight ahead. And William got the uncomfortable feeling that he had already explored the possibilities that the block offered. Yet he couldn't be sure. And he couldn't bring himself to ask him. Instead he walked along beside him, thinking desperately, We gotta move. I'll talk to Pink. We gotta move this time for sure.

That Sunday after Pink came home from church they looked for a new place. They went in and out of apartment houses along Seventh Avenue and Eighth Avenue, 135th Street, 145th Street. Most of the apartments they didn't even look at. They just asked the super how much the rents were.

It was late when they headed for home. He had irritably agreed with Pink that they'd better stay where they were. Thirty-two dollars a month was all they could afford.

"It ain't a fit place to live, though," he said. They were walking down Seventh Avenue. The street looked wide to him, and he thought with distaste of their apartment. The rooms weren't big enough for a man to move around in without bumping into something. Sometimes he thought that was why Annie May spent so much time away from home. Even at thirteen she couldn't stand being cooped up like that in such a small amount of space.

And Pink said, "You want to live on Park Avenue? With a

doorman bowin' you in and out? 'Good mornin', Mr. William Jones. Does the weather suit you this mornin'?' " Her voice was sharp, like the crack of a whip.

That was five years ago. And now again they ought to move on account of Pink not being able to stand the stairs anymore. He decided that Monday night after work he'd start looking for a place.

It was even hotter in the drugstore than it was in the street. He forced himself to go inside and put on a limp work coat. Then broom in hand he went to stand in the doorway. He waved to the superintendent of the building on the corner. And watched him as he lugged garbage cans out of the areaway and rolled them to the curb. Now, that's the kind of work he didn't want Sam to have to do. He tried to decide why that was. It wasn't just because Sam was his boy and it was hard work. He searched his mind for the reason. It didn't pay enough for a man to live on decently. That was it. He wanted Sam to have a job where he could make enough to have good clothes and a nice home.

Sam's being in the army wasn't so bad, he thought. It was his being in Georgia that was bad. They didn't treat black people right down there. Everybody knew that. If he could figure out some way to get him farther north, Pink wouldn't have to worry about him so much.

The very sound of the word Georgia did something to him inside. His mother had been born there. She had talked about it a lot and painted such vivid pictures of it that he felt he knew the place — the heat, the smell of the earth, how cotton looked. And something more. The way her mouth had folded together whenever she had said, "They hate niggers down there. Don't you never none of you children go down there."

That was years ago; yet even now, standing here on Fifth Avenue, remembering the way she said it turned his skin clammy cold in spite of the heat. And of all the places in the world, Sam had to go to Georgia. Sam, who was born right here in New York, who had finished high school here — they had to put him in the army and send him to Georgia.

He tightened his grip on the broom and started sweeping the sidewalk in long, even strokes. Gradually the rhythm of the motion stilled the agitation in him. The regular back-and-forth motion was so pleasant that he kept on sweeping long after the sidewalk was clean. When Mr. Yudkin, who owned the store, arrived at eight-thirty he was still outside with the broom. Even now he didn't feel much like talking, so he only nodded in response to the druggist's brisk "Good morning! Hot today!"

William followed him into the store and began polishing the big mirror in back of the soda fountain. He watched the man out of the corner of his eye as he washed his hands in the back room and exchanged his suit coat for a crisp white laboratory coat. And he thought maybe when the war was over Sam ought to study to be a druggist instead of a doctor or a lawyer.

As the morning wore along, customers came in in a steady stream. They got Bromo-Seltzers, cigarettes, aspirin, cough medicine, baby bottles. He delivered two prescriptions that cost five dollars. And the cash register rang so often it almost played a tune. Listening to it he said to himself, Yes, Sam ought to be a druggist. It's clean work and it pays good.

A little after eleven o'clock three young girls came in. "Cokes," they said, and climbed up on the stools in front of the fountain. William was placing new stock on the shelves and he studied them from the top of the stepladder. As far as he could see, they looked exactly alike. All three of them. And like

Annie May. Too thin. Too much lipstick. Their dresses were too short and too tight. Their hair was piled on top of their heads in slicked set curls.

"Aw, I quit that job," one of them said. "I wouldn't get up that early in the morning for nothing in the world."

That was like Annie May, too. She was always changing jobs. Because she could never get to work on time. If she was due at a place at nine, she got there at ten. If at ten, then she arrived about eleven. He knew, too, that she didn't earn enough money to pay for all the cheap, bright-colored dresses she was forever buying.

Her girl friends looked just like her and just like these girls. He'd seen her coming out of the movie houses on 125th Street with two or three of them. They were all chewing gum and they nudged each other and talked too loud and laughed too loud. They stared hard at every man who went past them.

Mr. Yudkin looked up at him sharply, and he shifted his glance away from the girls and began putting big bottles of Father John's medicine neatly on the shelf in front of him. As he stacked the bottles up he wondered if Annie May would have been different if she'd stayed in high school. She had stopped going when she was sixteen. He had spoken to Pink about it. "She oughtn't to stop school. She's too young," he'd said.

But because Annie May was Pink's sister's child, all Pink had done had been to shake her head comfortably. "She's tired of going to school. Poor little thing. Leave her alone."

So he hadn't said anything more. Pink always took up for her. And he and Pink didn't fuss at each other like some folks do. He didn't say anything to Pink about it, but he took the afternoon off from work to go to see the principal of the school. He had to wait two hours to see her. And he studied the pictures on the walls in the outer office, and looked down at his shoes while he tried to put into words what he'd say — and how he wanted to say it.

The principal was a large-bosomed white woman. She listened to him long enough to learn that he was Annie May's uncle. "Ah, yes, Mr. Jones," she said. "Now in my opinion —"

And he was buried under a flow of words, a mountain of words, that went on and on. Her voice was high-pitched and loud, and she kept talking until he lost all sense of what she was saying. There was one phrase she kept using that sort of jumped at him out of the mass of words — "a slow learner."

He left her office feeling confused and embarrassed. If he could only have found the words he could have explained that Annie May was bright as a dollar. She wasn't any "slow learner." Before he knew it he was out in the street, conscious only that he'd lost a whole afternoon's pay and he never had got to say what he'd come for. And he was boiling mad with himself. All he'd wanted was to ask the principal to help him persuade Annie May to finish school. But he'd never got the words together.

When he hung up his soiled work coat in the broom closet at eight o'clock that night he felt as though he'd been sweeping floors, dusting fixtures, cleaning fountains and running errands since the beginning of time itself. He looked at himself in the cracked mirror that hung on the door of the closet. There was no question about it; he'd grown older-looking since Sam had gone into the army. His hair was turning a frizzled gray at the temples. His jawbones showed up sharper. There was a stoop in his shoulders.

"Guess I'll get a haircut," he said softly. He didn't really need one. But on a Saturday night the barbershop would be crowded. He'd have to wait a long time before Al got around to him. It would be good to listen to the talk that went on — the arguments that would get started and never really end. For a little while all the nagging worry about Sam would be pushed so far back in his mind, he wouldn't be aware of it.

The instant he entered the barbershop he could feel himself begin to relax inside. All the chairs were full. There were a lot of customers waiting. He waved a greeting to the barbers. "Hot, ain't it?" he said, and mopped his forehead.

He stood there a minute, listening to the hum of conversation, before he picked out a place to sit. Some of the talk, he knew, would be violent, and he always avoided those discussions because he didn't like violence — even when it was only talk. Scraps of talk drifted past him.

"White folks got us by the balls —"

"Well, I dunno. It ain't just white folks. There's poor white folks gettin' their guts squeezed out, too —"

"Sure. But they're white. They can stand it better."

"Sadie had two dollars on 546 yesterday and it came out and —"

"You're wrong, man. Ain't no two ways about it. This country's set up so that —"

"Only thing to do, if you ask me, is shoot all them crackers and start out new —"

He finally settled himself in one of the chairs in the corner — not too far from the window and right in the middle of a group of regular customers who were arguing hotly about the war. It was a good seat. By looking in the long mirror in front of the barbers he could see the length of the shop.

Almost immediately he joined in the conversation. "Them Japs ain't got a chance —" he started. And he was feeling good. He'd come in at just the right time. He took a deep breath before he went on. Most every time he started talking about the Japs the others listened with deep respect. Because he knew more about them than the other customers. Pink worked for some navy people and she told him what they said.

He looked along the line of waiting customers, watching their reaction to his words. Pretty soon they'd all be listening to him. And then he stopped talking abruptly. A soldier was sitting in the far corner of the shop, staring down at his shoes. Why, that's Scummy, he thought. He's at the same camp where Sam is. He forgot what he was about to say. He got up and walked over to Scummy. He swallowed all the questions about Sam that trembled on his lips.

"Hiya, son," he said. "Sure is good to see you."

As he shook hands with the boy he looked him over carefully. He's changed, he thought. He was older. There was something about his eyes that was different than before. He didn't seem to want to talk. After that first quick look at William he kept his eyes down, staring at his shoes.

Finally William couldn't hold the question back any longer. It came out fast. "How's Sam?"

Scummy picked up a newspaper from the chair beside him. "He's all right," he mumbled. There was a long silence. Then he raised his head and looked directly at William. "Was the las' time I seen him." He put a curious emphasis on the word "las'."

William was conscious of a trembling that started in his stomach. It went all through his body. He was aware that conversation in the barbershop had stopped. It was like being inside a cone of silence in which he could hear the scraping noise of the razors — a harsh sound, loud in the silence. Al was putting thick oil on a customer's hair and he turned and looked with the hair-oil bottle still in his hand, tilted up over the customer's head. The men sitting in the tilted-back barber's chairs twisted their necks around — awkwardly, slowly — so they could look at Scummy.

"What you mean — the las' time?" William asked sharply. The words beat against his ears. He wished the men in the barbershop would start talking again, for he kept hearing his own words. "What you mean — the las' time?" Just as though he were saying them over and over again. Something had gone wrong with his breathing, too. He couldn't seem to get enough air in through his nose.

Scummy got up. There was something about him that William couldn't give a name to. It made the trembling in his stomach worse.

"The las' time I seen him he was O.K." Scummy's voice made a snarling noise in the barbershop.

One part of William's mind said, Yes, that's it. It's hate that makes him look different. It's hate in his eyes. You can see it. It's in his voice, and you can hear it. He's filled with it.

"Since I seen him las'," he went on slowly, "he got shot by a white MP. Because he wouldn't go to the nigger end of a bus. He had a bullet put through his guts. He took the MP's gun away from him and shot the bastard in the shoulder." He put the newspaper down and started toward the door; when he reached it he turned around. "They court-martialed him," he said softly. "He got twenty years at hard labor. The notice was posted in the camp the day I left." Then he walked out of the shop. He didn't look back.

There was no sound in the barbershop as William watched him go down the street. Even the razors had stopped. Al was still holding the hair-oil bottle over the head of his customer. The heavy oil was falling on the face of the man sitting in the chair. It was coming down slowly — one drop at a time.

The men in the shop looked at William and then looked

away. He thought, I mustn't tell Pink. She mustn't ever get to
know. I can go down to the mailbox early in the morning and I
can get somebody else to look in it in the afternoon, so if a notice comes I can tear it up.

The barbers started cutting hair again. There was the
murmur of conversation in the shop. Customers got up out of
the tilted-back chairs. Someone said to him, "You can take my
place."

He nodded and walked over to the empty chair. His legs
were weak and shaky. He couldn't seem to think at all. His
mind kept dodging away from the thought of Sam in prison.
Instead the familiar detail of Sam's growing up kept creeping
into his thoughts. All the time the boy was in grammar school
he made good marks. Time went so fast it seemed like it was
just overnight and he was in long pants. And then in high
school.

He made the basketball team in high school. The whole
school was proud of him, for his picture had been in one of the
white papers. They got two papers that day. Pink cut the pictures out and stuck one in the mirror of the dresser in their
bedroom. She gave him one to carry in his wallet.

While Al cut his hair he stared at himself in the mirror until
he felt as though his eyes were crossed. First he thought,
Maybe it isn't true. Maybe Scummy was joking. But a man
who was joking didn't look like Scummy looked. He wondered
if Scummy was AWOL. That would be bad. He told himself
sternly that he mustn't think about Sam here in the barbershop
— wait until he got home.

He was suddenly angry with Annie May. She was just plain
no good. Why couldn't something have happened to her? Why
did it have to be Sam? Then he was ashamed. He tried to find
an excuse for having wanted harm to come to her. It looked

like all his life he'd wanted a little something for himself and Pink and then when Sam came along he forgot about those things. He wanted Sam to have all the things that he and Pink couldn't get. It got to be too late for them to have them. But Sam — again he told himself not to think about him. To wait until he got home and in bed.

Al took the cloth from around his neck and he got up out of the chair. Then he was out on the street heading toward home. The heat that came from the pavement seeped through the soles of his shoes. He had forgotten how hot it was. He forced himself to wonder what it would be like to live in the country. Sometimes on hot nights like this, after he got home from work, he went to sit in the park. It was always cooler there. It would probably be cool in the country. But then it might be cold in winter — even colder than the city.

The instant he got in the house he took off his shoes and his shirt. The heat in the apartment was like a blanket — it made his skin itch and crawl in a thousand places. He went into the living room, where he leaned out of the window, trying to cool off. Not yet, he told himself. He mustn't think about it yet.

He leaned farther out of the window, to get away from the innumerable odors that came from the boxlike rooms in back of him. They cut off his breath, and he focused his mind on them. There was the greasy smell of cabbage and collard greens, smell of old wood and soapsuds and disinfectant, a lingering smell of gas from the kitchen stove, and over it all Annie May's perfume.

Then he turned his attention to the street. Up and down as far as he could see, folks were sitting on the stoops. Not talking. Just sitting. Somewhere up the street a baby wailed. A woman's voice rose sharply as she told it to shut up.

Pink wouldn't be home until late. The white folks she

worked for were having a dinner party tonight. And no matter how late she got home on Saturday night, she always stopped on Eighth Avenue to shop for her Sunday dinner. She never trusted him to do it. It's a good thing, he thought. If she ever took a look at me tonight she'd know there was something wrong.

A key clicked in the lock and he drew back from the window. He was sitting on the couch when Annie May came in the room.

"You're home early, ain't you?" he asked.

"Oh, I'm going out again," she said.

"You shouldn't stay out so late like you did last night," he said mildly. He hadn't really meant to say it. But what with Sam —

"What you think I'm going to do? Sit here every night and make small talk with you?" Her voice was defiant. Loud.

"No," he said, and then added, "but nice girls ain't runnin' around the streets at four o'clock in the mornin'." Now that he'd started he couldn't seem to stop. "Oh, I know what time you come home. And it ain't right. If you don't stop it, you can get some other place to stay."

"It's O.K. with me," she said lightly. She chewed the gum in her mouth so it made a cracking noise. "I don't know what Auntie Pink married a little runt like you for, anyhow. It wouldn't bother me a bit if I never saw you again." She walked toward the hall. "I'm going away for the weekend," she added over her shoulder, "and I'll move out on Monday."

"What you mean for the weekend?" he asked sharply. "Where you goin'?"

"None of your damn business," she said, and slammed the bathroom door hard.

The sharp sound of the door closing hurt his ears so that he winced, wondering why he had grown so sensitive to sounds in the last few hours. What'd she have to say that for, anyway, he asked himself. Five feet five wasn't so short for a man. He was taller than Pink, anyhow. Yet compared to Sam, he supposed he was a runt, for Sam had just kept on growing until he was six feet tall. At the thought he got up from the chair quickly, undressed, and got in bed. He lay there trying to still the trembling in his stomach; trying even now not to think about Sam, because it would be best to wait until Pink was in bed and sound asleep so that no expression on his face, no least little motion, would betray his agitation.

When he heard Pink come up the stairs just before midnight he closed his eyes. All of him was listening to her. He could hear her panting outside on the landing. There was a long pause before she put her key in the door. It took her all that time to get her breath back. She's getting old, he thought. I mustn't ever let her know about Sam.

She came into the bedroom and he pretended to be asleep. He made himself breathe slowly. Evenly. Thinking I can get through tomorrow all right. I won't get up much before she goes to church. She'll be so busy getting dressed she won't notice me.

She went out of the room and he heard the soft murmur of her voice talking to Annie May. "Don't you pay no attention, honey. He don't mean a word of it. I know menfolks. They's always tired and out of sorts by the time Saturdays come around."

"But I'm not going to stay here anymore."

"Yes, you is. You think I'm goin' to let my sister's child be turned out? You goin' to be right here."

They lowered their voices. There was laughter. Pink's deep

and rich and slow. Annie May's high-pitched and nervous. Pink said, "You looks lovely, honey. Now, have a good time."

The front door closed. This time Annie May didn't slam it. He turned over on his back, making the springs creak. Instantly Pink came into the bedroom to look at him. He lay still, with his eyes closed, holding his breath for fear she would want to talk to him about what he'd said to Annie May and would wake him up. After she moved away from the door he opened his eyes.

There must be some meaning in back of what had happened to Sam. Maybe it was some kind of judgment from the Lord, he thought. Perhaps he shouldn't have stopped going to church. His only concession to Sunday was to put on his best suit. He wore it just that one day and Pink pressed the pants late on Saturday night. But in the last few years it got so that every time he went to church he wanted to stand up and yell, "You goddamn fools! How much more you goin' to take?"

He'd get to thinking about the street they lived on, and the sight of the minister with his clean white collar turned hind side to and sound of his buttery voice were too much. One Sunday he'd actually gotten on his feet, for the minister was talking about the streets of gold up in heaven; the words were right on the tip of his tongue when Pink reached out and pinched his behind sharply. He yelped and sat down. Someone in back of him giggled. In spite of himself a slow smile had spread over his face. He stayed quiet through the rest of the service but after that, he didn't go to church at all.

This street where he and Pink lived was like the one where his mother had lived. It looked like he and Pink ought to have gotten further than his mother had. She had scrubbed floors, washed and ironed in the white folks' kitchens. They were

doing practically the same thing. That was another reason he
stopped going to church. He couldn't figure out why these
things had to stay the same, and if the Lord didn't intend it like
that, why didn't He change it?

He began thinking about Sam again, so he shifted his attention to the sounds Pink was making in the kitchen. She was
getting the rolls ready for tomorrow. Scrubbing the sweet po-
tatoes. Washing the greens. Cutting up the chicken. Then the
thump of the iron. Hot as it was, she was pressing his pants.
He resisted the impulse to get up and tell her not to do it.

A little later, when she turned the light on in the bathroom,
he knew she was getting ready for bed. And he held his eyes
tightly shut, made his body rigidly still. As long as he could
make her think he was sound asleep she wouldn't take a real
good look at him. One real good look and she'd know there was
something wrong. The bed sagged under her weight as she
knelt down to say her prayers. Then she was lying down beside
him. She sighed under her breath as her head hit the pillow.

He must have slept part of the time, but in the morning it
seemed to him that he had looked up at the ceiling most of the
night. He couldn't remember actually going to sleep.

When he finally got up, Pink was dressed and ready for
church. He sat down in a chair in the living room away from
the window, so the light wouldn't shine on his face. As he
looked at her he wished that he could find relief from the confusion of his thoughts by taking part in the singing and shouting that would go on in church. But he couldn't. And Pink
never said anything about his not going to church. Only sometimes like today, when she was ready to go, she looked at him a
little wistfully.

She had on her Sunday dress. It was made of a printed material — big red and black poppies splashed on a cream-colored background. He wouldn't let himself look right into her eyes, and in order that she wouldn't notice the evasiveness of his glance, he stared at the dress. It fit snugly over her best corset, and the corset in turn constricted her thighs and tightly encased the rolls of flesh around her waist. She didn't move away, and he couldn't keep on inspecting the dress, so he shifted his gaze up to the wide cream-colored straw hat she was wearing far back on her head. Next he noticed that she was easing her feet by standing on the outer edges of the high-heeled patent leather pumps she wore.

He reached out and patted her arm. "You look nice," he said, picking up the comic section of the paper.

She stood there looking at him while she pulled a pair of white cotton gloves over her roughened hands. "Is you all right, honey?" she asked.

"Course," he said, holding the paper up in front of his face.

"You shouldn't talk so mean to Annie May," she said gently.

"Yeah, I know," he said, and hoped she understood that he was apologizing. He didn't dare lower the paper while she was standing there looking at him so intently. Why doesn't she go, he thought.

"There's grits and eggs for breakfast."

"O.K." He tried to make his voice sound as though he were absorbed in what he was reading that he couldn't give her all of his attention. She walked toward the door, and he lowered the paper to watch her, thinking that her legs looked too small for her body under the vastness of the printed dress, that womenfolks were sure funny — she's got that great big pocketbook swinging on her arm and hardly anything in it. Sam used to love to tease her about the size of the handbags she carried.

When she closed the outside door and started down the stairs, the heat in the little room struck him in the face. He almost called her back so that he wouldn't be there by himself — left alone to brood over Sam. He decided that when she came home from church he would make love to her. Even in the heat the softness of her body, the smoothness of her skin, would comfort him.

He pulled his chair up close to the open window. Now he could let himself go. He could begin to figure out something to do about Sam. There's gotta be something, he thought. But his mind wouldn't stay put. It kept going back to the time Sam graduated from high school. Nineteen seventy-five his dark blue suit had cost. He and Pink had figured and figured and finally they'd managed it. Sam had looked good in the suit; he was so tall and his shoulders were so broad it looked like a tailor-made suit on him. When he got his diploma everybody went wild — he'd played center on the basketball team, and a lot of folks recognized him.

The trembling in his stomach got worse as he thought about Sam. He was aware that it had never stopped since Scummy had said those words "the las' time." It had gone on all last night until now there was a tautness and a tension in him that left him feeling as though his eardrums were strained wide open, listening for sounds. They must be a foot wide open, he thought. Open and pulsing with the strain of being open. Even his nostrils were stretched open like that. He could feel them. And a weight behind his eyes.

He went to sleep sitting there in the chair. When he woke up his whole body was wet with sweat. It musta got hotter while I slept, he thought. He was conscious of an ache in his jawbones. It's from holding 'em shut so tight. Even his tongue — he'd been holding it so still in his mouth it felt like it was glued there.

Attracted by the sound of voices, he looked out of the window. Across the way a man and a woman were arguing. Their voices rose and fell on the hot, still air. He could look directly into the room where they were standing, and he saw that they were half-undressed.

The woman slapped the man across the face. The sound was like a pistol shot, and for an instant William felt his jaw relax. It seemed to him that the whole block grew quiet and waited. He waited with it. The man grabbed his belt and lashed out at the woman. He watched the belt rise and fall against her brown skin. The woman screamed with the regularity of clockwork. The street came alive again. There was the sound of voices, the rattle of dishes. A baby whined. The woman's voice became a murmur of pain in the background.

"I gotta get me some beer," he said aloud. It would cool him off. It would help him to think. He dressed quickly, telling himself that Pink wouldn't be home for hours yet and by that time the beer smell would be gone from his breath.

The street outside was full of kids playing tag. They were all dressed up in their Sunday clothes. Red socks, blue socks, danced in front of him all the way to the corner. The sight of them piled up the quivering in his stomach. Sam used to play in this block on Sunday afternoons. As he walked along, women thrust their heads out of the opened windows, calling to the children. It seemed to him that all the voices were Pink's voice saying, "You, Sammie, stop that runnin' in your good clo'es!"

He was so glad to get away from the sight of the children that he ignored the heat inside the barroom of the hotel on the corner and determinedly edged his way past girls in sheer summer dresses and men in loud plaid jackets and tight-legged cream-colored pants until he finally reached the long bar.

There was such a sense of hot excitement in the place that he turned to look around him. Men with slicked, straightened hair were staring through half-closed eyes at the girls lined up at the bar. One man sitting at a table close by kept running his hand up and down the bare arm of the girl leaning against him. Up and down. Down and up. William winced and looked away. The jukebox was going full blast, filling the room with high, raw music that beat about his ears in a queer mixture of violence and love and hate and terror. He stared at the brilliantly colored moving lights on the front of the jukebox as he listened to it, wishing that he had stayed at home, for the music made the room hotter.

"Make it a beer," he said to the bartender.

The beer glass was cold. He held it in his hand, savoring the chill of it, before he raised it to his lips. He drank it down fast. Immediately he felt the air grow cooler. The smell of beer and whiskey that hung in the room lifted.

"Fill it up again," he said. He still had that awful trembling in his stomach, but he felt as though he were really beginning to think. Really think. He found he was arguing with himself.

"Sam mighta been like this. Spendin' Sunday afternoons whorin'."

"But he was part of me and part of Pink. He had a chance —"

"Yeah. A chance to live in one of them hell-hole flats. A chance to get himself a woman to beat."

"He woulda finished college and got a good job. Mebbe been a druggist or a doctor or a lawyer —"

"Yeah. Or mebbe got himself a stable of women to rent out on the block —"

He licked the suds from his lips. The man at the table nearby had stopped stroking the girl's arm. He was kissing her — forcing her closer and closer to him.

"Yeah," William jeered at himself. "That coulda been Sam on a hot Sunday afternoon —"

As he stood there arguing with himself he thought it was getting warmer in the bar. The lights were dimmer. I better go home, he thought. I gotta live with this thing some time. Drinking beer in this place ain't going to help any. He looked out toward the lobby of the hotel, attracted by the sound of voices. A white cop was arguing with a frowzy-looking girl who had obviously had too much to drink.

"I got a right in here. I'm mindin' my own business," she said with one eye on the bar.

"Aw, go chase yourself." The cop gave her a push toward the door. She stumbled against a chair.

William watched her in amusement. "Better than a movie," he told himself.

She straightened up and tugged at her girdle. "You white son of a bitch," she said.

The cop's face turned a furious red. He walked toward the woman, waving his nightstick. It was then that William saw the soldier. Tall. Straight. Creases in his khaki pants. An overseas cap cocked over one eye. Looks like Sam looked that one time he was home on furlough, he thought.

The soldier grabbed the cop's arm and twisted the nightstick out of his hand. He threw it half the length of the small lobby. It rattled along the floor and came to a dead stop under a chair.

"Now what'd he want to do that for?" William said softly.

He knew that night after night the cop had to come back to this hotel. He's the law, he thought, and he can't let — Then he stopped thinking about him, for the cop raised his arm. The soldier aimed a blow at the cop's chin. The cop ducked and reached for his gun. The soldier turned to run.

It's happening too fast, William thought. It's like one of those horse race reels they run over fast at the movies. Then he froze inside. The quivering in his stomach got worse. The soldier was heading toward the door. Running. His foot was on the threshold when the cop fired. The soldier dropped. He folded up as neatly as the brown-paper bags Pink brought home from the store, emptied, and then carefully put in the kitchen cupboard.

The noise of the shot stayed in his eardrums. He couldn't get it out. "Jesus Christ!" he said. Then again, "Jesus Christ!" The beer glass was warm. He put it down on the bar with such violence some of the beer slopped over on his shirt. He stared at the wet place, thinking Pink would be mad as hell. Him out drinking in a bar on Sunday. There was a stillness in which he was conscious of the stink of the beer, the heat in the room, and he could still hear the sound of the shot. Somebody dropped a glass, and the tinkle of it hurt his ears.

Then everybody was moving toward the lobby. The doors between the bar and the lobby slammed shut. High, excited talk broke out.

The tall thin black man standing next to him said, "That ties it. It ain't even safe here where we live. Not no more. I'm goin' to get me a white bastard of a cop and nail his hide to a street sign."

"Is the soldier dead?" someone asked.

"He wasn't movin' none," came the answer.

They pushed hard against the doors leading to the lobby. The doors stayed shut.

He stood still, watching them. The anger that went through him was so great that he had to hold on to the bar to keep from falling. He felt as though he were going to burst wide open. It was like having seen Sam killed before his eyes. Then he heard the whine of an ambulance siren. His eardrums seemed to have been waiting to pick it up.

"Come on, what you waitin' for?" He snarled the words at the people milling around the lobby doors. "Come on!" he repeated, running toward the street.

The crowd followed him to the 126th Street entrance of the hotel. He got there in time to see a stretcher bearing a limp khaki-clad figure disappear inside the ambulance in front of the door. The ambulance pulled away fast, and he stared after it stupidly.

He hadn't known what he was going to do, but he felt cheated. Let down. He noticed that it was beginning to get dark. More and more people were coming into the street. He wondered where they'd come from and how they'd heard about the shooting so quickly. Every time he looked around there were more of them. Curious, eager voices kept asking, "What happened? What happened?" The answer was always the same. Hard, angry. "A white cop shot a soldier."

Someone said, "Come on to the hospital. Find out what happened to him."

In front of the hotel he had been in the front of the crowd. Now there were so many people in back of him and in front of him that when they started toward the hospital, he moved along with them. He hadn't decided to go — the forward movement picked him up and moved him along without any intention on his part. He got the feeling that he had lost his identity as a person with a free will of his own. It frightened him at first. Then he began to feel powerful. He was surrounded by hundreds of people like himself. They were all together. They could do anything.

As the crowd moved slowly down Eighth Avenue, he saw that there were cops lined up on both sides of the street. Mounted cops kept coming out of the side streets, shouting, "Break it up! Keep moving. Keep moving."

The cops were scared of them. He could tell. Their faces were dead white in the semidarkness. He started saying the words over separately to himself. Dead. White. He laughed again. Dead. White. The words were funny said separately like that. He stopped laughing suddenly because a part of his mind repeated, Twenty years, twenty years.

He licked his lips. It was hot as all hell tonight. He imagined what it would be like to be drinking swallow after swallow of ice-cold beer. His throat worked and he swallowed audibly.

The big black man walking beside him turned and looked down at him. "You all right, brother?" he asked curiously.

"Yeah," he nodded. "It's them sons of bitches of cops. They're scared of us." He shuddered. The heat was terrible. The tide of hate quivering in his stomach made him hotter. "Wish I had some beer," he said.

The man seemed to understand not only what he had said but all the things he had left unsaid. For he nodded and smiled. And William thought this was an extraordinary night. It was as though, standing so close together, so many of them like this — as though they knew each other's thoughts. It was a wonderful thing.

The crowd carried him along. Smoothly. Easily. He wasn't

really walking. Just gliding. He was aware that the shuffling feet of the crowd made a muffled rhythm on the concrete sidewalk. It was slow, inevitable. An ominous sound, like a funeral march. With the regularity of a drumbeat. No. It's more like a pulse beat, he thought. It isn't a loud noise. It just keeps repeating over and over. But not that regular, because it builds up to something. It keeps building up.

The mounted cops rode their horses into the crowd. Trying to break it up into smaller groups. Then the rhythm was broken. Seconds later it started again. Each time the tempo was a little faster. He found he was breathing the same way. Faster and faster. As though he were running. There were more and more cops. All of them white. They had moved the colored cops out.

"They done that before," he muttered.

"What?" said the man next to him.

"They moved the black cops out," he said.

He heard the man repeat it to someone standing beside him. It became part of the slow shuffling rhythm on the sidewalk. "They moved the black cops." He heard it go back and back through the crowd until it was only a whisper of hate on the still hot air. "They moved the black cops."

As the crowd shuffled back and forth in front of the hospital, he caught snatches of conversation. "The soldier was dead when they put him in the ambulance." "Always tryin' to fool us." "Christ! Just let me get my hands on one of them cops."

He was thinking about the hospital and he didn't take part in any of the conversations. Even now across the long span of years he could remember the helpless, awful rage that had sent him hurrying home from this same hospital. Not saying anything. Getting home by some kind of instinct.

Pink had come to this hospital when she had had her last child. He could hear again the cold contempt in the voice of the nurse as she listened to Pink's loud grieving. "You people have too many children anyway," she said.

It left him speechless. He had his hat in his hand and he remembered how he wished afterward that he'd put it on in front of her to show her what he thought of her. As it was, all the bitter answers that finally surged into his throat seemed to choke him. No words would come out. So he stared at her lean, spare body. He let his eyes stay a long time on her flat breasts. White uniform. White shoes. White stockings. White skin.

Then he mumbled, "It's too bad your eyes ain't white, too." And turned on his heel and walked out.

It wasn't any kind of answer. She probably didn't even know what he was talking about. The baby dead, and all he could think of was to tell her her eyes ought to be white. White shoes, white stockings, white uniform, white skin, and blue eyes.

Staring at the hospital, he saw with satisfaction that frightened faces were appearing at the windows. Some of the lights went out. He began to feel that this night was the first time he'd ever really been alive. Tonight everything was going to be changed. There was a growing, swelling sense of power in him. He felt the same thing in the people around him.

The cops were aware of it, too, he thought. They were out in full force. Mounties, patrolmen, emergency squads. Radio cars that looked like oversize bugs crawled through the side streets. Waited near the curbs. Their white tops stood out in the darkness. "White folks riding in white cars." He wasn't aware that he had said it aloud until he heard the words go through the crowd. "White folks in white cars." The laughter that followed the words had a rough, raw rhythm. It repeated the pattern of the shuffling feet.

Someone said, "They got him at the station house. He ain't here." And the crowd started moving toward 123rd Street.

Great God in the morning, William thought, everybody's out here. There were girls in thin summer dresses, boys in long coats and tight-legged pants, old women dragging kids along by the hand. A man on crutches jerked himself past to the rhythm of the shuffling feet. A blind man tapped his way through the center of the crowd, and it divided into two separate streams as it swept by him. At every street corner William noticed someone stopped to help the blind man up over the curb.

The street in front of the police station was so packed with people that he couldn't get near it. As far as he could see they weren't doing anything. They were simply standing there. Waiting for something to happen. He recognized a few of them: the woman with the loose, rolling eyes who sold shopping bags on 125th Street; the lucky-number peddler — the man with the white parrot on his shoulder; three sisters of the Heavenly Rest for All movement — barefooted women in loose white robes.

Then, for no reason that he could discover, everybody moved toward 125th Street. The motion of the crowd was slower now because it kept increasing in size as people coming from late church services were drawn into it. It was easy to identify them, he thought. The women wore white gloves. The kids were all slicked up. Despite the more gradual movement he was still being carried along effortlessly, easily. When someone in front of him barred his way, he pushed against the person irritably, frowning in annoyance because the smooth forward flow of his progress had been stopped.

It was Pink who stood in front of him. He stopped frowning

when he recognized her. She had a brown-paper bag tucked under her arm and he knew she had stopped at the corner store to get the big bottle of cream soda she always brought home on Sundays. The sight of it made him envious, for it meant that this Sunday had been going along in an orderly, normal fashion for her while he — She was staring at him so hard he was suddenly horribly conscious of the smell of the beer that had spilled on his shirt. He knew she had smelled it, too, by the tighter grip she took on her pocketbook.

"What you doing out here in this mob? A Sunday evening and you drinking beer," she said grimly.

For a moment he couldn't answer her. All he could think of was Sam. He almost said, "I saw Sam shot this afternoon," and he swallowed hard.

"This afternoon I saw a white cop kill a black soldier," he said. "In the bar where I was drinking beer. I saw it. That's why I'm here. The glass of beer I was drinking went on my clothes. The cop shot him in the back. That's why I'm here."

He paused for a moment, took a deep breath. This was how it ought to be, he decided. She had to know sometime and this was the right place to tell her. In this semidarkness, in this confusion of noises, with the low, harsh rhythm of the footsteps sounding against the noise of the horses' hoofs.

His voice thickened. "I saw Scummy yesterday," he went on. "He told me Sam's doing time at hard labor. That's why we ain't heard from him. A white MP shot him when he wouldn't go to the nigger end of a bus. Sam shot the MP. They gave him twenty years at hard labor."

He knew he hadn't made it clear how to him the soldier in the bar was Sam; that it was like seeing his own son shot before his very eyes. I don't even know whether the soldier was dead, he thought. What made me tell her about Sam out here in the street like this, anyway? He realized with a sense of shock that he really didn't care that he had told her. He felt strong, powerful, aloof. All the time he'd been talking he wouldn't look right at her. Now, suddenly, he was looking at her as though she were a total stranger. He was coldly wondering what she'd do. He was prepared for anything.

But he wasn't prepared for the wail that came from her throat. The sound hung in the hot air. It made the awful quivering in his stomach worse. It echoed and reechoed the length of the street. Somewhere in the distance a horse whinnied. A woman standing way back in the crowd groaned as though the sorrow and the anguish in that cry were more than she could bear.

Pink stood there for a moment. Silent. Brooding. Then she lifted the big bottle of soda high in the air. She threw it with all her might. It made a wide arc and landed in the exact center of the plate-glass window of a furniture store. The glass crashed in with a sound like a gunshot.

A sigh went up from the crowd. They surged toward the broken window. Pink followed close behind. When she reached the window, all the glass had been broken in. Reaching far inside, she grabbed a small footstool and then turned to hurl it through the window of the dress shop next door. He kept close behind her, watching her as she seized a new missile from each store window that she broke.

Plate-glass windows were being smashed all up and down 125th Street — on both sides of the street. The violent, explosive sound fed the sense of power in him. Pink had started this. He was proud of her, for she had shown herself to be a fit mate for a man of his type. He stayed as close to her as he could. So in spite of the crashing, splintering sounds and the swarming, violent activity around him, he knew the exact moment when she lost her big straw hat; when she took off the high-heeled patent leather shoes and flung them away, striding swiftly along in her stockinged feet. That her dress was hanging crooked on her.

He was right in back of her when she stopped in front of a hat store. She carefully appraised all the hats inside the broken window. Finally she reached out, selected a small hat covered with purple violets, and fastened it securely on her head.

"Woman's got good sense," a man said.

"Man, oh, man! Let me get in there," said a raw-boned woman who thrust her way forward through the jam of people to seize two hats from the window.

A roar of approval went up from the crowd. From then on when a window was smashed it was bare of merchandise when the people streamed past it. White folks owned these stores. They'd lose and lose and lose, he thought with satisfaction. The words "twenty years" reechoed in his mind. I'll be an old man, he thought. Then: I may be dead before Sam gets out of prison.

The feeling of great power and strength left him. He was so confused by its loss that he decided this thing happening in the street wasn't real. It was so dark, there were so many people shouting and running about, that he almost convinced himself he was having a nightmare. He was aware that his hearing had now grown so acute he could pick up the tiniest sounds: the quickened breathing and the soft, gloating laughter of the crowd; even the sound of his own heart beating. He could hear these things under the noise of the breaking glass, under the shouts that were coming from both sides of the street. They forced him to face the fact that this was no dream but a reality from which he couldn't escape. The quivering in his stomach kept increasing as he walked along.

Pink was striding through the crowd just ahead of him. He studied her to see if she, too, were feeling as he did. But the outrage that ran through her had made her younger. She was tireless. Most of the time she was leading the crowd. It was all he could do to keep up with her, and finally he gave up the attempt — it made him too tired.

He stopped to watch a girl who was standing in a store window, clutching a clothes model tightly around the waist. "What's she want that for?" he said aloud. For the model had been stripped of clothing by the passing crowd, and he thought its pinkish torso was faintly obscene in its resemblance to a female figure.

The girl was young and thin. Her back was turned toward him, and there was something so ferocious about the way her dark hands gripped the naked model that he resisted the onward movement of the crowd to stare in fascination. The girl turned around. Her nervous hands were tight around the dummy's waist. It was Annie May.

"Ah, no!" he said, and let his breath come out with a sigh.

Her hands crept around the throat of the model and she sent it hurtling through the air above the heads of the crowd. It landed short of a window across the street. The legs shattered. The head rolled toward the curb. The waist snapped neatly in two. Only the torso remained whole and in one piece.

Annie May stood in the empty window and laughed with the crowd when someone kicked the torso into the street. He stood there, staring at her. He felt that now for the first time he understood her. She had never had anything but badly paying jobs — working for young white women who probably despised her. She was like Sam on that bus in Georgia. She didn't want just the nigger end of things, and here in Harlem there wasn't anything else for her. All along she'd been trying the only way she knew how to squeeze out of life a little something for herself.

He tried to get closer to the window where she was standing. He had to tell her that he understood. And the crowd, tired of the obstruction that he had made by standing still, swept him up and carried him past. He stopped thinking and let himself be carried along on a vast wave of feeling. There was so much plate glass on the sidewalk that it made a grinding noise under the feet of the hurrying crowd. It was a dull, harsh sound that set his teeth on edge and quickened the trembling of his stomach.

Now all the store windows that he passed were broken. The people hurrying by him carried tables, lamps, shoeboxes, clothing. A woman next to him held a wedding cake in her hands — it went up in tiers of white frosting with a small bride and groom mounted at the top. Her hands were bleeding, and he began to look closely at the people nearest him. Most of them, too, had cuts on their hands and legs. Then he saw there was blood on the sidewalk in front of the windows, blood dripping down the jagged edges of the broken windows. And he wanted desperately to go home.

He was conscious that the rhythm of the crowd had changed. It was faster, and it had taken on an ugly note. The cops were using their nightsticks. Police wagons drew up to the curbs. When they pulled away, they were full of men and women who carried loot from the stores in their hands.

The police cars slipping through the streets were joined by

other cars with loudspeakers on top. The voices coming through the loudspeakers were harsh. They added to the noise and confusion. He tried to listen to what the voices were saying. But the words had no meaning for him. He caught one phrase over and over: "Good people of Harlem." It made him feel sick.

He repeated the words "of Harlem." We don't belong anywhere, he thought. There ain't no room for us anywhere. There wasn't no room for Sam in a bus in Georgia. There ain't no room for us here in New York. There ain't no place but top floors. The top-floor black people. And he laughed and the sound stuck in his throat.

After that he snatched a suit from the window of a men's clothing store. It was a summer suit. The material felt crisp and cool. He walked away with it under his arm. He'd never owned a suit like that. He simply sweated out the summer in the same dark pants he wore in winter. Even while he stroked the material, a part of his mind sneered — you got summer pants; Sam's got twenty years.

He was surprised to find that he was almost at Lenox Avenue, for he hadn't remembered crossing Seventh. At the corner the cops were shoving a group of young boys and girls into a police wagon. He paused to watch. Annie May was in the middle of the group. She had a yellow fox jacket dangling from one hand.

"Annie May!" he shouted. "Annie May!" The crowd pushed him along faster and faster. She hadn't seen him. He let himself be carried forward by the movement of the crowd. He had to find Pink and tell her that the cops had taken Annie May.

He peered into the dimness of the street ahead of him, looking for her; then he elbowed his way toward the curb so that he

292 Miss Muriel and Other Stories

could see the other side of the street. He forgot about finding Pink, for directly opposite him was the music store that he passed every night coming home from work. Young boys and girls were always lounging on the sidewalk in front of it. They danced a few steps while they listened to the records being played inside the shop. All the records sounded the same — a terribly magnified woman's voice bleating out a blues song in a voice that sounded to him like that of an animal in heat — an old animal, tired and beaten, but with an insinuating know-how left in her. The white men who went past the store smiled as their eyes lingered on the young girls swaying to the music.

"White folks got us comin' and goin'. Backwards and forwards," he muttered. He fought his way out of the crowd and walked toward a no-parking sign that stood in front of the store. He rolled it up over the curb. It was heavy and the effort made him pant. It took all his strength to send it crashing through the glass on the door.

Almost immediately an old woman and a young man slipped inside the narrow shop. He followed them. He watched them smash the records that lined the shelves. He hadn't thought of actually breaking the records but once he started, he found the crisp, snapping noise pleasant. The feeling of power began to return. He didn't like these records, so they had to be destroyed.

When they left the music store there wasn't a whole record left. The old woman came out of the store last. As he hurried off up the street he could have sworn he smelled the sharp, acrid smell of smoke. He turned and looked back. He was right. A thin wisp of smoke was coming through the store door. The old woman had long since disappeared in the crowd.

Farther up the street he looked back again. The fire in the

record shop was burning merrily. It was making a glow that lit up that part of the street. There was a new rhythm now. It was faster and faster. Even the voices coming from the loudspeakers had taken on the urgency of speed.

Fire trucks roared up the street. He threw his head back and laughed when he saw them. That's right, he thought. Burn the whole damn place down. It was wonderful. Then he frowned. "Twenty years at hard labor." The words came back to him. He was a fool. Fire wouldn't wipe that out. There wasn't anything that would wipe it out.

He remembered then that he had to find Pink. To tell her about Annie May. He overtook her in the next block. She's got more stuff, he thought. She had a table lamp in one hand, a large enamel kettle in the other. The lightweight summer coat draped across her shoulders was so small it barely covered her enormous arms. She was watching a group of boys assault the steel gates in front of a liquor store. She frowned at them so ferociously he wondered what she was going to do. Hating liquor the way she did, he half expected her to cuff the boys and send them on their way up the street.

She turned and looked at the crowd in back of her. When she saw him she beckoned to him. "Hold these," she said. He took the lamp, the kettle and the coat she held out to him, and he saw that her face was wet with perspiration. The print dress was darkly stained with it.

She fastened the hat with the purple flowers securely on her head. Then she walked over to the gate. "Git out the way," she said to the boys. Bracing herself in front of the gate, she started tugging at it. The gate resisted. She pulled at it with a sudden access of such furious strength that he was frightened. Watching her, he got the feeling that the resistance of the gate had transformed it in her mind. It was no longer a gate — it had become the world that had taken her son, and she was wreaking vengeance on it.

The gate began to bend and sway under her assault. Then it was down. She stood there for a moment, staring at her hands — big drops of blood oozed slowly over the palms. Then she turned to the crowd that had stopped to watch.

"Come on, you niggers," she said. Her eyes were little and evil and triumphant. "Come on and drink up the white man's liquor." As she strode off up the street, the beflowered hat dangled precariously from the back of her head.

When he caught up with her she was moaning, talking to herself in husky whispers. She stopped when she saw him and put her hand on his arm.

"It's hot, ain't it?" she said, panting.

In the midst of all this violence, the sheer commonplaceness of her question startled him. He looked at her closely. The rage that had been in her was gone, leaving her completely exhausted. She was breathing too fast in uneven gasps that shook her body. Rivulets of sweat streamed down her face. It was as though her triumph over the metal gate had finished her. The gate won anyway, he thought.

"Let's go home, Pink," he said. He had to shout to make his voice carry over the roar of the crowd, the sound of breaking glass.

He realized she didn't have the strength to speak, for she only nodded in reply to his suggestion. Once we get home she'll be all right, he thought. It was suddenly urgent that they get home, where it was quiet, where he could think, where he could take something to still the tremors in his stomach. He tried to get her to walk a little faster, but she kept slowing down until, when they entered their own street, it seemed to him they were barely moving.

In the middle of the block she stood still. "I can't make it," she said. "I'm too tired."

Even as he put his arm around her she started going down. He tried to hold her up, but her great weight was too much for him. She went down slowly, inevitably, like a great ship capsizing. Until all of her huge body was crumpled on the sidewalk.

"Pink," he said. "Pink. You gotta get up," he said over and over again.

She didn't answer. He leaned over and touched her gently. Almost immediately afterward he straightened up. All his life, moments of despair and frustration had left him speechless — strangled by the words that rose in his throat. This time the words poured out.

He sent his voice raging into the darkness and the awful confusion of noises. "The sons of bitches," he shouted. "The sons of bitches."

Doby's Gone

WHEN DOBY FIRST CAME into Sue Johnson's life her family were caretakers on a farm way up in New York State. And because Sue had no one else to play with, the Johnsons reluctantly accepted Doby as a member of the family.

The spring that Sue was six they moved to Wessex, Connecticut — a small New England town whose neat colonial houses cling to a group of hills overlooking the Connecticut River. All that summer Mrs. Johnson had hoped that Doby would vanish long before Sue entered school in the fall. He would only complicate things in school.

For Doby wasn't real. He existed only in Sue's mind. He had been created out of her need for a friend her own age — her own size. And he had gradually become an escape from the very real world that surrounded her. She first started talking about him when she was two and he had been with her ever since. He always sat beside her when she ate and played with her during the day. At night he slept in a chair near her bed so that they awoke at the same time in the morning. A place had to be set for him at mealtime. A seat had to be saved for him on trains and buses.

After they moved to Wessex, he was still her constant companion just as he had been when she was three and four and five.

On the morning that Sue was to start going to school she said, "Doby has a new pencil, too. And he's got a red plaid shirt just like my dress."

"Why can't Doby stay home?" Mrs. Johnson asked.

"Because he goes everywhere I go," Sue said in amazement. "Of course he's going to school. He's going to sit right by me."

Sue watched her mother get up from the breakfast table and then followed her upstairs to the big front bedroom. She saw with surprise that her mother was putting on her going-out clothes.

"You have to come with me, Mommy?" she asked anxiously. She had wanted to go with Doby. Just the two of them. She had planned every step of the way since the time her mother told her she would start school in the fall.

"No, I don't have to, but I'm coming just the same. I want to talk to your teacher." Mrs. Johnson fastened her coat and deftly patted a loose strand of hair in place.

Sue looked at her and wondered if the other children's mothers would come to school, too. She certainly hoped so because she wouldn't want to be the only one there who had a mother with her.

Then she started skipping around the room holding Doby by

the hand. Her short black braids jumped as she skipped. The gingham dress she wore was starched so stiffly that the hemline formed a wide circular frame for her sturdy dark brown legs as she bounced up and down.

"Ooh," she said suddenly. "Doby pulled off one of my hair ribbons." She reached over and picked it up from the floor and came to stand in front of her mother while the red ribbon was retied into a crisp bow.

Then she was walking down the street hand in hand with her mother. She held Doby's hand on the other side. She decided it was good her mother had come. It was better that way. The street would have looked awfully long and awfully big if she and Doby had been by themselves, even though she did know exactly where the school was. Right down the street on this side. Past the post office and town hall that sat so far back with green lawn in front of them. Past the town pump and the old white house on the corner, past the big empty lot. And there was the school.

It had a walk that went straight down between the green grass and was all brown-yellow gravel stuff — coarser than sand. One day she had walked past there with her mother and stopped to finger the stuff the walk was made of, and her mother had said, "It's gravel."

She remembered how they'd talked about it. "What's gravel?" she asked.

"The stuff in your hand. It's like sand, only coarser. People use it for driveways and walks," her mother had said.

Gravel. She liked the sound of the word. It sounded like pebbles. Gravel. Pebble. She said the words over to herself. You gravel and pebble. Pebble said to gravel. She started making up a story. Gravel said to pebble, "You're a pebble." Pebble said back, "You're a gravel."

"Sue, throw it away. It's dirty and your hands are clean," her mother said.

She threw it down on the sidewalk. But she kept looking back at it as she walked along. It made a scattered yellow-brown color against the rich brown-black of the dirt path.

She held on to Doby's hand a little more tightly. Now she was actually going to walk up that long gravel walk to the school. She and Doby would play there every day when school was out.

The school yard was full of children. Sue hung back a little looking at them. They were playing ball under the big maple trees near the back of the yard. Some small children were squatting near the school building, letting gravel trickle through their fingers.

"I want to play, too." She tried to free her hand from her mother's firm grip.

"We're going inside to see your teacher first." And her mother went on walking up the school steps holding on to Sue's hand.

Sue stared at the children on the steps. "Why are they looking so hard?" she asked.

"Probably because you're looking at them so hard. Now come on," and her mother pulled her through the door. The hall inside was dark and very long. A neat white sign over a door to the right said FIRST GRADE in bold black letters.

Sue peered inside the room while her mother knocked on the door. A pretty lady with curly yellow hair got up from a desk and invited them in. While the teacher and her mother talked grown-up talk, Sue looked around. She supposed she'd sit at one of those little desks. There were a lot of them and she wondered if there would be a child at each desk. If so then Doby would have to squeeze in beside her.

"Sue, you can go outside and play. When the bell rings you must come in," the teacher said.

"Yes, teacher," Sue started out the door in a hurry.

"My name is Miss Whittier," the teacher said. "You must call me that."

"Yes, Miss Whittier. Good-bye, Mommy," she said, and went quickly down the hall and out the door.

"Hold my hand, Doby," she said softly under her breath.

Now she and Doby would play in the gravel. Squeeze it between their fingers, pat it into shapes like those other children were doing. Her short starched skirt stood out around her legs as she skipped down the steps. She watched the children as long as she could without saying anything.

"Can we play, too?" she asked finally.

A boy with a freckled face and short stiff red hair looked up at her and frowned. He didn't answer but kept ostentatiously patting at a little mound of gravel.

Sue walked over a little closer, holding Doby tightly by the hand. The boy ignored her. A little girl in a blue and white checked dress stuck her tongue out.

"Your legs are black," she said suddenly. And then when the others looked up she added, "Why, look, she's black all over. Looky, she's black all over."

Sue retreated a step away from the building. The children got up and followed her. She took another backward step and they took two steps forward. The little girl who had stuck her tongue out began a chant, "Look, look. Her legs are black. Her legs are black."

The children were all saying it. They formed a ring around her and they were dancing up and down and screaming, "Her legs are black. Her legs are black."

She stood in the middle of the circle completely bewildered. She wanted to go home where it was safe and quiet and where her mother would hold her tight in her arms. She pulled Doby nearer to her. What did they mean her legs were black? Of course, they were. Not black but dark brown. Just like these children were white some other children were dark like her. Her mother said so. But her mother hadn't said anyone would make her feel bad about being a different color. She didn't know what to do; so she just stood there watching them come closer and closer to her — their faces red with excitement, their voices hoarse with yelling.

Then the school bell rang. And the children suddenly plunged toward the building. She was left alone with Doby. When she walked into the school room she was crying.

"Don't you mind, Doby," she whispered. "Don't you mind. I won't let them hurt you."

Miss Whittier gave her a seat near the front of the room. Right near her desk. And she smiled at her. Sue smiled back and carefully wiped away the wet on her eyelashes with the back of her hand. She turned and looked around the room. There were no empty seats. Doby would have to stand up.

"You stand right close to me and if you get tired just sit on the edge of my seat," she said.

She didn't go out for recess. She stayed in and helped Miss Whittier draw on the blackboard with colored chalk — yellow and green and red and purple and brown. Miss Whittier drew the flowers and Sue colored them. She put a small piece of crayon out for Doby to use. And Miss Whittier noticed it. But she didn't say anything, she just smiled.

"I love her," Sue thought. "I love my teacher." And then again, "I love Miss Whittier, my teacher."

At noon the children followed her halfway home from school. They called after her and she ran so fast and so hard that the pounding in her ears cut off the sound of their voices.

"Go faster, Doby," she said. "You have to go faster." And she held his hand and ran until her legs ached.

"How was school, Sue?" asked her mother.

"It was all right," she said slowly. "I don't think Doby likes it very much. He likes Miss Whittier though."

"Do you like her?"

"Oh, yes," Sue let her breath come out with a sigh.

"Why are you panting like that?" her mother asked.

"I ran all the way home," she said.

Going back after lunch wasn't so bad. She went right in to Miss Whittier. She didn't stay out in the yard and wait for the bell.

When school was out, she decided she'd better hurry right home and maybe the children wouldn't see her. She walked down the gravel path taking quick little looks over her shoulder. No one paid any attention and she was so happy that she gave Doby's hand a squeeze.

And then she saw that they were waiting for her right by the vacant lot. She hurried along trying not to hear what they were saying.

"My mother says you're a little nigger girl," the boy with the red hair said.

And then they began to shout: "Her legs are black. Her legs are black."

It changed suddenly. "Run. Go ahead and run." She looked over her shoulder. A boy was coming toward her with a long switch in his hand. He raised it in a threatening gesture and she started running.

For two days she ran home from school like that. Ran until her short legs felt as though they couldn't move another step.

"Sue," her mother asked anxiously, watching her try to catch her breath on the front steps, "what makes you run home from school like this?"

"Doby doesn't like the other children very much," she said panting.

"Why?"

"I don't think they understand about him," she said thoughtfully. "But he loves Miss Whittier."

The next day the children waited for her right where the school's gravel walk ended. Sue didn't see them until she was close to them. She was coming slowly down the path hand in hand with Doby trying to see how many of the big pebbles they could step on without stepping on any of the finer, sandier gravel.

She was in the middle of the group of children before she realized it. They started off slowly at first. "How do you comb that kind of hair?" "Does that black color wash off?" And then the chant began and it came faster and faster: "Her legs are black. Her legs are black."

A little girl reached out and pulled one of Sue's braids. Sue tried to back away and the other children closed in around her. She rubbed the side of her head — it hurt where her hair had been pulled. Someone pushed her. Hard. In the middle of her back. She was suddenly outraged. She planted her feet firmly on the path. She started hitting out with her fists. Kicking. Pulling hair. Tearing at clothing. She reached down and picked up handfuls of gravel and aimed it at eyes and ears and noses.

While she was slapping and kicking at the small figures that encircled her she became aware that Doby had gone. For the first time in her life he had left her. He had gone when she started to fight.

She went on fighting — scratching and biting and kicking — with such passion and energy that the space around her slowly cleared. The children backed away. And she stood still. She was breathing fast as though she had been running.

The children ran off down the street — past the big empty lot, past the old white house with the green shutters. Sue watched them go. She didn't feel victorious. She didn't feel anything except an aching sense of loss. She stood there panting, wondering about Doby.

And then, "Doby," she called softly. Then louder, "Doby! Doby! Where are you?"

She listened — cocking her head on one side. He didn't answer. And she felt certain he would never be back because he had never left her before. He had gone for good. And she didn't know why. She decided it probably had something to do with growing up. And she looked down at her legs hoping to find they had grown as long as her father's. She saw instead that her dress was torn in three different places, her socks were down around her ankles, there were long angry scratches on her legs and on her arms. She felt for her hair — the red hair ribbons were gone and her braids were coming undone.

She started looking for the hair ribbons. And as she looked she saw that Daisy Bell, the little girl who had stuck her tongue out that first day of school, was leaning against the oak tree at the end of the path.

"Come on, let's walk home together," Daisy Bell said matter-of-factly.

"All right," Sue said.

As they started past the empty lot, she was conscious that someone was tagging along behind them. It was Jimmie Piebald, the boy with the stiff red hair. When she looked back he came up and walked on the other side of her.

They walked along in silence until they came to the town pump. They stopped and looked deep down into the well. And spent a long time hallooing down into it and listening delightedly to the hollow funny sound of their voices.

It was much later than usual when Sue got home. Daisy Bell and Jimmie walked up to the door with her. Her mother was standing on the front steps waiting for her.

"Sue," her mother said in a shocked voice. "What's the matter? What happened to you?"

Daisy Bell put her arm around Sue. Jimmie started kicking at some stones in the path.

Sue stared at her mother, trying to remember. There was something wrong but she couldn't think what it was. And then it came to her. "Oh," she wailed, "Doby's gone. I can't find him anywhere."